ZEN: DAWN I...

Jack Macdonald

RIDER

ZEN:

DAWN IN THE WEST

Roshi Philip Kapleau

with a Foreword by Albert Low

RIDER
London Melbourne Auckland Johannesburg

A RIDER BOOK

First published in Great Britain in 1980 by Rider, an imprint of Century Hutchinson Ltd,
Brookmount House, 62-65 Chandos Place, Covent Garden, London WC2N 4NW

Reprinted 1987

Century Hutchinson Australia Pty Ltd,
PO Box 496, 16-22 Church Street, Hawthorn, Victoria 3122,
Australia

Century Hutchinson New Zealand Ltd,
PO Box 40-086, Glenfield, Auckland 10,
New Zealand.

Century Hutchinson South Africa Pty Ltd,
PO Box 337, Bergvlei, 2012 South Africa

© Zen Center, Inc. 1978, 1979

Printed and bound in Great Britain by The Guernsey Press Co Ltd,
Guernsey, Channel Islands

ISBN 0 09 1406110

A NOTE ON THE TITLE PAGE ILLUSTRATION/Richard Wehrman's
drawing, "Carp Leaping Up a Waterfall to Become a Dragon," is taken from
traditional Zen imagery. In ancient China a popular fable was that of a carp
struggling to reach the crest of a waterfall. After repeated attempts, the carp
finally summons up all its energies and in one mighty leap to the top becomes a
dragon. Because in the Orient the carp is celebrated for its vigor, perseverance,
and courage—qualities indispensable for awakening—large wooden sculptures of
this fish are often found in Zen monasteries. The waterfall represents the spiritual
aspirant's daily life, and the dragon stands for realized Mind

Liang K'ai's drawing of Shakyamuni (p. vii) appeared in *Zen and Japanese Culture*
by D. T. Suzuki and is reprinted by permission of the author's estate

The photograph of the Sixth Patriarch (p. 129) is taken from *Ch'an and Zen Teaching
(Series Three)* by Charles Luk and is reprinted by permission of the author

Hakuin's drawing of Bodhidharma (p. 111) appeared in *Zen Dust* by Isshu Miura
and Ruth Fuller Sasaki, and is reprinted here with the permission of the Marquis
Hosokawa Moritatsu, from whose collection it is taken

Dedicated to those who wish

not to seek but to find.

After six years of inner struggle and hard search, Shakyamuni ascended to the highest peak of Mind and saw into the innermost meaning of birth and death, becoming the Buddha, or Awakened One. After first relishing this sublime state and then pondering whether men and women still mired in the mud of greed, anger, and delusion could understand the profound truth realized by him, he descended from this highest of mountains into the world of suffering and began to teach the cause of suffering and the way to overcome it.

The painting radiates a deep stillness, accentuated by the fluttering drapery of Shakyamuni's garments and the oblique line of the mountain. The atmosphere conveys the profundity of enlightenment even as the features of Shakyamuni reflect great serenity, wisdom, and compassion. There is nothing other-worldly or mystical here; the Buddha is shown in concrete human form. True awakening, the painting implies, is not a "high" which keeps one, full of wonder and joy, in the clouds of an abstract oneness, but a realization that brings one solidly down to earth into the world of toil and struggle. The ascent is for oneself, the descent for others.

"Shakyamuni Descending the Mountain," by Liang K'ai (thirteenth century), one of the great Chinese Zen painters of the Southern Sung period.

CONTENTS

PART ONE / FLASHES OF ZEN

PART TWO / THE SECLUDED TRAINING PERIOD (SESSHIN)

INTRODUCTION

I / *ENCOURAGEMENT TALKS AND COMMENTARIES*

PART THREE / DEVOTIONS

ILLUSTRATIONS /

FOREWORD / *ZEN: DAWN IN THE WEST*

is a companion volume to *The Three Pillars of Zen*. First published in 1965, *The Three Pillars of Zen* has sold some 150,000 copies in English. To date it has been translated into German, Spanish, and French, and is now being translated into Portuguese, Dutch, and Turkish. It is undoubtedly a classic of its kind and will continue to serve as a manual for Zen practitioners in years to come.

When it was published, *The Three Pillars* sounded a clarion call. From the middle sixties through the middle seventies, Roshi Kapleau crossed the length and breadth of America responding to invitations to talk to people in all walks of life. He spoke at colleges, universities, growth centers, and symposia; he appeared before human-potential groups, religious organizations, and encounter groups; he traveled to Canada, Mexico, Costa Rica, Germany, and even Poland. His presence—his down-to-earth approach, common sense, and humor—confirmed what had been promised in *The Three Pillars:* He was a Westerner fully and naturally at home with Zen. Furthermore, he showed through his actions and manner that he had penetrated deeply into Zen and had struggled through and resolved much that balked and frustrated those who were listening to him. The result was that first a steady trickle, then a stream, then a flood of people came to Rochester to study and practice with him at the Zen Center he had founded.

For many years Roshi Kapleau has conducted workshops and *sesshins,* has given talks, has counseled his Zen students, and has met with all kinds of people who have come to him for advice and guidance. From this experience he now draws to write *Zen: Dawn in the West.*

In 1966 the Center held its first sesshin; in 1968 a catastrophic fire broke out and burned all but the shell of the building of the Center. With skills learned on the job the members struggled for two years with themselves, with each other, and with obstinate material to renovate and resurrect the shell into a Zen temple. The Center has been enlarged considerably since then and many improvements have occurred. However, in spite of fires, construction projects, and constant changes, the basic work of Zen— *zazen,* sesshin, workshops, ceremonies, and devotional rituals— has been carried on. Many of the traditional ceremonies have been adapted and adjusted to meet the requirements of our time and culture, but Roshi Kapleau has tenaciously and unremittingly preserved the spirit of Zen as passed to him from his teachers Harada-roshi and Yasutani-roshi.

The demands that Roshi Kapleau makes upon those who work with him are as great as the demands made at Hosshin Monastery where he trained. He does not tolerate self-indulgence or self-pity, nor does he allow excuses or special pleading. He expects commitment and hard work. "If a student cannot equal or surpass his teacher," he says, "they have both failed."

Here is a Westerner, both enlightened and articulate, aware of the doubts, concerns, and hopes of contemporary, technologically oriented people. Such a combination of qualities is rare.

The reader should be aware of the true purpose of this book: Just as a sesshin is dedicated to the awakening of the participants, so a book written by an enlightened teacher has in the end one aim—the eventual awakening of the reader.

Albert Low, author of *Zen and Creative Management*

PREFACE / My first book, *The Three Pillars of Zen*, set forth the principles and methods of Zen Buddhism through the words of the Japanese Zen masters, both ancient and modern, and provided the reader with a map and compass charting every step on the journey to Self-realization. A familiarity with these teachings and practices, which incorporate elements of Indian and Chinese Zen as well, is, I believe, essential if one is to see in proper perspective the new Buddhism evolving in the West. At the same time it must be recognized that since the Buddhism of Japan and other Asian countries inevitably is blended with the cultures unique to their civilizations, the essence must be distilled from the cultural accretions. This is no simple task.

ZEN: DAWN IN THE WEST offers the old wine in new bottles. It reflects the impact of Zen on North and South Americans and Europeans—their intimate and varied reactions—within their own cultural milieu. It answers, in the Zen manner, their eager, probing questions and their outspoken doubts.

This book also enables the reader to participate vicariously in sesshin, the intensive training period in seclusion that is the heart of Zen discipline, and gives more than a hint of the wonder and joy of awakening, vividly described by a number of Western-ers who have had this unique experience.

Few books on Zen give adequate expression to the significance of devotions and rituals, which are indispensable ingredients of spiritual training. An attempt is made here to fill this lacuna, not didactically but through letters and dialogues which bring to focus the reservations of many beginners in these areas. To provide meaningful expression for such devotions, new English translations of key Zen texts, expressly adapted for chanting, are included.

It has been said that Zen is above morality but morality not below Zen. This paradoxical statement, together with Zen's sin-gular freedom from sentimentality and moral preachments, has given rise to the mistaken notion that Zen defies morality and ignores social responsibility. The truth, as the reader will dis-cover, is quite the contrary. Zen fosters moral, responsible behav-ior by quelling the flames of greed, anger, and deluded thinking that scorch the human mind, thus liberating the compassion and love within every heart.

The extensive literature on Zen in the English language not-withstanding, Zen Buddhism remains for many an inscrutable oriental religion. It is hoped that the Zen here presented, having been filtered through the experience of a Western teacher in his encounters with Western Zen students and enthusiasts, will speak directly to contemporary men and women in the West in the familiar accents of our time and culture.

The reader will note that in the rendering of foreign names, especially those of Chinese masters, inconsistency abounds. In Japan, Indian and Chinese Buddhist names have been given Japanese readings, a custom I could not justify adhering to in a book in English, even though Japanized names are relatively easy for Westerners to pronounce. But neither did it seem en-tirely fair to those readers familiar with Japanized foreign names (most Zen texts in English have been translated by Japanese writers) to leave all such names in their original transliteration, especially when Chinese names in particular pose a formidable pronunciation barrier to the average Western reader. As a compromise I have adopted the practice—likely to satisfy neither the Chinese nor the Japanese nor the Indian reader—of using a Japanized name when it seemed more familiar or manageable, and keeping the Chinese or Indian pronunciation in cases where it had gained familiarity.

Behind this book are the innumerable helping hands of *bodhisattvas* past and present, without whose inspiration and active support it would never have come into being. The following most readily come to mind:

My teachers, the memory of whose tireless efforts and countless benefactions has inspired this work throughout.

Bodhin, a Zen monk at the Rochester Zen Center, collaborated with me on every aspect of the book. Without his linguistic skill and dedication, my task of selecting, editing, and organizing the material that went into this volume would have been immeasurably more difficult.

Albert Low graciously consented to write the Foreword, read the manuscript several times, and offered many suggestions that made this a better book than it would otherwise have been.

Gail Graef, my secretary, tactfully prodded and cajoled, not allowing the work pace to slacken. Her mindful attention to detail, as well as her typing and other skills, were immensely helpful.

Tina Kjolhede gave freely of her time and editorial skills. With a sharp eye and painstaking care she pruned away much excessive verbiage that would have been a burden to the reader.

Toni Packer, a senior teacher at the Zen Center, read the manuscript with a critical eye and made many recommendations that greatly improved the quality of the book.

Richard Wehrman generously contributed his time and talent in designing the cover jacket, the carp drawing on the title page, and the three drawings in the "Devotions" section.

Rafe Martin, owner of the OxCart Bookshop, was a valued collaborator in the preparation of the section on recommended books.

Richard Clarke's translation of the popular *Affirming Faith in Mind* was helpful in the preparation of the final version.

Polly Papageorge uncomplainingly shouldered much of the typing load and prepared heavenly meals as well. Into her devoted and capable hands fell the task of meeting the many daily needs so essential to a supportive work atmosphere.

To all the aforementioned, as well as to the members of the Rochester Zen Center, who accepted my absences from the daily schedule with sympathetic forbearance, I express my heartfelt gratitude, hands palm to palm.

Rochester, New York   Philip Kapleau
April 8, 1978

ZEN: DAWN IN THE WEST

PART ONE / FLASHES OF ZEN

DIALOGUES / INTRODUCTION /

Zen has long been known as a "transmission outside the *sutras,* without reliance on words and letters." Ever since Shakyamuni Buddha held up a flower before the assembly of monks on Vulture Peak and Maha-kashyapa smiled back knowingly,[1] Zen has blossomed most fragrantly, not in words but in action. With this in mind the reader might at first wonder what role the following dialogues serve in conveying the spirit of Zen.

It would be a wonderful thing indeed if those who came to a Zen teacher brought with them the receptivity and understanding of Maha-kashyapa, but such is not the case, and so a teacher must resort to expedient means, stepping down to the level of verbal communication in order to reach the listener. Especially in our Western culture, where even the most rudimentary principles of Buddhism are still largely unknown—or misunderstood—the teacher is obliged to speak to beginners in a language they can understand. For a hesitant beginner, whose mind is a mass of questions, to respond unquestioningly to the command "Sit and you will understand!" requires too demanding a leap of faith in his True-nature. Like an elephant, which, it is said, will not walk over an unknown surface until it has first tested it to be sure it will bear its weight, the Zen newcomer needs to feel his way slowly, first satisfying his intellect that he is traveling in the right direction and then gaining the faith and confidence to go eventually he "knows not where by a road he knows not of."

Questions from the heart, not the head, are the lifeblood of a Zen teacher. But theoretical questions have their place too, restricted though it is, for more than anything else they reveal exactly where the questioner stands and how firmly he is rooted there. This knowledge is useful to the teacher.

The material for the dialogues that follow was drawn over the last twelve years from a variety of sources, but primarily from lectures given at colleges and universities and at spiritual and other types of growth centers. Another source was introductory workshops conducted regularly at the Zen Center in Rochester.

On campuses the format invariably included a Friday evening lecture open to the public; these talks were attended not only by students and professors but also by men and women of widely varying background from the surrounding area. There were always opportunities to ask questions, as there were in the full workshop that usually came the next day.

On the whole, the lectures and workshops held at auditoriums, libraries, and other public places, as well as those given on the private grounds of special groups, have drawn fewer serious-minded people than the workshops at the Center. One who has a casual interest in Zen, perhaps an intellectual curiosity, can with little effort attend a free Zen seminar given at his campus or in his hometown. Consequently, theoretical questions—for example, relating to Zen in comparison with other traditions—were more numerous in such a setting, particularly at talks before university students and teachers, than in the discussion periods at Rochester workshops.

The groups that gathered for workshops at the Rochester Zen Center were kaleidoscopic in their composition. A typical one would include a management consultant, dance instructor, truck driver, banker, cook, and psychiatric aide, as well as artists and musicians, housewives and mothers, writers, and performers, doctors, psychologists, students, and teachers. Most traveled from homes in the eastern half of the country, but several came from as far as Oregon, Nova Scotia, Mexico, Germany, and Switzerland. Ages also covered a wide range, from eighteen to eighty.

It is often said that the well does not go to the thirsty, the thristy go to the well. Although it seemed worthwhile in the past to accept invitations from various groups to conduct Zen workshops in other cities, most of my time is now spent with those who come to the Rochester Center. The men and women who over the past twelve years have expended the time, energy, and money to travel to Rochester from often distant points have come for various reasons: some out of mere curiosity, some to discuss, some to argue. But underneath there is always a gnawing dissatisfaction with their lives and a desire, however faint, to overcome this dis-ease.

Not all of the questions were raised by the audience and answered from the podium. Usually after the formal discussion period had ended, refreshments were served and a group of especially involved participants would gather around me. It was usually here and in the free-wheeling discussions that ensued that the most thoughtful questions would emerge, questions that for one reason or another participants had not wanted to ask before the audience.

None of the following dialogues should be confused with what takes place in *dokusan*, the student's face-to-face encounter with the roshi in private. Questions raised at workshops are in an altogether different sphere from those brought up in dokusan.

Workshop participants have no formal relationship with me as do those who are accepted for dokusan. Besides having had experience with any number of the current array of body-mind therapies and systems, those who attend workshops may still have an off-and-on tie to another spiritual tradition and even profess allegiance to someone they consider their teacher. The most notable common denominator among workshop participants is the absence of any firm commitment. They may quite fairly be called "seekers," as distinguished from the "practicers" who come before me for dokusan.

Recognizing the severe limitations in the receptivity and understanding of an audience at a lecture or workshop and their lack of familiarity with Zen and a Zen teacher's methods, I cannot in fairness to such an audience operate in a traditional Zen way.

A typical workshop question, if brought up in dokusan, would be answered with one or two words, perhaps a blow, or silence. A long verbal response to a complex question, however, is not contrary to Zen teaching, for the Buddha himself emphasized the need to adapt anwers to the comprehension of the questioner.

Some readers may be confused to find similar questions eliciting different replies in different dialogues. Yet there is a great deal to every question that lies behind its wording. In listening to a question a teacher must ascertain where the questioner stands, so to speak, so that he knows how best to direct his answer. Just as truth itself is not static but dynamically alive, so the "right" answer can never be fixed. For this reason, a reply that does not reflect the questioner's particular needs is a mere abstraction.

In most cases the dialogues were recorded from notes taken during the workshops by disciples who accompanied and assisted me. At some out-of-town workshops tapes were made and mailed to the Center. Finally, to avoid repetition some vital questions raised in workshops that were answered in the *The Three Pillars of Zen* have been excluded from these dialogues.

If the material in this section has the power to inspire in a unique way, it is perhaps because it is taken directly from the volleying of live questions and live answers—from the problems and doubts, the curiosities and challenges of businessmen, teachers, students, workers, and many others in our contemporary Western society.

THE DIALOGUES / 1 / WHERE DID ZEN ORIGINATE—IN INDIA, CHINA, OR JAPAN? / A group of students from the Asian Studies Department of the University of Rochester visited the Zen Center one day. After having been shown the meditation hall *(zendo)* and other facilities, they were invited to make comments.

JAPANESE STUDENT: Excuse me for my impoliteness, but I noticed in the meditation room that you had straw matting on the wall. This was strange for me. We Japanese never put straw matting on the wall. In Zen temples in Japan I never saw it used that way either. May I ask why you do that?

ROSHI: It serves our purpose by providing a neutral-colored, undistracting surface to the wall.

CHINESE STUDENT [to Japanese]: You seem to think that the correct Zen way is what the Japanese do. Don't forget that Ch'an, which you Japanese call Zen, came to Japan from China.

INDIAN STUDENT [to Chinese and Japanese]: Both of you seem to forget that the Buddha Shakyamuni was Indian, not Chinese or Japanese. Buddhism didn't begin in China or Japan—it began in India.

ROSHI: And the three of you need to be reminded that our American tradition is to use all traditions freely. Each of your countries has poured the waters of its own Buddhist culture into the ocean of Buddhism. These waters are now quenching the spiritual thirst of many Americans. The Buddha's Way is universal, transcending all cultures. The Buddha isn't found just in India or China or Japan but wherever men and women revere him and live according to his teachings.

BURMESE STUDENT: In that case Lord Buddha is mostly found in my country. We have about ninety thousand Buddhist monks in Burma and our people respect them very much. We worship Lord Buddha at pagodas and in our homes. We venerate him as the greatest saint who ever lived.

ROSHI [to Burmese]: Do you meditate?

BURMESE STUDENT: Well, no, sir, I have a very heavy schedule of courses at the university and can't find time for it. I wish I could.

ROSHI: The Buddha may be found in Burma, but *you* have yet to find him.

[to Chinese] What about you?

CHINESE STUDENT: I would like to meditate, but I have a small room and my roommate plays records day and night. He hardly ever studies. He drives me crazy. I wish *he* would meditate.

ROSHI: The Buddha is a stranger to you too.

[turns to Indian student]

INDIAN STUDENT: My family is Hindu, but we regard the teachings of Lord Buddha as no different from our own.

ROSHI: Isn't there meditation in Hinduism?

INDIAN STUDENT: Yes, sir, but I don't have time for it because I do hatha yoga.

ROSHI: Did Shakyamuni Buddha teach hatha yoga? [to Japanese] Do you do zazen?

JAPANESE STUDENT: No, sir, I don't know how. Please teach me.

ROSHI: You've had your first lesson!

2 / IF I SPEAK OF ZEN, IT WON'T BE ZEN I'M SPEAKING OF / (Appearance before a group of psychoanalysts)

INSTITUTE DIRECTOR [after some introductory remarks]: Roshi Kapleau will now tell us what Zen is.

[The students accompanying roshi place two mats with cushions on the floor. Roshi seats himself on one. One student prostrates before roshi, then seats himself on the other cushion, about a foot away.]

STUDENT: What is Zen?

[Roshi produces a ripe banana, peels it, and begins eating it.]

STUDENT: Is that all? Can't you show me anything else?

ROSHI: Come closer, please.

[Student moves closer. Roshi takes rest of banana and thrusts it into student's face. Student prostrates and leaves.]

SECOND STUDENT [addressing audience]: Do you all understand?

[No response]

You have just witnessed a first-rate demonstration of Zen. Are there any questions?

[A long silence]

QUESTIONER: Roshi, I am not satisfied with your demonstration. You have shown us something that I am not sure I understand. It must be possible to *tell* us what Zen is.

ROSHI: If you insist on words, Zen is an elephant copulating with a flea.

QUESTIONER: I understand that better. . . .

[Laughter]

SECOND QUESTIONER: How about a more detailed statement on Zen?

ROSHI: If I speak of Zen it won't be Zen I'm speaking of.

3 / WHY DO ZEN MASTERS ANSWER IN A SNOTTY TONE? /

QUESTIONER: Why is it that Zen masters don't bother to explain things to people who ask questions showing they are genuinely troubled? Instead the masters answer in what seems to be a flippant or outright snotty tone.

ROSHI: If you're hungry and I offer you only a menu, will that satisfy you?

QUESTIONER: Of course not. Why do you ask?

ROSHI: Every explanation, no matter how detailed and subtle, is looking from one small side at that which has infinite dimensions. There I go adding another head to the one you already have.

QUESTIONER: See, that's just what I mean about being nasty.

ROSHI [laughing]: You must be joking.

QUESTIONER: No, I'm serious.

ROSHI: A student once asked a master, "What is buddha?" To this he replied, "Who are you?" Would you call that a nasty answer?

QUESTIONER: I certainly would.

ROSHI: Suppose I tell you that the student came to awakening as a result of this exchange. Would you still find fault with the answer?

QUESTIONER: Yes. Not only the words themselves but also the tone in which you spoke them—which I presume reflects the master's tone—make it a nasty answer. The master could have gotten his point across in a nicer way had he wanted to be civil.

ROSHI [throwing up hands and laughing]: Zen is not for you, friend!

4 / IF AMERICANS SPEND THEIR TIME MEDITATING, ENERGETIC SOCIE-TIES WILL OUTPRODUCE AND EVEN "BURY" US /

QUESTIONER: During one of the breaks in this workshop I no-ticed some interesting decorations on the walkway connecting the main building with the Buddha Hall. I asked a Center mem-ber about them and he said that they were clouds and water. When I asked him their significance, he said that novices in Zen training are often called *unsui,* meaning "cloud-water," be-cause in Zen the aim is to produce a person who "drifts like clouds and flows like water."

That answer bothers me. I am a plant manager and I came to this workshop to find out whether Zen methods can help our workers become more alert and active. What will happen to our country if a philosophy of drifting like clouds takes over? What, for example, will happen to our food production, upon which so much of the world depends, and of other goods we make for ourselves and other countries? If Americans spend their time meditating instead of working, energetic societies like the Russian and the Chinese will outproduce and even "bury" us, as Khrushchev once threatened.

ROSHI: We're more likely to be "buried" by the Japanese than by the Russians or the Chinese. Japan today is the largest pro-ducer in Asia and, according to an article in *Time* [March 28, 1977], posted the second highest gross national product in the free world, behind only the United States.

In 1966, when I was leaving Japan after thirteen years of train-ing there, a farewell party was given me by a group of Japanese Zen friends. At one point a businessman, the owner of a large factory, came up to me and whispered confidentially, "Kapleau-*san,* if you go to Washington and see your President Johnson, tell him that we Japanese have a secret weapon that will enable us to outproduce the United States."

"Really? What is it?"

"Zen!"

This man's firm, like many Japanese corporations today, was regularly sending its employees into Zen monasteries.[2] The purpose is not only to develop in them greater self-discipline and awareness, but also to teach them that whether work is dreary or rewarding depends not on the work itself but on their mind state while doing it.

QUESTIONER: I still can't see a philosophy of "drifting like clouds" being of any use to a technologically oriented society like ours.

ROSHI: All right, let's talk about that a little further. Tell me, what do clouds do?

QUESTIONER: They just drift, but I don't believe people should be aimless drifters.

ROSHI: Clouds move freely—that is, no-mindedly—forming and reforming according to atmospheric conditions and their own nature. Water adapts itself to all circumstances, becoming round when put into a round vessel and square when put into a square one. But it always retains its identity. Temporarily it may turn into vapor or ice when obliged to by certain conditions, but always it returns to water, resuming its flow, for nothing can stop it from eventually reaching its source, the sea. "Water is yielding but all-conquering. It never attacks but always wins the last battle," to quote an ancient Chinese sage.

Clouds and water are symbolic of the perfected Zen man, whose life is characterized by freedom and spontaneity plus the resilience to adapt himself to changing circumstances. So he lives without strain or anxiety. That is why Zen trainees are called "cloud-water."

QUESTIONER: Maybe I'm dense, but I still don't see the connection between clouds and water and working productively.

ROSHI: Productivity requires energy, and energy flows most freely in the worker who is able to adapt easily to new obstacles and other changing conditions. If you are locked into rigid notions of how things *ought* to be, conflict is inevitable and the resulting frustration saps your energies and interferes with a wholehearted effort.

What measures are plant managers taking to make factory work more challenging, more spiritually rewarding for their workers?

QUESTIONER: Our firm has tried company-paid courses in TM and Silva Mind Control, but frankly, neither of these has helped much. Other large concerns have been subsidizing courses in psychology and other self-improvement subjects for their employees.

ROSHI: From the Zen standpoint these are only stopgap measures, because they deal with the leaves and branches and not with the root cause. They do no more than paper over the gulf separating the worker from his job. So long as managers do not adapt work to the human needs of their workers but insist that workers adjust to the demands of the machine, the laborer will not identify with his work; he will see it as no more than a means to earn money with which to buy more material things for himself and his family, and he will feel alienated. In other words, managers must make work more fulfilling for their workers by involving their workers' hearts and minds and not just their limbs. For their part, workers owe it to themselves to learn how to experience work as a means to personal salvation.

QUESTIONER: What do you mean by "salvation"?

ROSHI: Liberation from the bind of ego, from the deluded notion of a separate reality called "I." From the Zen viewpoint, then, work has a far deeper purpose than simply turning out a product or rendering a service useful to society. Rightly regarded, it is a vehicle for Self-realization. But if work is to serve that function, workers must train themselves not to evaluate their jobs as boring or enjoyable, for one can only make such judgments by "stepping back," thus separating himself from his work. They must also learn to relate to their jobs single-mindedly, with nothing held back—in other words, with no "thought gaps" between themselves and their work. Performed this way, work acts as a cleanser, flushing away random, irrelevant thoughts, which are as polluting to the mind as physical contaminants are to the body. Thus work becomes an expression of True-mind, creative and energizing. This is the true nobility of labor. To work this way is called in Zen working for oneself.

QUESTIONER: Working for yourself while working for the company—that should make everybody happy.

ROSHI: Amen!

5 / ZEN AND PSYCHOTHERAPY—ARE THEY COMPATIBLE? /

QUESTIONER: Is it advisable to do zazen while you are in psychotherapy?

ROSHI: Are you in therapy now?

QUESTIONER: Yes.

ROSHI: Are you doing zazen?

QUESTIONER: Very little. I've hesitated to do more because I'm not sure what effect it would have on my therapy.

ROSHI: Why don't you take this up with your therapist and be guided by what he says?

QUESTIONER: He told me he doesn't think much of meditation or zazen. I know he doesn't do it himself.

ROSHI: That's a pity. There are a number of psychologists and psychiatrists at our Center who have been doing zazen for many years, and even recommend it to their patients. Still, if you have confidence in your therapist and wish to continue with him, you ought to do what he tells you. Should you lose faith in him and still feel the need for further therapy, pick a therapist who has a broader background that includes, if not a practicing familiarity with Zen, then at least a recognition of its value.

SECOND QUESTIONER: Can a neurotic or psychotic person do zazen?

ROSHI: People who are highly nervous or seriously disturbed cannot do zazen. You don't appear to fall in either category.

SECOND QUESTIONER: I wasn't thinking of myself.

ROSHI: A mentally disturbed person who straightens himself out can benefit enormously from zazen, but he, even more than others, would need to work with a teacher.

SECOND QUESTIONER: Do you know anything about Morita Therapy? I understand it combines Western psychiatric methods with elements of Zen. Do we have anything like it in our country?

ROSHI: Morita, a Japanese psychiatrist told me, had studied traditional Western psychiatry and had had Zen training—how much is in question—so naturally he used both in treating patients. His therapy leans heavily on the strong Japanese family system and group-oriented culture.

While in Japan I knew two psychiatrists with training in both Morita Therapy and Zen. One was doing zazen under Yasutani-roshi, next to whose temple, in a small village, he had his clinic. Each of his patients lived with a family, partaking of the work and social activities of the family. This was part of the treatment. Patients who were only mildly disturbed did zazen in the roshi's temple, and one or two even attended sesshin.

In this country many psychiatrists, analysts, and psychologists are practicing Zen. Those who have been doing so for a long time often use Zen principles and methods in treating patients. Perhaps the closest thing to a system of psychotherapy utilizing elements of Zen is Eric Fromm's. Fromm evidently thinks highly of Zen. A Center member told me that at the 1965 *Pacem in Terris* Conference in Switzerland, sponsored by the Center for the Study of Democratic Institutions, he had a conversation with Fromm in which he asked Fromm whether mental health could be attained through Zen. "It's the only way to mental health," Fromm answered.

THIRD QUESTIONER: Where does Zen begin and psychotherapy leave off, or psychotherapy begin and Zen leave off?

ROSHI: When I asked a psychiatrist with long experience in Zen a similar question, he replied, "I feel that my job is to clear up the confusion and mental instability of my patients so that they can one day be ready for Zen."

Does that answer your question?

THIRD QUESTIONER: I guess so.

SECOND QUESTIONER: Roshi, what do you do when someone comes to your Center who is obviously neurotic or schizophrenic yet who wants to do zazen?

ROSHI: Persons mildly anxious or depressed who have a sincere wish to practice are allowed to stay. After all, in the profoundest sense, who isn't neurotic? Who until awakening doesn't view the world myopically from the dualistic standpoint of self-and-other? Seriously disturbed individuals, however, could become worse through zazen and disturb others doing zazen. For these reasons they are advised to see a psychotherapist in whom they have confidence.

6 / HOW DO THE PSYCHOPHYSICAL THERAPIES AND ZEN DIFFER? /

QUESTIONER: There are so many spiritual paths, disciplines, and therapies these days—it's very bewildering. How do you decide whether to go into Zen or Chinese or Tibetan Buddhism or Yoga or Sufism or Hare Krishna or the Divine Light Mission or the Unification Church or TM or est or scientology or Arica; or psychophysical therapies like Gestalt, rolfing, bioenergetics, biofeedback, psychoanalysis, transactional analysis, psychodrama, Silva Mind Control, psychosynthesis—

ROSHI: Stop, that's enough [laughing]!

First you must decide what it is you want and what you are prepared to work hard for. Ask yourself, "Will I be satisfied with anything short of full awakening even if it takes several lifetimes? Do I really yearn to know who I am, why I was born, why I must die, what the meaning of my life is? Or is my aim simply to tone up my body, improve my concentration, or learn to relax?"

SECOND QUESTIONER: I heard you tell someone during the break—I hope you don't mind my repeating it—that you didn't think much of the new body-mind disciplines that are springing up everywhere. Yet many of these therapies are now incorporating meditation, which is, after all, the basis of Zen. Can there be that much difference between types of meditation?

ROSHI: You misunderstood me. As a way to enlightenment I would not recommend those therapies or the atmosphere prevailing at many encounter groups. Enlightenment aside, these groups do have a worthwhile function when conducted not simply by someone who has "graduated" from a short course, but by one who with years of training in his field may justly be called a bonafide teacher. There can be many reasons, however, for practicing meditation. In the psychophysical therapies meditation is essentially a means to attain relaxation and to quiet random thoughts so that one functions more effectively on a psychophysical level. But when meditation is not fueled by the desire for religious awakening and is divorced from the teaching that no man is an island unto himself, it can easily degenerate into a self-satisfied numbness to the pain of others.

In his article entitled "The New Narcissism" [*Harpers*, October 1975] Peter Marin comes down heavily on the trend in therapy toward what he calls "the deification of the isolated self," and speaks of the "ways in which selfishness and moral blindness now assert themselves in the larger culture as enlightenment and psychic health. . . ."

My own experience conducting workshops at the invitation of encounter and therapy groups would tend to bear out Marin's contentions. After one particularly vexing weekend during which it was impossible to quiet the participants for zazen, it struck me that instead of socking egos I was massaging them by acquiescing in the atmosphere of fun and relaxation that prevailed among the participants. That this was the very tone the sponsors sought was dramatically brought home at the beginning of one workshop when an official of the sponsoring organization, a psychologist who had himself led encounter groups, asked, "Roshi, before you start, do you mind if I warm everyone up with a few simple techniques? It will only take a few minutes."

"Go right ahead," I replied.

First he asked that everyone pair off back to back. The men quickly tried to find the most attractive women, and vice versa. Then he announced, "Assume that each of you is being introduced to the person you are with and that for some reason you don't like them. Show your dislike with your backs and faces." Obligingly, they all wriggled their shoulders and contorted their faces into exaggerated frowns.

Then the leader said, "This time when you are introduced you enjoy meeting each other. Now act out the emotion of pleasure." At this all slowly rubbed their back against their partner's and smiled broadly. After some five minutes the leader called a halt, then turned to me. "Thank you, Roshi—I hope you don't mind this little introduction of mine."

With the participants now laughing and joking, the leader had created precisely the atmosphere I had hoped to avoid as a backdrop for the workshop.

Clearly, these men and women hadn't come to the workshop because of a burning desire to find out who they were or what their relation to their fellow beings was. They sought not spiritual awakening but self-glorification in a spiritually perfumed atmosphere, though of course they would not admit it to themselves. Having come, they could tell themselves with a certain satisfaction that they were in step with the new-age higher consciousness.

THIRD QUESTIONER: Socrates himself said, "Know thyself." Doesn't each person, then, have to focus on himself?

ROSHI: At an early stage in spiritual training a concern with self is valid. But this concern is no more than a night's lodging on the way to true Self-realization and not a long-term resting place, as it seemed to have become for them. Yet behind their clamorous activities was the longing, fundamental to every human being, for intimacy and sharing, for wholeness and Self-knowledge. Most had intimations of a world of freedom still out of their reach for want of a purer aspiration and a willingness to accept discipline. It was their attachment to material things and their clinging to the pleasures of the senses that barred acceptance of this necessary discipline. The inability to resolve this fundamental conflict between a deep longing for liberation and the desire for pleasure generated frustration and pain in them. Of course, they felt the dis-ease, but the source of the conflict creating it remained unacknowledged. It was easy to blame the ego, that black magician. But ego is an abstraction, while the body, its most visible manifestation, is concrete. So like the activists in the sixties who smashed physical objects, wanting in reality to destroy their oppressive sense of self-and-other but not yet spiritually oriented to know how, these seekers grappled with the body.

So one weekend it was hatha yoga, the next perhaps *tai chi* or rolfing or bioenergetics or Arica or est, or whatever. The body had to be stretched, twisted, jerked, jabbed, pounded. Still missing, though, was the faith that ego could be overcome in this manner. And there was no faith because there was no real desire to banish this openly despised but secretly cherished guardian deity. Nor was there the desire to hear, "True awakening and liberation from bondage to the ego-self demand self-sacrifice and a disciplined life." Whenever it was pointed out by me that serious involvement in Zen Buddhism demanded this kind of dedication and that Zen was, moreover, a religious tradition with rites and ceremonies and a compassionate concern for one's fellow creatures, invariably an embarrassed silence followed.

Not surprisingly, a number who came to my workshops claimed to have gained enlightenment at one of the encounter groups they had previously attended. Of those I tested not one had had genuine enlightenment. Obviously they were confusing expansion of consciousness with *kensho*.

FOURTH QUESTIONER: But Roshi, doesn't expansion of consciousness have value?

ROSHI: It does, but expansion of consciousness is a limited objective, for without awakening, such expansion is still within the bounds of ego; the dualism or fundamental neurosis of "myself and others" remains unaffected. Only genuine awakening can dissolve it.

FIFTH QUESTIONER: Will you elaborate on the difference between expansion of consciousness and enlightenment?

ROSHI: Enlightenment, or seeing into one's True-nature, is much more than an expansion of consciousness or a heightened awareness. True awakening takes place when both the conscious and subconscious minds—or the eight levels of consciousness, to use Buddhist terminology—have been "broken through" and the mind emptied of all fantasies, images, thought forms, and blissful feelings.

The difference between mind expansion and *satori* can be illustrated with a wristwatch. The watch face, with its numbers, hands, and movement, corresponds to relativity, our life in time and space, birth and death, cause and effect, *karma*. The reverse side of the watch, which is blank, corresponds to the changeless, undifferentiated aspect of our life. Of this absolute realm nothing can be posited. One whose understanding is on the level of the discriminating intellect is like a person who sees the face but is unaware of the back of the watch. Expansion of consciousness can be likened to enlarging the face; but no matter how much you enlarged it you would still be dealing with the face alone. Satori is like this [suddenly flipping over watch]. Now for the first time you realize that a watch actually consists of a face *plus* a back. In the same way, with awakening comes the understanding that relative mind and absolute mind are two aspects of our True-nature.

SIXTH QUESTIONER: Why is it so hard to understand Zen? Why are there so many interpretations of it?

ROSHI: Actually Zen is simple and down-to-earth: When hungry you just eat, when tired you just sleep, when working you just work. But without training you can't do that because your mind is like a motor that won't be turned off, and that "just" mocks you. Most people who write or talk about Zen lack the opened eye of Zen, so their words muddy what is naturally like a crystal-clear pond. Words and concepts are like magic tricks: Unless you've seen what lies behind them they can bewilder you. In fact, on the level of words it is easy to confuse enlightenment with megalomania or narcissism.

As an illustration, consider the following two quotations:

1. "He considered himself the universe's unique sentient center, the sole authentic incarnate will it contained or had ever contained. . . . 'I am, none else besides me.' "

2. "Throughout heaven and earth I am the most honored One!"

One of these is by the Buddha, the other pertains to Hitler. Can you distinguish them?

[A number of replies are called out.]

The first is a passage from Richard Hughes' *The Fox in the Attic* and refers to Hitler. In the second quotation the Buddha is speaking. How chillingly similar the words, yet how diametrically opposed the meanings!

Or consider this definition of narcissism, found in *Time* magazine [September 20, 1976]: "Total narcissim is generally taken to mean an inability to distinguish the self from the outside world, as an infant makes no distinction between himself, his mother, and a bottle of milk."

If the word "narcissism" were replaced with "enlightenment," that statement could *almost* be a description of the awakened mind. I say "almost" because the enlightened, while they do make distinctions, do not make them from the dualistic standpoint of self-and-other. A bird is a Bird is a BIRD. How many of you understand that?

A VOICE: It's as clear as mud!

ROSHI [laughing]: Words, words, words! Listen to Chuang-tzu: "Words exist for meaning, but once you understand the meaning you can throw away the words. But where can I find a man with whom I can converse without words?"

7 / IS IT WISE TO COMBINE HATHA YOGA OR TAI CHI OR KARATE WITH ZEN? /

QUESTIONER: Is it wise to combine hatha yoga or tai chi or karate with Zen?

ROSHI: Both hatha yoga and tai chi, provided you separate them from their philosophic aspects and do not devote more time to them than to Zen, go well with zazen and in fact strengthen it.

QUESTIONER: Do you do any of these, Roshi?

ROSHI: Yes, I do hatha yoga for about an hour daily.

QUESTIONER: What time of the day do you do it?

ROSHI: In the morning. First we have zazen, then chanting, and then yoga. It is an excellent way to start the day. My teachers, Harada-roshi and Yasutani-roshi, both did calisthenics for an hour every day until the age of about eighty-five.

SECOND QUESTIONER: I'm one of those guys who doesn't like any physical exercise outside of a walk now and then. But I do go to a chiropractor once a week for manipulations and occasionally have a thorough masage by a professional. These treatments make me feel as good as the exercise would. Do you see any conflict between these treatments and zazen?

ROSHI: No. If they make you feel better they will aid rather than hinder your zazen. You would be helping yourself more, though, if you disciplined yourself in hatha yoga or tai chi or jogging or swimming, or practiced some other sport, for then you would also be exercising your subjectivity, your autonomy as a free-acting human being. During a chiropractic treatment

or a massage you are being *acted upon*. You become a passive
object instead of an active subject. There is a world of difference
between the two.

8 / WHAT ARE UNWHOLESOME THOUGHTS? /

QUESTIONER: Earlier in the workshop you mentioned unwholesome thoughts. Would you give some examples of unwholesome
thoughts?

ROSHI: Notions of good and evil, daydreams, "I love this, I
hate that," angry or resentful thoughts, stubborn opinions, needless judgments, unnecessary evaluations and conclusions, pointless discriminations, covetous and jealous thoughts.

SECOND QUESTIONER: How is it possible to avoid making judgments and having opinions?

ROSHI: Note the word "needless." Teachers, parents, critics,
judges must make judgments—that's their job. But we are speaking of *gratuitous* evaluations that the ordinary person makes dozens of times a day and that parents unwittingly compel their
childen to make. For example, asking a child, "Which do you
like more, roses or daisies?" invites a response such as, "I like
roses better than daisies." Asking someone by the way of conversation, "What do you think of so-and-so?" solicits a judgment
and this separates the individual from the person or thing he
judges. Equally harmful are self-judgments, labeling one's own
actions "good" or "bad." This evaluating attitude is found in
the Bible itself, which tells us that after God created the world
he looked at it and called it "good."

SECOND QUESTIONER: I still don't see what is basically wrong
with judgments and opinions.

ROSHI: Once you form an opinion you're stuck with it. You
then feel compelled to defend it, becoming argumentative and
aggressive. "Opinion," said Voltaire, "has caused more trouble
on this earth than all the plagues and earthquakes."

9 / IS THERE A SPECIAL ZEN DIET? /

QUESTIONER: Is there a special Zen diet?

ROSHI: No, it would be a contradiction in terms. As soon as you postulate a Zen diet you enslave yourself to it. Zen teaches the freedom to accept or reject without compulsion or remorse. How then could there be a "Zen macrobiotic" or other Zen diet? It is one thing to say that it is easier to discipline oneself in Zen and come to awakening when your basic vitality is strong, and that a moderate diet of nutritious, unrefined, and unprocessed foods will help bring this about. It is quite another to insist upon a Zen diet.

It is surprising how few people are aware that even good food can be harmful when prepared and served by one who is anxious or fearful, or whose mind is dominated by anger or resentment. The chemical changes produced in the body by these impure vibrations have the power to "poison" food handled by such an individual, and to cause in sensitive persons who eat it such reactions as headaches, stomach upsets, and similar ailments. That is why in Zen monasteries only those advanced in their practice, whose minds are purest and most equable, are allowed to prepare and handle food. It goes without saying that one's own mind state when eating food also has an effect on its digestibility.

QUESTIONER: But if you're eating at a restaurant how can you know the mental state of the cooks?

ROSHI: You can't, and that's why one who is seriously involved in spiritual practice would do well to avoid the ordinary "greasy spoon" restaurant whenever possible.

QUESTIONER: What about restaurants run by religious groups?

ROSHI: When food is seen as an offering, as it ideally is in such places, it is prepared and served with love and dedication; it therefore becomes infused with these purer vibrations.

QUESTIONER: I noticed that the lunch you served today consisted of natural, vegetarian food. I would expect this at a Zen center, but what seems interesting is how many other people are into natural foods these days. Even our school cafeteria has put in a health-food bar. What is the significance of this trend?

ROSHI: The wish to purify the body really reflects a subconscious longing for Self-fulfillment. But many get bogged down in physical health and it becomes an end in itself. They become so enamored of food charts, of counting *yins* and *yangs*, and of exercising the body that they never go beyond a concern with the body to achieve true spiritual emancipation. In such people there is still no conscious awareness of their alientation from Self, no strongly felt ego pain to propel them into asking searching questions about the meaning of life and death. Awakening implies the *dropping* of body and mind.

THIRD QUESTIONER: Should one also avoid meat to be a good Buddhist?

ROSHI: There are far more fundamental requirements than the eating or not eating of meat. In any case, it's not a simple matter of should or should not. As one's practice deepens, subconscious fears and compulsive habits gradually fade and the body-mind acquires an increasingly keen sensitivity and subtlety, so that one naturally develops a preference for vegetarian food over coarse foods like meat.

There is much to be said for a simple diet. Most people overeat, and Seneca's observation that men do not die naturally but kill themselves with their knives and forks is as true today as it was in his time. No one who is troubled by indigestion, chronic constipation, and kindred ills resulting from eating too much or eating too-rich foods can carry on Zen practice effectively. Especially if one has a sedentary job, exercises little, and meditates long, to eat little is better than to eat much. A sparse diet helps zazen in yet another way by muting sexual desire and the fantasies that it spawns. In fact, during the deepest states of *samadhi* the body requires little or no food but seems to extract a different kind of nourishment from the atmosphere.

Until you reach this point, however, it is unwise to give up meat and fish and poultry all at once, for this abrupt withdrawal may bring about illness and put an end to zazen. Introduce any dietary changes gradually, giving the body's chemistry time to adjust to them.

The truth is that we are depleted more by our angry, lustful, and greedy thoughts than by insufficient quantities of protein or vitamins. Zazen by focusing and controlling the mind strengthens concentration and purifies the emotions, enabling one eventually to banish harmful, extraneous thoughts. The spiritually healthy person is one who has developed this capacity, has seen into the true nature of things, and is able creatively to adapt to his environment—that is, to respond freely and fully to changing circumstances without anxiety. Ultimately, behind all chronic illness lies spiritual dis-ease. The gnawing sense of unfulfillment sickens the body, and a sick body makes a perturbed mind sicker.

10 / READING ABOUT ENLIGHTENMENT IS LIKE SCRATCHING AN ITCHY FOOT THROUGH YOUR SHOE /

QUESTIONER: I'm probably sticking my neck out, but I have to ask this anyway. Often after reading about enlightenment I seem to understand quite clearly what it is, and many times I've definitely felt the oneness of all life. But what is the difference between this kind of understanding and Zen awakening?

ROSHI: Reading about enlightenment is like reading about nutrition when you're hungry. Will that fill your belly? Obviously not. Only when you taste, chew, and swallow the food do you feel satisfied, and this is comparable to enlightenment, or awakening. But even then the food you have eaten will not nourish you until digestion and assimilation have taken place. In the same way, until you have integrated into your daily life what you have perceived, your awakening is not working for you yet— it will not transform your life. And just as the final step in nutrition is elimination, so one must eventually rid himself of the notion "*I* am enlightened." Only then can you "walk freely between heaven and earth."

Now suppose your foot itches. Does it feel better to scratch your bare foot or to scratch the itch through your shoe?

QUESTIONER: To scratch your bare foot, naturally.

ROSHI: Reading about enlightenment is like scratching an itch through your shoe.

11 / TO READ OR NOT TO READ? /

QUESTIONER: There are two points concerning reading that puzzle me. You said that to come to awakening one needs to give up thinking in terms of self-and-other and to stop playing with concepts, and you implied that reading, which breeds concepts and random thoughts, should be abandoned. I've read that there were many scholarly Zen monks in ancient China and Japan, so they obviously must have done a lot of reading.

My second point is a personal one. I'm studying to be a psychiatrist and have no choice but to do much reading, not only in my own field but in related areas.

ROSHI: What is this reading "in related areas"?

QUESTIONER: For example, in order to understand the problems of people in different countries, it helps to be familiar with their ways of expression and thought patterns. That involves reading. But if reading is detrimental to my zazen and I abandon every kind of reading, including technical journals, how will I grow and be able to better help my patients?

ROSHI: What I said was that *indiscriminate* reading must be abandoned, not all reading. Students like you and certain professionals need to read and study; these activities should be considered part of your zazen. And regular sitting, by strengthening concentration and calming your mind and emotions, will better enable you to study as well as to retain what you learn. Many of our members are students, teachers, and professional people.

QUESTIONER: How do you define indiscriminate reading?

ROSHI: Indiscriminate reading is the intemperate reading of newspapers, magazines, novels, and similar matter not essential or related to your work or studies. Note the word "intemperate." Have you ever watched people in a bus station, an airport, or on a plane? More often than not, if they're by themselves, as soon as they are seated out comes the newspaper or magazine or book. Very few can meditate or just sit quietly. Reading consumes energy, whereas zazen conserves and focuses it. If in zazen you allow your center of gravity to settle in the area a hand's width below the navel, you establish a well of energy there that vitalizes your entire being. You can compare this process to that of a generator charging a battery.

My teacher used to tell his students that the less reading they did of books on philosophy or *about* Zen the more quickly they would awaken. Why so? Because he knew that this kind of reading especially clogs the mind with sticky concepts and notions. Harada-roshi, himself a former professor, once said that the Sixth Patriarch's unique experience of satori upon hearing the Diamond sutra recited by an itinerant monk [3] could be attributed in part to his illiteracy—that is, to the fact that his mind was free from the idle speculations fostered by extensive reading and study.

Novices in Zen monasteries are encouraged to read only the life stories of the masters and patriarchs, although they also memorize certain sutras for the purpose of chanting. Having access to a teacher, from whom they can directly hear the truth, they need not take it devitalized from the printed page. Zen emphasizes, "Hear the truth, believe it, practice it." *Hear* the truth, for the truth spoken by one who has experienced it vibrates with a power unmatched by the most eloquent written word.

Be aware that excessive reading of any kind, like massive doses of drugs, burdens the mind and blunts its capacity for creative thinking. Indiscriminate reading can also foster a greed for useless facts and a pride in their possession, qualities not conducive to spiritual progress. True wisdom, in the end, consists in the ability to read unwritten books. Nietzsche wrote that when his eyesight became so poor that he could no longer read books, he began at last to read himself.

Reading and zazen do not complement each other. Long stretches of reading, especially of facts and theories, tire the brain and enervate the body, paralyzing the desire for zazen. After zazen, on the other hand, your mind will feel so clean and alert that you won't want to cloud it with reading of any kind.

SECOND QUESTIONER: But I should think it would be inspiring to read the masters' sayings and also helpful to study the principles of Buddhism.

ROSHI: If you are working closely with a teacher, you can deduce the principles from zazen itself. The freer your mind of facts and theories, the purer it will be to receive the teaching and the faster your progress. After awakening, however, reading the sutras and the sayings of the masters can be very helpful. What has just been said applies to those with a spiritual teacher. If you haven't one, then for you the best kind of reading is that which strengthens faith and conviction. Don't fall into the habit of reading every new book on Zen or yoga, or whatever tradition you're interested in. With or without a teacher you need to discover the meditation mat and learn how to discipline yourself. And once you are convinced of the need for spiritual discipline and training, find a teacher and begin walking the Way.

THIRD QUESTIONER: What about reading novels for sheer pleasure?

ROSHI: It all depends how eager you are for awakening. If you're thirsting for Self-realization, you'll get up at 3 A.M., not to reach for a novel but to head for the sitting mat, and nothing will tear you loose from it.

FOURTH QUESTIONER: What sort of books are best to read when you want to live a spiritual life?

ROSHI: Emerson said, "That book is good which puts me in a working mood." If you want to realize your True-nature—and not merely speculate about it—that book is good which has the deep ring of truth discovered through personal experience. The good book stirs the heart, fires the imagination, and leads to the resolve to let nothing stand in the way of full awakening. In short, it gets you out of the armchair and onto the sitting mat.

FIFTH QUESTIONER: Are there any books that you specifically recommend?

ROSHI: I annotated a list of books that I myself have found inspiring and instructive. [See "Annotated Reading List."] A few excellent titles are omitted because they are no longer in print.

Do not think that you need to read each of these recommended books, or any of them. Even of those you do read, depending on your aspiration and spiritual development, a tip-of-the-tongue taste will suffice for some, others might be rolled over the tongue like a fine liqueur, and a few savored and swallowed with the relish of one who hasn't eaten in several days.

Each of these books, let me emphasize, carries a label: "Warning: May be habit-forming. Harmful if taken in large doses."

12 / WHAT IS REALLY REAL? /

QUESTIONER: If I understood you correctly, and I think you were quoting the Buddha, you said that nothing exists.

ROSHI: You didn't get that straight. I quoted the Buddha as saying that things neither exist nor nonexist. That is quite different from what you said.

QUESTIONER: All right, I stand corrected. But if things neither exist nor nonexist, what is real—what is really real?

ROSHI: Step up here, please.

[Questioner goes up to platform. Roshi leans over and whispers in his ear. Both laugh and shake hands.]

Only *that* is really real!

13 / HOW DO YOU FIND YOUR TEACHER? /

QUESTIONER: You said earlier in the workshop that it's not advisable to have more than one teacher. I read where an Indian guru on the West Coast said, "One can be committed to more than one spiritual teacher at a time. A bee takes honey from several flowers, and a person can learn medicine from one teacher and law from another. There's no conflict." Why don't you agree with him?

ROSHI: Are you committed to a teacher now?

QUESTIONER: No. I am a bee buzzing from flower to flower.

ROSHI: When will you start producing honey?

QUESTIONER: Soon I hope. I'm still gathering nectar wherever I can find it.

ROSHI: Don't forget that a bee produces honey only after it stops buzzing from flower to flower. And you don't get pure clover honey, for instance, from a bee that has also been into buckwheat or linden blossoms.

To get back to my earlier statement: What I said was, "It's all right to 'court' many teachers *before* asking for the helping hand of one, but once you commit yourself formally as a student you shouldn't cast sheep's eyes at other teachers." However, after having trained with one teacher and awakened under him, you can benefit from contact with other enlightened teachers.

QUESTIONER: What do you mean by "cast sheep's eyes"?

ROSHI: Don't cheat on him. Spiritual adultery is no better than the physical kind. If you chase after other teachers like a weather vane turning with every fresh wind, you will succeed only in confusing yourself, with no gain.

QUESTIONER: Does that mean one should unquestioningly submit to the teacher?

ROSHI: No. You must learn to think independently and to rely on your own intuitions and life experiences. Just before he passed away the Buddha told his disciples gathered around him, some of whom were weeping at the thought of losing their beloved master: "Be ye lamps unto yourselves . . . seek salvation alone in the *dharma*. Look not for assistance to anyone besides yourselves."

In Zen, the roshi's aim, apart from bringing a student to enlightenment, is to preserve the student from his influence. He doesn't wish to control the student's life but only to make him strong enough to be master of his life instead of its slave. In certain other spiritual traditions, as you know, the guru virtually rules his students' lives, even to the extent of telling them whether to marry and have children. His word is law. If his spirituality is deep, there is little danger. If it is not, God help the student!

Shun any teacher who says, "I am enlightened." Beware of any guru who claims to be an avatar, an incarnation of a god or buddha. Above all, avoid the "master" who allows his followers to shout his praises with arms upraised at mass rallies, and to laud him as the holiest of holies. He is the greatest menace.

How does a genuine master react to praise? When the Buddha's attendant Ananda told him one time, "Methinks that in the past there has never been a master as great as the World-honored One, nor will there be one as great in the future," the Buddha replied, "Have you known all the buddhas of the past?"

"No, World-honored One."

"Well, have you the power to know all the buddhas of the future?"

"No, World-honored One."

"Then surely, Ananda, you thoroughly know the Tathagata's mind?"

"No, World-honored One, not even that."

"How, then," asked the Buddha, "can you speak so boldly?"

SECOND QUESTIONER: Does a roshi get a certificate, something like an academic degree, certifying that he can teach?

ROSHI: There is a calligraphic acknowledgment that a master gives his student when he sanctions his enlightenment, but that can hardly be called a teaching certificate, because real Zen training begins after enlightenment. Students who complete work on all the koans prescribed by their teacher receive what is called *inka*, but inka in itself does not make one a qualified teacher any more than graduation from medical school makes one a full-fledged doctor. In Zen, as in other Asian traditions, a disciple is ready to teach when his teacher says he is. This naturally places a great deal of responsibility in the hands of the master. If he is wise, with high standards, his seal of approval is the public's safeguard. If he is mediocre, inka or not, his disciple will leave much to be desired.

SECOND QUESTIONER: That's confusing. Isn't a roshi by definition a master and therefore wise?

ROSHI: There's a good deal of misunderstanding about the meaning of the terms "roshi" and "master." The literal translation of roshi is "venerable teacher"—that is, one who commands respect and reverence by reason of age or great dignity. The abbot of a monastery, the chief priest of a temple, or a lay teacher beyond the age of, say, fifty could be addressed as roshi and the title would simply imply deep respect. In Japan "roshi" is an honorific used for the most part by a teacher's own disciples and followers; it is not a title signifying completion of a prescribed course of study or in recognition of high spiritual accomplishments.

The title "master" conveys something quite different. A Zen master is a person of deep spiritual insight and wisdom who has experienced the emptiness and impermanence of all things, and whose lifestyle reflects such awareness. In his book *Points to Watch in Buddhist Training*, written in 1235, Zen master Dogen defined a master as one who is fully enlightened, who lives by what he knows to be the truth, and who has received the transmission from his own teacher. By these criteria only a few roshis anywhere can be considered masters. The terms, though, are often used interchangeably.

THIRD QUESTIONER: Whether a roshi is a master or not, certainly he is wise enough to know whether a student is capable of teaching, isn't he?

ROSHI: You would think so, wouldn't you?

THIRD QUESTIONER: Then why would he allow a student to teach prematurely?

ROSHI: Roshis have human failings—although certainly far fewer than the average person—and they can make errors in judgment.

FOURTH QUESTIONER: But doesn't enlightenment clear away imperfections and personality flaws?

ROSHI: No, it shows them up! Before awakening one can easily ignore or rationalize his shortcomings, but after enlightenment this is no longer possible; one's failings are painfully evident. Yet at the same time a strong determination develops to rid oneself of them. Even opening the Mind's eye fully does not at one fell swoop purify the emotions. Continuous training after enlightenment is required to purify the emotions so that our behavior accords with our understanding. This vital point must be clearly understood.

In the West a roshi is expected to be buddha-like, his conduct flawless. In one sense this is a compliment to Zen training. But this idealistic view can blind one to the merits of a teacher. In Japan I knew a roshi who drank heavily, although he was seldom drunk. He had many followers who respected him highly. I asked one of them, a doctor, "Doesn't it ever bother you that your roshi drinks so much?"

"No—why should it? He is a wise and compassionate man in spite of his drinking."

"But isn't he addicted to alcohol?"

"No, he can either take it or leave it; he prefers to take it."

I mentioned this incident to a few of my disciples. Several of them asked in surprise, "How could any roshi reconcile heavy drinking with the fifth precept, 'not to take liquor that confuses the mind'? We could understand his taking a drink now and then but not drinking constantly. What kind of example is he to his students?"

Asians are more tolerant in such matters than Westerners, so they do not categorically reject a teacher whom they discover to be less than buddha-like, for they know that a man may be a fine teacher and yet not have purged himself of all defilements. A Japanese long experenced in Zen once told me, "My roshi does have character flaws, yet of the teachers [4] I have had he is the only one who has taught me real Zen and I am exceedingly grateful to him. But, alas, his karmic load is heavy."

THIRD QUESTIONER: I once heard a guru say, "The real teacher is your own heart."

ROSHI: That itself is teaching, isn't it?

THIRD QUESTIONER: All the same, what can a roshi give you?

ROSHI: He can't give you anything you don't already have, but he can take away much that is foreign to your True-nature: the sticky beliefs, chesty opinions, petty rationalizations, illusory ideals, and deluded thoughts, all of which imprison you as in a cocoon. And when your mind is ripe the roshi can, through words or actions, nudge that mind into awakening. At that point he's like a hen that pecks on the shell of the egg when the chick is ready to hatch.

A roshi gives you himself, which is a great deal and at the same time nothing. An outstanding Zen monk once said, "Empty-handed I went to my teacher and empty-handed I returned."

When another was asked by a master, "What have you brought with you?" he replied, "That which had never been lost even before I went to my old teacher."

"If that is the case, why did you go to him at all?"

"If I had not gone to him, how could I realize that it had never been lost?"

So you need a teacher to learn that there is nothing to learn. And why is there nothing to learn? Because it was all learned

aeons and aeons ago. Nonetheless a roshi is essential. Even the
Buddha had teachers. A fully developed roshi personifies openness, compassion, and wisdom, qualities you hope to actualize
in yourself. Remember, too, he has struggled through the pain,
frustration, and despair you feel. In your moments of brooding
doubt, when you are enveloped in darkness and feel hopeless
about your practice, the roshi can give you an infusion of courage
and turn you once more in the direction of the sun.

Another of his vital roles is to test you when you think you
have come to awakening. Zen masters have devised a thorough
testing procedure, for nothing can be more harmful than to
think you have awakened when you have merely experienced
ecstasy, visions, trances, or hallucinations, which in Zen are called
makyo, experiences short of true awakening. And even when the
enlightenment is genuine a teacher is necessary to dispel the
subtle pride that arises, the feeling, "I have become enlightened." The roshi's testing is also a means of measuring the
depth of realization, for there is shallow awakening (kensho)
and deep (satori).

THIRD QUESTIONER: How does a serious seeker distinguish a
genuine teacher from a charlatan?

ROSHI: During the period I was living in ashrams and meditation centers in Southeast Asia I heard it said that no matter
what superior qualities a guru may possess, if he is obviously
seeking name and fame, is after money, or is carrying on with
his female students, these impurities will corrupt his teaching;
a prospective student would therefore do well to avoid him.

FOURTH QUESTIONER: Suppose a roshi has none of these failings. If you are a beginner, how can you be sure he is enlightened
and spiritually developed?

ROSHI: Unless you've had long spiritual training yourself, you
can't be certain. The only thing you can be sure of is whether
you have a rapport with him or her. That's important, but by
itself not enough to go on, because while you may feel comfortable with someone posing as a teacher, that person may actually
have had little or no training. You may have to rely on the
advice of knowledgeable friends.

What a wit once observed about marriage applies equally to
the master-disciple relationship: Before entering into it keep

both eyes open—afterward only one. But even with both eyes open you can't expect perfection from a teacher.

THIRD QUESTIONER: What exactly does "keep both eyes open" mean in this context?

ROSHI: That you shouldn't hesitate to ask a teacher who his teacher was and how long he trained under him. Read his books if he has written any. If you like what he has written and what you sense between the lines, arrange to meet him. Ask him questions, intuit his spirit, savor his silences.

THIRD QUESTIONER: Let's say that a roshi I'm interested in is enlightened. How can I be sure he is the teacher for *me?*

ROSHI: A roshi may be deeply enlightened, with many followers, and yet be the wrong teacher for you. Why? Because he fails to arouse in you feelings of confidence and devotion so that you can willingly bow down before him and, childlike, receive his teaching. You must be able to say with conviction, "He is the teacher for me—the one I've been searching for!" And yet it is also true that the moment you spontaneously cry out, "Oh help me! I need help!" you open yourself to the teacher right for you.

FIRST QUESTIONER: To go back to the guru's statement that you can learn medicine from one teacher and law from another—why isn't that true?

ROSHI: You are talking about law and medicine, not spiritual training. The relationship between a master and a disciple, in any tradition, is different from that between an academic teacher and his student.

FIRST QUESTIONER: What is the difference?

ROSHI: In this discussion I have been using the terms "student," "disciple," "teacher," and "master" loosely. Properly, a student is associated with a teacher, a disciple with a master. In the ideal teacher-student relationship the student respects the teacher as the possessor of a certain body of knowledge or of a skill that he would like to acquire, while the teacher values the student for his eagerness and ability to absorb the knowledge he is trying to impart to him. Their relationship is largely impersonal and limited; what sustains it is their common interest in this study. The master-disciple relationship, on the other hand, is personal and deep because grounded in a karmic affinity. What moves the disciple in the direction of the master is not the latter's knowledge, not even his wisdom, but his character and personality, for the disciple senses that it is through these that he will be able to complete himself.

In our center we have three categories of affiliation: member, personal student, and disciple. Each of these relationships has responsibilities and privileges different from those of the other two.

FOURTH QUESTIONER: What responsibilities does a personal student have?

ROSHI: His primary responsibility is to be faithful to his teacher, which is nothing more than being true to his own deepest feelings, and not to go around playing footsie with other roshis or gurus or *lamas*. In making a formal commitment you are promising yourself as well as your teacher to make a sincere, all-out effort under his guidance.

FIRST QUESTIONER: Why isn't a student twice as well off with two teachers?

ROSHI: Actually he's worse off. Sooner or later he's bound to become confused, with the result that he will either neglect both teachers or drop them. The student who tries to serve two masters fails both. And he is the loser, for neither one will treat him as a serious aspirant. Lukewarm students invite a lukewarm response from a teacher.

Even within the same tradition teachers have different methods, depending on the training they themselves have received, their personalities, and the depth of their awakening. The first may tell you one thing and the other say what seems to be the opposite. They are not contradicting each other; if they are both spiritually developed, each of their instructions is valid. But for the novice the seeming contradiction may pose problems of such an imposing nature that they discourage him and sap his energies.

Differences between traditions may seem even more contradictory. Let's say you are the student of a Zen master and at the same time have a swami as a teacher. Your guru might tell you, for example, "Don't give yourself to the phenomenal world: it is *maya*, unreal. Only *brahma* is real." But your Zen teacher might say, "Involve yourself in the world of form so completely that you transcend it." An enlightened person would have no trouble understanding both statements and reconciling them. For a beginner, though, the confusion can be ruinous—like a chameleon trying to make good on a scotch plaid.

14 / THERE ARE NO TEACHERS OF ZEN /

QUESTIONER: This is not meant to be a rude question, but would you tell us the qualifications of a Zen master or teacher?

ROSHI: I am not a Zen master, much less a teacher, so I don't know.

QUESTIONER: What are you doing now if not teaching?

ROSHI: Can one really teach anybody anything? It is rank conceit to think so.

QUESTIONER: You seem to be doing a pretty good job of it.

ROSHI: In the book of koans called *The Gateless Barrier (Mumonkan)* [5] there is a verse that reads, "Without raising a foot we are there already; the tongue has not moved, but the teaching is finished."

Get it?

QUESTIONER: No. What does it mean?

ROSHI: If there is nothing outside us, where is there to go and what is there to know?

QUESTIONER: But don't you have students at your center in Rochester whom you teach?

ROSHI: I merely share with them what I do seriously for myself.

QUESTIONER: What about your own teachers? In *The Three Pillars of Zen* you say you had three Zen masters as your teachers. Didn't they teach you anything? You stayed with them, I think, for thirteen years. You must have felt you were learning something to stay that long.

ROSHI: If I learned anything from them it was that there is nothing to learn. So I didn't learn, I unlearned. I didn't gain, I lost—a lot of mental confusion and false notions.

QUESTIONER: I still don't understand why you say you are not a teacher.

ROSHI: This story may help you understand. A famous Zen master, once said to his students, "If I went around from temple to temple on useless pilgrimages the way you do, where would I be today? Don't you know that in all of China there are no teachers skilled in Zen?"

A monk asked, "How can you say there are no teachers of Zen when there are thousands of monks in countless temples?"

"I don't say there is no Zen, only that there are no teachers of Zen."

QUESTIONER: Is that a koan?

ROSHI: Yes, *yours!*

15 / TRANSCENDENTAL MEDITATION: WHO TRANSCENDS WHAT? /

QUESTIONER: What do you think of TM [Transcendental Meditation]?

ROSHI: Do you do TM yourself?

QUESTIONER: I've been considering it.

ROSHI: It's all right as far as it goes—it just doesn't go very far.

QUESTIONER: Is it possible to come to enlightenment through TM?

[Roshi smiles.]

SECOND QUESTIONER: I read in *Science* magazine [January 1976] that a group of psychologists from the University of Washington in Seattle did an experiment with five TM meditators, four of whom were teachers of TM, and found that during half their meditation time they were sleeping and not meditating.

THIRD QUESTIONER (to second questioner): Is any single experiment conclusive? Other studies have shown the value of TM. Anyway, if you fall asleep while meditating, that's because your body needs sleep.

ROSHI: That's absolutely so. But why does it need sleep?

THIRD QUESTIONER: Because you're tired.

ROSHI: And why do you become tired and sleepy? Usually because your eyes are closed and you are not sitting in a stable, erect posture, not breathing properly, and not using your mind correctly. Done the right way, meditation is rejuvenating, not exhausting. Your mind becomes razor-sharp, with a heightened sense of awareness. A slouching, limp body induces a dull, sleepy mind.

Tell me, how long have you been doing TM?

THIRD QUESTIONER: About a year.

ROSHI: Then you ought to be able to' answer this question: In Transcendental Meditation who transcends what?

[No answer]

16 / BIOFEEDBACK MACHINES: ELECTRIC ZEN? /

QUESTIONER: Are you familiar with biofeedback machines? I've heard them called "electric Zen." How do they work?

ROSHI: The idea of biofeedback, according to its sponsors, is to teach a person to become aware of his or her own brain-wave patterns by observing them on a chart or hearing them translated into sound, and in this way learn to elicit at will alpha brain rhythms, which are said to be relaxing and calming. But what is so special about alpha waves? A Center member who builds alpha machines tried one on himself during zazen as an experiment and found that ten minutes after beginning he was already registering steady alpha waves on the machine. He later said that on that occasion he actually felt less concentrated than usual in his zazen.

QUESTIONER: During the break I was talking with one of your students about biofeedback machines. He mentioned that you had had an interesting experience with one. Would you mind telling us about it?

ROSHI [hesitating]: Well, it was quite some time ago.

QUESTIONER: Couldn't we hear it anyway?

ROSHI: All right. It happened at a national convention of the Humanistic Psychology Association in Florida, to which I had been invited to hold a workshop on Zen. One of my students, a clinical psychologist, said he had a close friend, an engineer, who would very much like me to test a biofeedback machine of his design that had just been put on the market. So we went to a private room, where there were some ten or fifteen persons waiting to view the test. The device was small enough to fit into your hand and sold, I think, for two-hundred dollars.

They strapped a leather band, mounted with electrodes, around my head and plugged me in. Then earphones were added. Soon I could hear "beep, beep," first in spurts, then in a steady flow. I must have gotten into a samadhi-like state, for the next thing I remember hearing was a voice exclaim, "Why, he's gone off the machine! It's never happened before!" After unplugging me the engineer and his assistant, looking glum, remarked, "Back to the drawing boards!"

I hesitated to recount this incident because it sounds boastful, but what happened to me was not remarkable—it could happen to any experienced meditator, and actually did to one other person tested with me.

QUESTIONER: Did you feel relaxed?

ROSHI: Certainly, but who wouldn't after sitting quietly for twenty or thirty minutes? You can achieve relaxation, and far more, with zazen—without spending two hundred dollars for a mechanical toy. Toys are for children, not for adults!

SECOND QUESTIONER: I read somewhere that brain-wave feedback will bring the same results after just a few weeks or months that requires years of effort in Zen.

ROSHI [laughing]: You must be kidding! To claim that spiritual awakening and a transformation of personality can be accomplished at all—let alone more quickly—simply by hooking up to a machine is ridiculously naïve. Even if one is able while "plugged in" to ease into a relaxed state, this hardly brings deep calm or lasting peace of mind; it does not answer fundamental questions of existence; it does not transform one's life in any real way, all of which Zen awakening does.

A psychologist at the same convention demonstrated a large biofeedback machine that was intended for use with hospitalized or bedridden patients to help reduce high blood pressure and cure other ailments. That seemed a valid use of a biofeedback machine.

An article someone sent me on biofeedback machines quotes

Dr. Frederick Gibbs, of the University of Illinois Medical School, as saying that the "high" derived from alpha feedback machines is "cerebral masturbation"—an apt description. One who regularly plugs into a machine to relax loses the ability to act out of his own deepest resources and instead of being master of the machine becomes its slave. This is not Zen. Zen develops freedom, not a neurotic dependence.

17 / CAN I PRACTICE ZEN AND BE A GOOD JEW (OR CATHOLIC)? /

QUESTIONER: I am a Jew and proud of it. Can I practice Zen and be a good Jew at the same time?

ROSHI: What were you before you were a Jew?

QUESTIONER: I don't know.

ROSHI: Find out! Then your Jewishness won't be uppermost in your mind.

QUESTIONER: How do I find out?

ROSHI: Question yourself day and night with the yearning to know and the conviction that you can know. Learn to live the way a fish swims or a bird flies—unself-consciously. Let go of ambition—it leads to aggression. Be aware and responsive. In whatever your right hand finds to do involve also your left. Avoid unnecessary judgments. Be modest and unassuming; offer your opinion only when it is asked for. Forget your good deeds and confess your bad ones. And never fail to relate every effect to the cause that produced it.

QUESTIONER: Can't I do all that as a practicing Jew?

ROSHI: If you can, fine. If not . . .

QUESTIONER: Can I practice Zen and be a good Catholic?

ROSHI: If you practice Zen you can, but if you practice Zen Buddhism you can't.

QUESTIONER: Why not?

ROSHI: To practice Zen Buddhism means to transcend your self, and to transcend your self means to forget your self. When that happens, you are neither a good Catholic nor a good Zen Buddhist.

QUESTIONER: What am I then?
ROSHI: Yes, what are you then?

18 / WHAT IS THE VALUE OF A "HOLY" MOUNTAIN FOR ZAZEN? /

QUESTIONER: I plan to take off three months to meditate by myself and am wondering what kind of place is best to go to. I have read that Zen monks used to go to the mountains, but I know people who say the vibes are good in the desert or by the sea. What is your opinion?

ROSHI: In the beginning any quiet place, outdoors or in, where the vibrations help you to focus inward is best for zazen; this certainly would include the mountains and the desert. But it is well not to stay too long in such an "ideal" environment, for without difficulties to struggle with one builds up a false strength, a seeming calm and steadfastness that crumble in the face of the demands of life. Just as in track hurdlers are said to develop greater all-around strength than sprinters, in the same way one who has learned to concentrate and unify the mind in the midst of clamor and activity has far greater stability and resilience than one who has spent years alone in the mountains or desert or elsewhere.

In my experience, there was little solitude or "peace and quiet" at monasteries and meditation centers where the training was rigorous. Only in romantic novels about the East, or in their movie counterparts, are monasteries set in lush valleys aglow with heavenly peace, the white-bearded sage with flowing robes, his staff in hand, gently saying, "My sons . . ." to the sweet-faced disciples gathered round him while gems of wisdom tumble from his lips and a magnificent sun sinks into the horizon behind him. The reality, believe me, is far less romantic.

How well I remember my six-week stay in a Buddhist monastery in Rangoon in the late fifties. My arrival coincided with a drive by the recently installed military government to rid Rangoon of its large canine population. Under the Buddhist Prime Minister U Nu the animals had not been molested, but with the ascendancy of the Army they were being rounded up and shot.

The Buddhist Center comprised some five hundred acres and a number of individual meditation houses. In these units *bhikshus* and *bhikshuni* (that is, celibate Buddhist monks and nuns) as well as laymen meditated, ate, and slept. With an instinct for survival the dogs fled to the monasteries for sanctuary, and each of these houses found itself with a complement of ten or fifteen dogs, headed by a leader and with a definite hierarchy. After meals the dogs lined up according to rank and were fed the leftovers. There was the usual jockeying for position among the hungry dogs, and periodically the leader had to fight off atempts by younger dogs to oust him. Occasionally dogs from one house tried to muscle into the chow line of another house and were snarlingly repulsed. At times the howling-yapping-snarling was fierce. An Englishman recently arrived from London complained bitterly, "I came here expecting to find the quiet that was impossible in London, but look what I came to! How could *anyone* meditate in the middle of this bloody racket?"

The Japanese monasteries were not free of outside distractions either. One in which I had spent three years before going to Rangoon had a strikingly similar animal problem. Villagers surreptitiously brought unwanted puppies and kittens to the monastery at night, releasing them underneath the monastery building in the hope that the monks would somehow be able to provide for them. These animals grew up semiwild in the open space between the earth and the floor of the building. The monks would leave food for them, but only at night did the animals come out to eat or prowl. Then with the approach of daylight they would slink back to the den where they slept, played, and fought. Invariably during the early-morning sitting and evening zazen the animal cave, as the monks called it, erupted into a cacophony of yelps, yaps, howls, growls, barks, snarls, whines, meows, and hisses that could be clearly heard in the zendo. With a strengthening of concentration, after two or three months of zazen, this jam session, surprisingly, often acted as a spur instead of a hindrance, for the strong effort to transcend the disturbance unlocked energies not usually available. When one succeeded in focusing on his practice, the clamor, through some mysterious alchemy, became a harmonious chord.

There were other intrusive sounds. At daybreak three times a week railroad cars loaded with cattle for slaughter would stop for half an hour in the yard of a nearby railroad station. These animals, sensing they were going to be slaughtered, rent the air with pitiful wailing, which could plainly be heard in the monastery zendo. Learning to cope with this distraction proved to be excellent training.

QUESTIONER: You said that it is unwise to remain for long in the mountains, but didn't the old Zen masters in China and Japan live and do zazen in the mountains for many years?

ROSHI: That is true, but few continued to live as hermits or ascetics. After leading a solitary life for a time, most joined a monastic community on the mountain. Some communities had hundreds of monks. In Dharmsala in the hills of northern India today you will find communities of Tibetan monks and lay people that are probably similar to those in ancient China.

Since ancient times Zen monks and lay people have favored the mountains over the desert or the sea. But you should be aware that there are ordinary mountains and there are holy mountains.

QUESTIONER: What do you mean "holy mountains"?

ROSHI: Mountains that come to be known as holy are centers of cosmic energies, forces with the power to evoke awe and reverence. More than that, the energy of these mountains turns one inward and activates the subtlest vibrations within oneself. To respond fully to this high energy requires openness and a purified body-mind. Spiritually oriented persons come to a holy or sacred mountain with what might be called a measure of grace—that is, purity—and are uplifted by the invisible forces of the mountain and their own reverence and awe. Through religious rites and ceremonies the self is transcended and the gap between devotee and mountain disappears. Then the mountain is no longer a mountain, it is a two-legged individual looking remarkably like oneself yet so much grander!

One holy mountain I have experienced is in Mexico. At first encounter this mountain seemed to be a city of temples built into rock. That sight was so moving that I found myself crying in a kind of dazed joy. Unlike the Alps and the Rockies, which are towering and remote in their majesty, this mountain is more man-sized, drawing one toward it with its very accessibility and intimacy. One had the same feeling about Arunachala, Sri Ramana Maharshi's holy mountain in India.

With two of my senior students I did zazen in a large cave in the bowels of this Mexican holy mountain. It was obvious that extensive religious ceremonies had been held there, for the vibrations of such rites could still be felt. Later we learned that in ancient times Mayans, Toltecs, and Aztecs had come long distances to participate in these rituals.

SECOND QUESTIONER: What social value is there in going off to meditate on a mountain or in a desert?

ROSHI: In the case of a spiritually developed person the social value is great. Ask yourself why a Zen master, who is nothing if not compassionate, would isolate himself on a mountain unless he knew that by so doing he could aid many people. In the Zen tradition, as you've heard, masters and other enlightened individuals have gone to live in solitude because then, unburdened by the demands of the world, they could spend long hours in zazen, chanting the sutras, and engaging in other devotions. In effect they become powerful broadcasting stations, transmitting the buddha truth to the minds of people everywhere, not unlike a radio or TV transmitter.

SECOND QUESTIONER: For TV or radio reception you need a receiving set tuned to a broadcast. How can people "tune in" when they are not even aware that someone is beaming mental vibrations at them?

ROSHI: They are already "tuned in" whether they know it or not, for they are all part of one Mind. In the Buddhist view, individual consciousness is a "knowing" energy force, the sum total of a constantly changing series of sense impressions, perceptions, thoughts, tendencies, and memories, all of which are fundamentally empty. As a changing aspect of Mind, consciousness is coextensive with similar and higher energy forces—for instance, buddhic—with which it constantly interacts on individual and cosmic levels, conscious as well as subconscious. But human beings, misled by their bifurcating intellects, lose awareness of this basic communion. Out of this estrangement grows the unconscious longing for reconciliation, a longing that is nourished by the solitary devotions of the masters, who with their disciplined, purified, and awakened minds can freely absorb high energies and transmit them to other minds. Fundamentally the communion is never lost, and because of this the "signal" gets through and eventually effects a turnabout in the deepest seat of consciousness. That all of this occurs on an unconscious level doesn't make it any the less real.

THIRD QUESTIONER: Is there any scientific proof that what you have just told us does actually happen?

ROSHI: Why when we can transmit an electromagnetic impulse thousands of miles through space to alter the course of a space-craft—a feat that should be no more awe-inspiring than the mind that made it possible—is what you have just heard impossible to accept without scientific proof? Don't you know that psychokinesis, the ability to move or distort physical objects by mind processes alone, or to influence another's mind from a remote point, is a well-established phenomenon in parapsychology?

SECOND QUESTIONER: Could you tell us the techniques by which these masters transmit their own vibrations and the energies of the mountain?

ROSHI: There are no techniques but there are different modes of zazen to accomplish different ends. If the aim is to help people in extreme suffering—for example, as a consequence of an earth-quake, flood, or other disaster—a master might focus his consciousness on such a place.

SECOND QUESTIONER: How exactly would he do that?

ROSHI: During the first few minutes of his zazen he might, for example, allow his mind to dwell on mental images of victims of these calamities, after which he might project feelings of sympathy and compassion toward them. Having in this way established a rapport with them, he would then empty his mind of those images and feelings, and every other kind, to reach a state of no-mindness. It is at this point of absolute oneness, where awareness of the mountain, oneself, and every image or thought disappears, that the transmission takes place. But you need not be a master, nor need you do zazen on a mountain, holy or otherwise, to help yourself and others. In the words of Zen Master Dogen, "One person sitting egolessly in zazen beomes imperceptibly one with all visible and invisible worlds, throughout past, present, and future, carrying on the ceaseless work of leading beings to enlightenment."

FOURTH QUESTIONER: I read that a few years ago the American authorities in Moscow discovered the Russians were beaming microwaves into the American embassy, and it was believed that these were causing the abnormal sickness, fatigue, and mental confusion occurring then among members of the embassy staff. I also read that the CIA was involved in experiments to manipulate human behavior by remote control so as to render a person subservient to some imposed will.

My question is: Is there any real difference between that kind of mind manipulation and what you have been talking about? Granting that the objective is different, can't any kind of mind control be dangerous, especially in the hands of the wrong people?

ROSHI: It certainly can. From what you say it appears that we are entering a new and dangerous era of undeclared warfare. But please understand that there is a vast difference between the altruistic efforts of masters, whose sole aim is to enlighten—not control—the unconscious minds of those in darkness and despair, and the actions of psychics or military technologists manipulating consciousness for purposes that are dubious at best.

FOURTH QUESTIONER: Roshi, can zazen make one's mind invulnerable to remote control?

ROSHI: Anyone who practices Zen seriously knows that zazen develops a strong mind under natural control, able to neutralize any attempts at manipulating it.

FOURTH QUESTIONER: Can zazen also protect us against microwaves?

ROSHI: I don't know. Apart from screening or jamming devices, there may be no long-term protection except the deterrent of mutual fear of retaliation. Yet here, too, those practiced in Zen or similar systems of body-mind spiritual training won't get nervous or frantic when they hear about these things. And when they have to die they will be able to do so with composure.

FIFTH QUESTIONER: May I bring up another subject? The term "vibrations" bothers me, because I don't understand it and people toss it around as though they can feel something that insensitive clods like me can't. What is it supposed to mean, anyway?

ROSHI: We know from physics that all matter, animate and inanimate, has electromagnetic properties whose nature is determined by the rate of vibration of its atomic particles. When the vibrations of a person or place are in harmony with our own, we feel comfortable and our reaction is a positive one; when they are not, we feel uncomfortable and say, "I don't like his vibes" or "I don't care for the vibrations here." Stated differently, it's an invisible atmosphere or quality surrounding a person or place.

FIRST QUESTIONER: What about the desert or the sea as a place to do zazen?

ROSHI: Having never tried zazen in the desert, I can't speak from personal experience. But members of our Center who have done so have given conflicting reports.

Zazen by the ocean has its merits, but a beach where many people come to swim and sunbathe is not conducive to serious zazen. Also bear in mind that when you're sitting high up on a mountain and gazing on a vast expanse of scenery, you may well be tempted to philosophize on the beauty or evanescence of life; the same is true of zazen by the sea or in the desert. Such contemplation can hinder your zazen.

FIRST QUESTIONER: From your experience, what is the best time to meditate in mountains or elsewhere?

ROSHI: Generally speaking there are four times of the day and night when the body-mind is most favorably disposed to zazen or meditation: dawn, noon, dusk, and midnight. As for mountains, I have found the best time for zazen to be before sunup.

FIRST QUESTIONER: Why is that?

ROSHI: After a mountain has absorbed *prana*—that is, the cosmic energies from the sun and the atmosphere and the earth—it evidently "digests" and assimilates these intangible nutrients during the night so that early in the morning, before sunrise, the mountain is robust and vital, its energies flowing freely. This, plus the coolness of the air at that hour, enables you more easily to put aside all thoughts and cares, become one with the mountain and absorb its emanations. In the hot afternoon, especially in tropical countries, the mountain's energies become muted, as though the monster rock were taking its own siesta. But in the evening once again it revivifies, taking on a cool glow. This, too, is a felicitous time for zazen. But nothing equals zazen on a mountain during the full moon.

SIXTH QUESTIONER: What about meditating in a cave? Didn't you say you meditated in a cave on that Mexican holy mountain?

ROSHI: A cave is fine if it's not a "cave of Satan."

SIXTH QUESTIONER: What's that?

ROSHI: "Cave of Satan" is a Zen expression for a serene, blissful state that becomes a kind of hell when, thinking it is genuine awakening, one wants to stay within its womblike confines.

SIXTH QUESTIONER: Why would anyone want to leave?

ROSHI [to everybody]: *That's* why it's called the "cave of Satan"!

19 / WHAT IS SATORI? /

QUESTIONER: What is satori?

ROSHI: When a Zen master was asked, "What is Buddhism?" he replied, "I don't understand Buddhism."

Me, I don't understand satori.

QUESTIONER: If you don't understand, who does?

ROSHI: Why don't you ask someone who says, "*I* am enlightened"?

20 / ARE YOU ENLIGHTENED? /

QUESTIONER: Are you enlightened?

ROSHI: If I say "Yes, *I* am enlightened," those of you who know will walk out in disgust. If I say, "No, I'm not enlightened," those of you who misunderstand will walk out disappointed.

So . . .

21 / CAN ENLIGHTENMENT COME WITHOUT TRAINING? /

QUESTIONER: Roshi, aren't there cases where enlightenment has come about suddenly and spontaneously? What precipitates it, and how is it different from Zen enlightenment?

ROSHI: Strictly speaking, every kind of awakening is sudden in the sense that it occurs abruptly, like water coming to a boil; what is "gradual" is the long training that usually precedes it. By "spontaneous" you mean enlightenment that comes without spiritual training, is that right?

QUESTIONER: Yes.

ROSHI: The question is always, "How genuine are so-called spontaneous enlightenments?" In the past twelve years I've tested dozens of persons who claimed to be enlightened and found only one who I felt had had a genuine awakening without prior training. Without training, however, one's life won't be appreciably transformed, for one won't be able to operate out of that enlightenment and in time it'll become merely a cherished memory.

If you study the cases of those who have truly and deeply awakened, you will find that in virtually every case the awakening came after much soul-searching, prompted either by a gnawing dissatisfaction with one's life or by personal anguish growing out of a traumatic emotional experience.

QUESTIONER: Why do some come to awakening relatively quickly and others take years?

ROSHI: Who can say, except that karmically the impelling drive for liberation is stronger in some than in others. Zen masters have said, "The quickest way to awakening is to struggle with a 'doubt-mass.'" In Zen "doubt" does not imply skepticism or reservation. A doubt-mass is a fundamental, perplexing problem that allows you no rest, such as, "If, as the Buddha and the Zen masters have said, the world is inherently whole and undefiled, why then do we see so much evil and suffering around us?" Obviously if you have the absolute faith that they were not mistaken, you will be driven to resolve the contradiction between what you believe as a matter of faith and the evidence of your senses. Depending on how deeply and persistently this perplexity grips you, and how tirelessly you seek an answer, awakening takes a shorter or longer time.

Such questioning is zazen. And if you were to persevere as though your life depended on finding the answer, you would need to do nothing else. "To come to full awakening," as one Zen master put it, "you must act like a man who has fallen into a hundred-foot-deep pit. His thousand, his ten thousand thoughts are reduced to the single thought: 'How can I get out of the pit?' He keeps it up from morning to night and from night to the following morning with no other thought." But how many are *driven* in this way? No more than a handful.

Formal Zen training is basically nothing more than the master's effort to stimulate this intense questioning, this doubt-mass, when it does not arise spontaneously. The indispensable preconditions of such an inquiry, however, are the unwavering conviction that one can dissolve the doubt-mass and the grim determination to do so. A student with a genuine thirst for Self-realization is usually assigned a koan. If he grapples with it seriously—and his involvement depends on how intensely he feels life's pain and how urgent is his desire to be free of it—then he will awaken. Moreover, his awakening will come more quickly with a koan which, more than any other practice, evokes and focuses the doubt-mass.

SECOND QUESTIONER: In college I studied philosophy to find out what the greatest minds have thought about human existence and because I wanted to know the meaning of my own life. That study not only didn't lead to enlightenment, it didn't even satisfy me intellectually.

ROSHI: How did you ask those questions about human existence? Like a child, out of curiosity, or did you question with all your heart and soul? Intellectual questions elicit intellectual answers; they won't transform your life. Only when you are driven to cry from your guts, "I must, I *will* find out!" will your question be answered. And that will be your awakening, for in the profoundest sense the question and answer are not two; they only appear so because of your discriminating intellect, which divides what is essentially indivisible.

Let me tell you a case of spontaneous awakening told me

by a plumber from Brooklyn, New York. He had no formal education beyond elementary school and no spiritual bent or religious affiliation. During World War II he spent four years in the Pacific, where he saw a great deal of fighting, and by the end of the war was utterly spent and exhausted.

When he returned to Brooklyn he couldn't, in his own words, "work, play, or make love. Everything appeared useless. One question kept bugging me: What is reality? I had never studied philosophy and I wasn't religious. I don't know where that question came from, but it wouldn't let go of me. I would be walking along the street and the only thing in my mind was, 'What is reality?' Sometimes I would bump into people or buildings, I was so dazed by the question. Even at night the question never left me. I remember waking up sometimes at two or three in the morning, unable to sleep, and the first thing that popped into my mind was, 'What is reality?'

"This went on for about six months. Then one day an explosion took place inside me and I was filled with a joy I had never felt before in my life. The question just evaporated in the air and I could work again and do the things people usually do.

"This elation—sometimes I felt as though I could leap over a ten-foot wall—lasted about four months. All that spoiled it was a new nagging question: 'What has happened to you? All this joy and ease aren't normal for you!' I began feeling bad just because I felt so good.

"My family and friends said, 'You ought to see a psychiatrist. You've had some pretty brutal war experiences and these feelings may be the first symptoms of something worse underneath.'

"The psychiatrists at the VA [veterans' hospital] were very much interested in my case. They put me through routine tests, gave me a few drugs, and began questioning me every day, asking about my war experiences in detail and about my life after I got back to America. I had a private room, and unlike a lot of patients had free run of the hospital. This special treatment felt good for a month or so, but then I began to get restless and tired of the whole rigamarole, and told one of my psychiatrists, 'Look, how much longer do I have to stay here? When are you going to decide what's wrong with me?'

" 'Tomorrow we are having a conference on your case and

you will hear from me after I get all the data together,' he told me.

"A few days later I got the word: 'You've had a conversion experience.' I didn't know what I had been converted from or to, but I was so anxious to leave the hospital that I didn't question their diagnosis, and let it go at that.

"It must have been ten years later, after a friend lent me your book *The Three Pillars of Zen*, that I finally realized what had happened to me: I had had a kensho or satori experience."

FIRST QUESTIONER: Did you feel, Roshi, that he had had a genuine enlightenment?

ROSHI: Before this man came to Rochester he had written me a lengthy letter in which he mentioned all that you have just heard. In reply he was advised to come to a workshop, at which time he could talk with me about his case and, if he wished, be tested as to the authenticity of his experience. After the workshop we reviewed together all the circumstances, particularly the immediate incidents, leading to the "explosion" and what he had seen and felt during his cataclysmic upheaval.

As he relived the events of that experience his eyes shone with a radiance that had been noticeably absent during the workshop, for I had observed his face and manner very carefully.

"Tell me, what is reality?" I asked him.

He hesitated, smiled, and replied, "My whole life."

"You said that at the time of your 'explosion' that question disappeared. Did anything take its place?"

"I don't remember. Nothing, I guess. All I can tell you is that I never felt better in my life. It was like being reborn—I felt like a baby. All questions and problems dropped away, and for the first time since I had gone into the Army I had lots of energy and drive."

"After that what happened?"

"Slowly the glow and bliss faded and that superenergy drained away. Now that I've read your book and come to this workshop, I know the importance of zazen. But will zazen bring back that wonderful joy?"

"Forget the joy," he was told. "Do zazen regularly, be aware and fully involved in your daily life, and you will have greater clarity, vitality, and feelings of profound gratitude. These will affect your life more positively than the ecstasy you experienced."

SECOND QUESTIONER: Roshi, were you satisfied with his answers?

ROSHI: No. My feeling was that what had happened to him was real enough, but it had happened many years earlier and was no longer operating in his life; it was now only a happy memory. Had he had a practice at the time to sustain and deepen it, he would have answered my questions differently.

FIRST QUESTIONER: Does the joy of satori last?

ROSHI: No. If you want to remain on Cloud Nine forever, there's something wrong with your realization. With true satori, Awareness does not fade. You need the zazen—that is, the samadhi power growing out of it—to enable you to live in accordance with your single vision, for habit forces of the past continue to draw you back into old patterns.

Those of you who read *The Three Pillars* may recall in the introductory lectures the parable of Vajradatta, who was half insane. He liked nothing more than to look in the mirror. One day he didn't see his head in the mirror and ran around crying frantically, "I've lost my head! I've lost my head! Where can it be?" How great was his joy when, after being clouted on the head and crying out in pain, he was told, *"There's* your head," and he realized that he had always had it. The head in this parable corresponds to our True-nature, and its discovery to awakening. Isn't it weird, though, to be overjoyed at discovering that which you have never been without? The point is that after awakening, spontaneous or otherwise, we can't live a natural life as long as we cling to this tremendous elation.

FIRST QUESTIONER: Suppose that someone like this plumber has had deep and painful war experiences and afterward gets into zazen. Would these experiences actually help him come to a deep and lasting enlightenment more quickly than otherwise?

ROSHI: The combination of traumatic experience and thorough Zen training might well produce a deep and lasting awakening. A Japanese doctor I knew who was a member of a certain zazen group in Japan is a good example. Once he was asked by me, "What brought you to Zen?" This is the story he told:

"Toward the end of World War II, having just completed my medical training, I was drafted into the Army. We Japanese were taking a terrible beating. Our men were dying like flies and there was little we few doctors could do to save them. Together with other doctors I was working day and night with the wounded and dying. Once I went an entire week without any sleep, tending to the wounded.

"After the war I couldn't go back to medicine. I kept asking myself, 'Why should I practice medicine and try to save people's lives? They're going to die anyway.' At this time a friend urged me to try Zen, and I became a disciple of Yasutani-roshi. He promised me that if I worked hard and came to kensho, my life would take a 180-degree turn and I would not only want to help people as a doctor but also would again feel compassion and love for everyone.

"So for the next three years I did zazen with great zeal and devotion, spurred on by the roshi's words of encouragement and my own unbearable confusion. I went to many sesshins. Then it happened: an inner explosion that annihilated all my ideas about suffering and death—and everything else. I perceived that superficially there was nothing but birth and death, but that at the same time in True-mind there is no birth and no death."

"Was that gnawing question, 'Why should I practice medicine?' ever answered?" I asked.

"Yes. With awakening came the simple answer: 'Because you are a doctor!' "

22 / IS THERE A DIFFERENCE BETWEEN PSYCHIC INSIGHTS AND SATORI? /

QUESTIONER: Is there a difference between psychic insights and satori?

ROSHI: They have their origin in a common ground—the Mind. Everyone, without exception, has this Mind as a birthright. But while the enlightened have awakened to it, the ordinary psychic has not. The important difference is in the *degree* of awareness or knowledge. The psychic is in touch with an area of mind inaccessible to ordinary consciousness; the awakened has seen into Mind itself. Since the fully awakened Mind perceives unlimited dimensions of consciousness, it naturally encompasses psychic perceptions.

SECOND QUESTIONER: What about Edgar Cayce? Wasn't he enlightened?

ROSHI: Cayce had extraordinary powers, but it is highly doubtful that he was awakened.

THIRD QUESTIONER: Speaking of Cayce, I have heard that he made a prediction that sometime within the next forty years California will be destroyed by an earthquake or flood. Do you place any stock in such prophecies?

ROSHI: Unless a psychic can give the *precise* time of a future occurrence—that is, pin it down to the exact year and day and hour—I would place little faith in his prediction. This is not to say that he is a charlatan, but that whatever powers he possesses are limited.

Let me continue. Although the psychic is able to contact dimensions inaccessible to the ordinary person, he has no real understanding of the source of this power. Moreover, his "gift" does not effect in him an attrition of ego or transformation of personality. He is still dominated by the notion of a self opposed by other selves. By contrast, with genuine enlightenment the notion of an ego-I is dispelled and the dualistic distinction of self and not-self is transcended. The consequences of this are enormous.

SECOND QUESTIONER: From the Zen viewpoint, then, is there no value in psychic experiences?

ROSHI: Certain psychic perceptions, by removing doubts as to rebirth and the validity of karma, are indeed valuable. Can you imagine anyone able to regress to past lifetimes, and to retain memory of them, who would not be convinced beyond a shadow of a doubt of the cyclic character of life? This conviction frees one from the mania of "You only live once, so eat, drink, and be merry" by dissolving the death anxiety it masks.

The realization, stemming from remembrances of past lives, that death, like life, is a temporary point between what precedes and what follows would also have a profound effect on one's behavior in this existence. Who but a fool or a madman would willfully hurt or destroy life if he were absolutely certain that karmic retribution in the form of a hellish existence will follow in this or a subsequent lifetime? Who wouldn't want to atone for his past transgressions if he were convinced that death is not the end but only a continuation, and that for his reckless dance he will surely have to pay the fiddler, if not now then in a subsequent existence?

Let me tell you a story that bears on the difference between the psychic and the Self-realized. It was related to me by an American professor whom I met in Japan. This professor had gone to India to find an enlightened master. One day in his search for the elusive guru he came upon a crowd in a small village. Edging his way toward the center he saw an ordinary-looking Indian giving a demonstration of psychic powers. Seeing the American, the psychic proceeded to give him a life reading, telling him things about himself and his wife and children that he could not have known beforehand. It was the professor's first direct experience with extrasensory perception, and he was dumfounded. Another unusual thing happened: The psychic would not accept a donation from the professor as he had from others to whom he gave readings.

After the demonstration the psychic called the professor aside and told him the following:

"Have you not come to India to seek Self-realization?"

"Yes."

"You are different from most foreigners I have met in India, so permit me to give you some heartfelt advice. You were impressed by my power to know your past and present, but for me this is nothing remarkable. I have had these *siddhis* [psychic powers] since I was a child, and my father before me had them. Believe me when I tell you that when I was a young man I had deep religious aspirations like yourself. But because people flocked to me for readings—and my father encouraged me to use my powers to help support our large and poor family—

my yearning for spiritual liberation fell by the wayside. Now I am an old man and despite my natural psychic intuitions no closer to Self-realization than I was forty-five years ago.

"In India you will find many psychics who pose as realized holy men, but you must not be deceived by them. The psychic has merely been in touch with the subtle manifestations of God's presence. The holy man has seen God himself. There is a sure way to distinguish an authentic master from a bogus one: He will not tolerate in his disciples an interest in or display of siddhis."

THIRD QUESTIONER: Are there any dangers in trying to develop psychic powers?

ROSHI: The story you have just heard makes clear the threat to Self-realization of a preoccupation with psychic powers. But there are other dangers. People who strive to develop psychic powers often do so at the expense of other areas of their personality. They can become one-sided and conceited, feeling that because of their unusual and rare abilities they deserve special recognition. Psychic powers are also seductive—the more one becomes involved with them the harder it is to become disentangled, until eventually one is caught as in a net.

Anyone who does zazen seriously will in time develop psychic abilities to one degree or another. The Buddha himself possessed numerous psychic perceptions, including the ability to recall past lifetimes, see into the future, and read others' minds. But never did he encourage his followers to develop psychic powers as a means to enlightenment, or to make a vain display of any they already had.

There is one more anecdote that illustrates the value Zen masters place on magical powers. One day a renowned Zen master of ancient China was traveling on a pilgrimage and came to the edge of a wide river. As he was standing there a strange character, appearing from nowhere, joined him and said, "Let's cross together." Not wishing to cross, the master said, "Brother, if you want to cross go by yourself." The monk walked over the water as though walking on solid ground, and turning his head said, "Come along." The master, replied, "Show-off! Had I known you were going to do that I would have cut off your shins!"

23 / NO PAIN, NO GAIN /

QUESTIONER: I had never done zazen before this workshop and had no idea it could be so uncomfortable. It seemed as though that second round of sitting would never end! Why is it necessary to put up with such discomfort to purify the mind?

ROSHI: Through erroneous thinking and laziness we have allowed our minds to be taken over by all manner of useless thoughts; all day long idle thoughts fly in and out like bees at a hive. The worst ones, however, are the permanent squatters, the fixed concepts. These become entrenched in the mind, helping the ego to solidify its position of dominance.

The fixed concepts are like stubborn stains. Because of them our minds have become an Augean stable of opinions and notions of right and wrong and of how things ought to be, as well as of desires, prejudices, and resentments growing out of greed, anger, and wrong thinking. It took Hercules with his superhuman strength to clean the Augean stables of their thirty years' accumulation of manure; so only a strong, concentrated exertion can rid the mind of a lifetime of mental garbage.

SECOND QUESTIONER: I found myself becoming very restless, which was painful in another way. I guess I'm just not used to sitting without moving.

ROSHI: Few are. At a workshop I recently conducted in Chicago one of the participants, a professor, was moving constantly during the formal sitting. Although everyone had been instructed how to sit with the knees touching the mat, a position that establishes physical and mental stability, for some reason he sat with raised knees. This awkward posture placed a strain on his body, causing him to move continually. After warning him several times to stop moving, because of the disruption to his own and others' concentration, I stood behind him with my stick and shuffled my feet to let him know I was there. He managed to sit still until the round ended, but then could hardly get up. Limping over to where I was standing he groaned, "That was the hardest work I've ever done. The worst part of it was the humiliating discovery that I could not keep count of my breaths beyond the number two. But I'm grateful that you didn't make it easy for me. In those twenty minutes of painful sitting I learned more about myself than through anything else I've ever attempted."

The reason many find it uncomfortable to sit quietly is that they are used to dispersing their energies in useless activities to avoid confronting their life problems. Sitting not only restrains them from scattering their energies, it also forces them to look inward and face themselves nakedly—face the problems they are trying to escape. And because zazen exposes the problems, they resent it, and they resent the teacher, who they feel is responsible for their being in that predicament. Thus sitting becomes one big "pain."

This point, however, is a crossroads, a time when one's determination is tested. Will you follow your old way of life—the easy, wasteful way—or will you embark upon the path of liberation? If you have truly realized that your life up to now has been leading you to a dead end, and your faith in the reality of your True-nature is strong, your determination to attain freedom will be equal to the task. And if you persevere in the struggle, fighting off all temptations to escape, you will come to a deep understanding and acquire a calmness and clarity charged with vitality.

SECOND QUESTIONER: How long does it take before one is able to sit in one of the lotus postures without pain? [6]

ROSHI: It depends on the flexibility of the mind and the ligaments. Mind, though, is foremost. A resilient mind—which is to say one not rigid or stubborn—produces a resilient body. Still, simple leg-stretching exercises can be helpful. Once a certain amount of flexibility is attained, you will be comfortable in these postures and experience a deep feeling of well-being. To come home from a day's work and sit on a couch in the quarter- or half-lotus position induces a deep repose not easily attainable otherwise. For studying or reading, one's concentration is far stronger in a lotus position than in a chair.

SECOND QUESTIONER: Why is that?

ROSHI: To draw the extremities together toward the center, as in this posture, is to unify and focus the mind, which then functions with one-pointed equilibrium. [7]

Don't feel discouraged if in the beginning you experience discomfort, because learning to do zazen is like learning anything valuable. It calls for perseverance. Remember, we have been misusing our bodies and minds for a long time. Instead of sitting and walking erectly, for instance, we slump, placing a strain on all our organs and impairing breathing. Just as we must learn to sit and walk properly, we must train our minds to function centripetally—that is, inwardly—as well as centrifugally. It is a strain at first to reverse this long-standing process, but if you persist with zazen you will begin to experience greater clarity, ease, and energy in your daily life.

THIRD QUESTIONER: Isn't it masochistic to put up with pain when you can avoid it?

ROSHI: The Buddha said that pain is a condition of life and that if we try to avoid it we condemn ourselves to a shallow existence, for pleasure and pain are two sides of the same coin. And pain is everywhere, isn't it? Birth itself is pain, for the child as well as for the mother. Sickness involves pain, as do the many infirmities of old age. To be with people one doesn't like is painful; to be separated from those one loves is equally painful. And what about the suffering of so many of the human race who live in misery and near starvation? What thoughtful person will not agree that our times of pain and sorrow outnumber those of joy and happiness?

FOURTH QUESTIONER: So why add to our pain by sitting in the lotus posture?

ROSHI: The lotus postures are not the only ones in which to do zazen. There are other positions, which are described and illustrated in *The Three Pillars of Zen.*

Since pain in general can be avoided only at the expense of a full, rich life, isn't it wise to come to grips with it? If you don't it will forever confront you. In every first-rate monastery or center or ashram I've been to in Asia it was said, "No pain, no gain."

FOURTH QUESTIONER: But how do you come to grips with pain?

ROSHI: In Zen training you are taught many methods of dealing with pain. Here is one used in some monasteries in Japan: In warm weather when mosquitoes are thickest, early in the morning and at dusk, the head monks normally place mosquito-repellent coils between every two sitters. From time to time, however, these coils are not set out and the mosquitoes, like a horde of angry invaders, rush in for the feast. You don't dare lift a hand to brush them away, for the head monks are standing behind you to see that you don't move. All manner of thoughts assail the mind. You suddenly remember having read that mosquitoes carry malaria and that if they sting you en masse you may contract this disease. Actually, whatever pain you feel comes from the *thought* of what might happen to you rather than from the bites themselves. But there is no escaping the mosquitoes, and after a few agonizing moments you do what the head monks are urging you to do—become one with the biting. Then lo, a miracle takes place! You no longer feel them. They are biting but no one is being bitten. You have disappeared—there is nothing to bite!

From this you learn that nothing can menace your peace of mind if you become one with it. In time you become less attached to the body as the truth sinks in that the more you pursue and cling to the pleasures of the senses the more pain you must eventually suffer.

FOURTH QUESTIONER: Granting that it is necessary for us to learn how to deal with pain, aren't there ways to do it without risking your health?

ROSHI: The "mosquito method" is only one among many. If you expose yourself to pain out of an ascetic desire to toughen yourself so you will be stronger than others, or from an equally impure motive, the discomfort is pointless. But if your objective is a high and pure one and there is no way to achieve it except through pain, then you must take the pain.

FOURTH QUESTIONER: Roshi, didn't you feel any resentment toward those monks for the pain they put you through when you were training in Japan?

ROSHI: Pain is a strange thing. The teachers you remember with gratitude are not those who made it easy for you but the ones who compassionately gave you a hard, painful time. After twenty-five years I still feel grateful to a certain head monk who stayed up one whole night during sesshin encouraging me with the stick. The encouragement stick is a wooden paddle two to three feet long that has been used in Chinese and Japanese Zen monasteries and temples for centuries to rouse the energies of a sitter, allowing him to make his strongest concentrative effort. Each shoulder is struck twice on acupuncture meridians that stimulate psychic energy. I had been in the monastery for about six months and this was the sixth and last night—the climax—of a sesshin. After formal zazen had ended at 9 P.M. I found a rickety chair and took it to the bathhouse to do *yaza* (late-night sitting). Hardly had I settled in when the stick landed with a loud crack on my shoulder. Standing over me was one of the head monks, a man who had looked after me since my arrival at the monastery and with whom I felt especially close. Although because of his demanding duties he, like the other head monks, usually went to bed at 10 or 11 P.M., tonight out of the deepest compassion he was giving, up his sleep to spur me on with the stick. The first hour passed and the second, but he did not let up. As the night wore on he stuck with me, working tirelessly, while the pain in my legs, which were braced around the sharp legs of the chair, grew even worse than the pain in my shoulders and back. Finally overcome by the strain and exhaustion, I passed out. Upon opening my eyes there was the monk standing beside me holding, instead of the stick, a bowl of raw eggs. I gulped them down.

"The next day begins in half an hour," he said. "You can rest until then." We looked at each other and silently embraced.

After the sesshin I asked this head monk, "What if I had had a weak heart and dropped dead from that all-night stick ordeal? Can't you see the papers abroad reporting, 'Middle-aged American beaten to death in Zen monastery in Japan'? Zen in the West might have been set back fifty years, not to mention the repercussions in Japan. Weren't you taking a big risk?" He smiled broadly. "Kapleau-san, you more strong than you think." That was all he said.

Something else this head monk once did is still fresh in my memory. During sesshin he was acting as English interpreter for the roshi. The procedure for going privately to the roshi (dokusan) was the following: At a given signal you lined up in the outer hall, sitting on your heels. When the roshi, in an inner room, rang his handbell to dismiss the person with him, you struck a bell in front of you with a wooden mallet and proceeded to his room.

When my turn came, waiting with this monk-interpreter still behind me, I struck the bell upon the roshi's signal, put down the mallet, and stood up to go before the roshi. At that moment the monk, without warning, struck me violently behind the ear with his open hand. In pain and rage—and ego—I turned and swung at him. He ducked, grabbed me by the waist, swung me around, and shoved me in the direction of the dokusan room. When I came before him, the roshi cried, *"Yosh! Yosh!"* (Good! Good!)—the first words of approval from him since my arrival at the monastery. Up until this time my manner at dokusan had always been halting and my answers to his questions intellectual. But now I found myself responding no-mindedly—from the guts, not the head—and the roshi was obviously pleased.

This episode had lasting benefits. I found myself operating on a higher energy level, and at dokusan was no longer afraid of the roshi. In other situations, too, I was able to respond with a keener awareness.

There are many other painful episodes that helped me greatly, but I won't burden you with them.

FIFTH QUESTIONER: But couldn't you have been helped without having to go through all that pain?

ROSHI: Before coming to Zen I was a self-indulgent, self-centered person. I did what pleased me, indifferent to the effect my pursuit of pleasure had on the lives of others. Instead of being the master of my life I was its slave, and didn't know it. But my Zen teachers knew it and, keen judges of character that they were, they gave me precisely the kind of treatment I needed. Besides bringing home truths about myself never before realized, this treatment gave me a sorely needed measure of humility. More than anything else, pain can do this for you provided you don't resent it.

SIXTH QUESTIONER: Roshi, knowing what you know now would you do it again?

ROSHI: Understand that if there was no karmic necessity for me to go to Japan I wouldn't have gone, nor would I have stayed as long as I did. And you wouldn't be here today if it weren't your karma—and mine too. In the same way that I know now, and must have sensed then, that that pain was necessary for my growth and development, all of you must feel the need for Zen discipline and training.

SIXTH QUESTIONER: Roshi, do you ever recommend going to Japan to study Zen?

ROSHI: In this country today there are competent Zen teachers and fine Zen training centers. In 1953, when I went, I knew of no such places in the West.

A VOICE: You must have had pretty bad karma to have needed to go to Japan and take all that pain.

A VOICE: Karma or no karma, I'd never go and suffer like that.

ROSHI: Because I went none of you needs to go.

24 / WHAT IS EMPTINESS? /

QUESTIONER: What is Buddhist emptiness? I know what the books say: It's the void, *sunyata,* and all that. But what is meant by "Form is only emptiness, emptiness only form"?

ROSHI: Suppose you are a craftsman working in silver, and you want to make a small figure of a buddha. When your silver is molten and flowing it has the possibility of actualizing itself into any object—that's emptiness, no-thingness. Then you pour the molten metal into the mold and it hardens—that's form. But now let us say that after you have formed your buddha you are dissatisfied with it and wish to make something else with the same silver. So you melt down the figure, and the silver returns to formlessness. In essence, then, this emptiness is no different from the form.

All this, don't forget, is only a conceptual model, not the real thing. So tell me, how would you take hold of emptiness as a concrete fact? Come forward and show me!

QUESTIONER [approaching the roshi]: This way [clutching at space]!

ROSHI: No, *this* way [indicating]!

QUESTIONER: Ouch!

ROSHI: Emptiness, after all, is only form, isn't it?

25 / WHAT, IF ANYTHING, SURVIVES BIOLOGICAL DEATH? /

QUESTIONER: Recently there have been a number of studies conducted and books written on the subject of life after death. Yet many people are skeptical; they maintain that there is no scientific proof of this. What does Zen say about the possibility of life in some form continuing after death?

ROSHI: One can only wonder how it could be doubted. Birth, growth, decay, disintegration, rebecoming—isn't this the cycle of natural events? Anyone who doubts it denies the evidence of his own senses and intellect, his deepest intuitions. Have you ever asked yourself, "What happens to the life force, the energy behind the activities constituting my 'self' after disintegration of my body?" The law of the conservation of energy states that energy is never lost, only transformed, so how is it possible for this life force permanently to disappear?

QUESTIONER: I'd like to believe it doesn't. But has anyone ever come back from the dead to tell us what it's like?

ROSHI: There isn't anyone in this room who *hasn't* come back— thousands of times! All life is life after death.

QUESTIONER: Do you really mean that, Roshi?

ROSHI: Why is it more surprising, as Voltaire pointed out, to be born twice than it is to be born once?

SECOND QUESTIONER: Can you tell me what I'll be like in my next lifetime?

ROSHI: Don't ask me; just look in a mirror.

SECOND QUESTIONER: What do you mean?

ROSHI: The Buddha said, "If you want to know the past— that is, cause—look at your present, which is its effect. If you want to know the future—effect—look at your present, its cause. In other words, what you are thinking and doing now is determining what you'll be like in your next life—so take care!"

THIRD QUESTIONER: There have been many accounts of people who technically died but were then brought back to life. Those who returned from the "dead" describe their out-of-body experience as so beautiful that they wished they had not returned to their painful bodies.

FOURTH QUESTIONER (to third questioner): You're referring to people whose hearts stopped and showed no signs of life for a short time but were soon revived. That's quite different from people who die and whose bodies are buried or cremated.

ROSHI: Let me say something about those out-of-body experiences. What has been described as beautiful is only the *first* stage. For one lacking the specific preparation of spiritual training, what follows the initial entry can be frightening, even terrifying, depending on one's karma. These later stages were described in detail in two texts[8] by Vasubandhu, a Buddhist philosopher of the fourth century. *The Tibetan Book of the Dead* is based on these works of his.

FIFTH QUESTIONER: Why is spiritual training necessary? Why can't you prepare yourself for these ordeals through reading and study?

ROSHI: If in the intermediate realm between decease and rebirth you were confronted with terrifying demonic images or other frightful apparitions, would it really help you to have read that they were only projections of your own consciousness, self-created phantoms? Like the hallucinations in bad acid trips, these visions have the power to terrify you because you don't understand their nature or how they can be banished.

Now suppose that in your zazen you had hallucinations of one kind or another again and again, and each time had been instructed by your teacher why they arise and how to deal with them. You would have learned *experientially* not to fear them, and that experience would be of immense help to you in the after-death existence. And if this training has been thorough, it is not likely that the trauma of death will dislodge this awareness.

SIXTH QUESTIONER: Is this intermediate realm the same as the *bardo* mentioned in *The Tibetan Book of the Dead?*

ROSHI: Yes.

SEVENTH QUESTIONER: Can you tell us more about this intermediate existence?

ROSHI: According to Vasubandhu, in this realm the intermediate being has intellect, emotion, and will—all of a tenuous nature—and even perceptions of a kind. And like an electric current, it is said to have the power to pass through material objects and to travel hundreds of miles instantaneously.

SEVENTH QUESTIONER: How long does it take for the future being to reincarnate?

ROSHI: Usually rebirth takes place within a forty-nine-day period. But this figure is not fixed. It can occur in a day or a week or not until many years later. Presumably the time of rebirth is determined, among other factors, by the attraction of the being to parents with whom it has a karmic affinity. The figure forty-nine, by the way, is seven times seven. In many religious systems, including Buddhism, the number seven is symbolically the cornerstone of the universe.

Buddhism speaks of two kinds of birth and death: continuous and "regular." Continuous birth and death—that is, creation and destruction—take place every millionth of a second, or some such phenomenal speed, as old cells die and new ones come into being. So, we can say that a new self is constantly being born, and that a man of sixty is not the same as, yet not different from, the person he was at thirty or at ten. Living is thus dying, and dying living. In fact, with every inhalation you are being reborn and with each exhalation you are dying.

"Regular" birth and death can also be referred to as "corporeal" when it pertains to the physical body and its processes as a whole, its coming into being and its extinction at the end of a lifetime. At decease one's life energy, or karma, is transmitted to this intermediate being, and its existence, too, is subject to continuous and "regular" birth and death, except that in this realm "regular" death and rebirth take place in seven-day periods as the intermediate being awaits the opportunity to be conceived. This intermediate being, according to Vasubandhu, has the mysterious capability of becoming aware of the sexual intercourse by which it will be conceived.

SEVENTH QUESTIONER: How does this karma energy pass from the dying individual to the intermediate being?

ROSHI: Many analogies have been used to describe the transmission process. My teacher used to liken it to impressing a seal on mud. Our present life is the seal and intermediate being the mud. The seal's design is karma. At the moment the seal is impressed on the surface of the mud, its design, or karmic pattern, is precisely transposed.

Others have compared it to playing a game of billiards. You hit a cluster of balls with your cueball, scattering them in all directions but leaving the cueball at a dead stop upon impact. What "thing" passed over? Was it any more than a certain force or momentum or energy? The direction the balls take depends on the *way* you strike the cueball—for example, whether you use spin on it or not—and also on the force of the momentum it generates in the other balls. Similarly, when you impress a seal onto mud and the impression remains after the seal is withdrawn, has any substance passed over? Wasn't it simply the *character* of the seal, its transposition to the mud, that remained?

SEVENTH QUESTIONER: But some thing or substance must pass over. Otherwise how can you say that what we become in our next incarnation depends on the kind of life we have led in this one?

ROSHI: Rebirth does not involve the transfer of a substance but the continuation of a process. The Buddha said, "Rebirth arises from two causes: the last thought of the previous life as its governing principle and the actions of the previous life as its basis. The stopping of the last thought is known as decease, the appearance of the first thought as rebirth."

SIXTH QUESTIONER: Suppose you had led an evil life but repented on your deathbed and cleared the slate through last rites or other means. Could you cheat your karma this way, or else by carefully guarding your last thought?

ROSHI: No. The average person's inevitable burden of guilt and his clinging to life is such as to make it impossible for him to resist the momentum of his karma. For such a person to succeed would be as unlikely as, say, smuggling a trunkful of narcotics into a foreign country without thinking of your cargo as you approach the customs check. In terms of easing passage from this life to the next, however, last rites administered by a clergyman can relieve the dying of guilt feelings arising from past transgressions, which, it is said, come up with great force and weigh heavily on the mind at the moment of death.

EIGHTH QUESTIONER: At a Buddhist funeral does the priest perform much the same function as a minister or a rabbi?

NINTH QUESTIONER: I went to a Buddhist funeral once. It was very different from other funerals I've been to. Instead of praising the character of the departed, the priest spoke directly to the spirit of the deceased. Why was he doing that?

ROSHI: The primary purpose of the Buddhist funeral is not

to console the family—although this has its place—but to awaken
the intermediate being to the true nature of existence. Remember, in the after-death existence the being is free of the limitations of body and of what we ordinarily conceive of as mind,
so its perceptions are magnified immensely. The funeral and
subsequent services thus represent literally a "once in a lifetime"
opportunity to awaken the deceased and thereby liberate him
from the binding chain of birth-and-death. If the priest or roshi,
who is usually the deceased's spiritual mentor, is realized himself
and has strong samadhi power, the service is both majestic and
awe-inspiring. In fiery, thundering tones he expounds the
dharma to the intermediate being, and this sound, propelled
by the force of his enlightened mind, has the power to penetrate
all realms. Bells are also rung, gongs struck, cymbals crashed,
and drums beaten in a solemn and rousing rhythm, after which
the Heart of Perfect Wisdom sutra,[9] whose substance is "Form
is only emptiness, emptiness only form," is chanted over and
over in a dynamic and unremitting effort to awaken the mind
of the intermediate being. Also included are supplications,
prayers, and other ceremonies during and before the funeral
as well as during subsequent memorial services. Since the crucial
period is the first forty-nine days, services are held every day
for the first seven days and then once a week, through the seven-
week period, on the death day. After that they are extended
into the third year, the seventh, the thirteenth, and so on, up
to fifty years.

TENTH QUESTIONER: What about Zen masters? If funeral services are held for them, too, who conducts them?

ROSHI: Usually a person of similar spiritual power or rank.

TENTH QUESTIONER: But since he is already awakened, what
purpose does the funeral serve?

ROSHI: Enlightenment is not a static condition; it is capable
of endless enlargement. Funeral and subsequent memorial services also allow respect and reverence to be shown to the deceased, and serve as a means of preserving and extending the
link between the deceased and the living.

ELEVENTH QUESTIONER: If one takes into his next lifetime everything he has learned in this lifetime, why does he have to learn
again how to relate to the objective world?

ROSHI: The answer to your question requires a lengthy explanation. According to Buddhist psychology, the whole universe is nothing but consciousness; nothing exists outside of Mind. Consciousness is divided into nine levels. The first six are the root consciousness of seeing, of hearing, of tasting, of smelling, of touching, and of thinking. Seeing includes the eye, the objects of sight and the sense of sight; thinking includes the brain, its thoughts, and the process of thought; and similarly with the other four senses. Together these six faculties comprise the individual-empirical consciousness, the body-mind that is born and dies.

The seventh, eighth, and ninth levels of consciousness do not perish with the death of the physical body. The seventh level (*manas* consciousness) is the persistent self-awareness consciousness. At this level, all sense data gathered at the first six levels are conveyed to the eighth level (relative *alaya* consciousness), the repository, or seed, consciousness, where every action, thought, and sense impression is recorded moment after moment.

The ninth level (absolute alaya consciousness) is the pure, formless Self-consciousness—our True-nature. It is related to the eighth level so intimately that there is almost no difference between the two. It can be compared to a limitless ocean, in which each individual life is a wave on the surface.

Please look at this chart: [10]

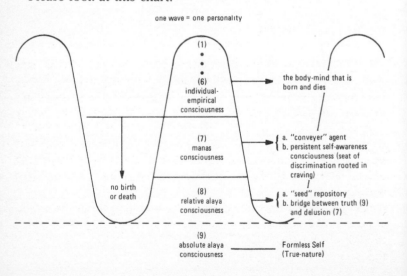

one wave = one personality

(1)
•
•
•
(6)
individual-
empirical
consciousness

the body-mind that is born and dies

no birth or death

(7)
manas
consciousness

a. "conveyer" agent
b. persistent self-awareness consciousness (seat of discrimination rooted in craving)

(8)
relative alaya
consciousness

a. "seed" repository
b. bridge between truth (9) and delusion (7)

(9)
absolute alaya
consciousness

Formless Self
(True-nature)

In a sense the eighth level, or "storehouse" of experiences, is the basis of personality and character since it continuously seeds new actions, giving rise to different thoughts and varying behavior. But then these thoughts and behavior in turn change the quality of the repository consciousness as they are instantaneously impressed upon it to become new seeds of action. Karma—which means action and reaction—develops as the ever-accumulating seed-experiences, in response to causes and conditions, blossom forth as new actions—which are not only effects but also causes of seeds. This process, even while it is fragmented, is continuous and endless. Vasubandhu described it as a "continuous sweep like a waterfall: The seed brings about the present action; the present action impresses itself on the seed; the triangle is completed; cause and effect are one."

This chart will make it clearer:

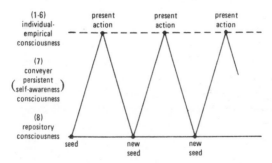

In relation to your question, although our individuality carries over into the next lifetime in terms of karmic propensities, bents, and talents, in the ordinary person there is no *conscious* memory of past lives or the details connected with them. It is simply buried in the subconscious, where it may or may not be later dredged up into waking consciousness. That is why children need to spend their childhood relearning how to relate to the objective world. In many ways they are strangers in a strange world.

ELEVENTH QUESTIONER: Yet there are certain little children who appear to have an ageless wisdom about them. They are referred to, I think the expression is, as "old souls." What makes them this way?

ROSHI: They carry over into this life more of the memory of a past life or lives than does the ordinary child. Having greater awareness or wisdom, they do not need to relearn as much.

TWELFTH QUESTIONER: What you've been telling us is interesting enough, but in your book *The Three Pillars of Zen* you mention somewhere that the Buddha refused to answer questions about what happens after death because they had nothing to do with enlightenment or the religious life. Why have you been doing what the founder of your religion wouldn't do?

ROSHI: If you reread that passage in *The Three Pillars*, you'll see that it was the *saint*—that is, a fully emancipated person, not the ordinary individual we have been discussing—whom the Buddha wouldn't say exists or does not exist after death. Why would he not say? Here is the answer in his own words [leafing through notes]: "Terms such as 'reborn' or 'not reborn' or 'both reborn and not reborn' or 'is neither reborn or not reborn' do not fit the case. . . . The saint, being released from what is styled form, is immeasurable, hard to fathom, like the great ocean."

You have a point nonetheless. It is misguided, grandmotherly kindness for me to entertain questions on life after death from this audience; it is far more important to find out who you are now than to know what happens after you die. For that matter, it's no less misguided for me to think I can succeed in conveying to you the real spirit of Zen in this setting. Why do I say that? Because the cards are stacked against me here. When students come to the Center in Rochester they come hat in hand, so to speak. They are humble and open, and because they respect my authority they will accept my treatment of them; otherwise they would leave. If they didn't feel an urgent need to transform their lives, they wouldn't have come. This need, and the humility and openness it generates, enables me to help them.

But when I come before you students and professors, I come to an audience that is for the most part merely curious about Zen. I am obliged to operate within the confines of an atmosphere created by academic, not Zen, standards. Suppose, for example, I refused to answer your questions on rebirth, or stood silent in response to other questions that "bake no bread." Might not Professor S—, who invited me here, grumble that he's not getting his money's worth? "Did we contribute an honorarium to the roshi's Center just to have him sit before us like a mute?" he might ask. Or, if I lashed out at your egos, he might reprove me with, "I didn't invite you here to insult and abuse my students."

TWELFTH QUESTIONER: What about Bodhidharma? [11] He went to China all the way from India. In your book you say he went by boat—a slow boat to China, no doubt. [Laughter] It was a lot more hazardous for him to do that than for you to come to this seminar.

A VOICE: So why did Bodhidharma go to China and why did you come here?

ROSHI: I don't know.

26 / ARE YOU ALIVE OR ARE YOU DEAD? /

QUESTIONER: There is much debate in medical circles these days about how to determine when a person is dead. Some say that it is when the heart stops beating, others say when the brain waves stop. What is the Buddhist viewpoint?

ROSHI: The Buddha said that cessation of the last thought is known as decease and the appearance of the first thought as rebirth. So tell me, right now are you alive or are you dead?

QUESTIONER: I'm alive—at least I hope I am.

A VOICE: He's dead from the neck up.

[Laughter]

ROSHI: You're both wrong! Now think carefully about the following dialogue:

An ancient Zen master took his disciple with him when he went to console a family grieving over the recent death of one of its members. When they arrived at the house the disciple knocked on the coffin and asked his teacher, "Master, is he alive or is he dead?"

The master replied, "I won't say he's alive, I won't say he's dead."

The disciple persisted, "Why won't you tell me one way or the other?"

"I won't say. I won't say," repeated the master.

On the way back to the temple the disciple, still deeply troubled by this question of life and death, suddenly turned to the master and demanded, "I must know! If you don't tell me, I won't be responsible for what I do to you."

"Do whatever you like," the master retorted, "but you won't get an answer from me." So the disciple struck him.

Years later, after the master had passed on, the disciple visited another master who had once been a disciple of the first master, and told him about the incident. Then the disciple asked, "Was he alive or was he dead?"

The master answered, "I won't say he was alive, I won't say he was dead."

Disciple: "Why won't you tell me?"

Master: "I won't say. I won't say."

The disciple suddenly had an awakening.

Now quick, tell me: why wouldn't either master answer the disciple's question?

[Various answers are called out.]

ROSHI: You're all out in left field.

This related anecdote may help you. At the funeral of one of his monks a famous Zen master joined the procession and remarked, "What a long procession of dead bodies follows the wake of a single living person."

SECOND QUESTIONER: Why don't you tell us what these dialogues mean?

ROSHI: If I explain you'll be robbed of the experience of coming to your own realization of their meaning. Can't you see that it was impossible for the master to answer?

THIRD QUESTIONER: If even the disciple couldn't understand at first what the master meant, how do you expect us to understand?

ROSHI: When your concern with life and death becomes as concrete and compelling as that monk's, you will find the answer to the meaning of life and death, and that will be your awakening.

27 / ZEN SAYS, "DON'T SUPPRESS THE EMOTIONS." BUT WHAT ABOUT ANGER? /

QUESTIONER: I asked this question during the [workshop] break and was told to take it up in the question period so that everyone could hear it. This morning at the beginning of zazen you told us that if we felt like crying to go ahead and cry, that in Zen you don't suppress the emotions. Suppose I get so mad at someone that I want to yell at him or hit him. Do I let go? I might feel better if I did, but what about the other guy?

ROSHI: No, you don't let go. Anger is one of the most destructive emotions, so you need to make an effort to control it. Unchecked, it can seriously undermine your practice; that is why the ninth precept [12] admonishes not to give way to anger.

QUESTIONER: How do you control it?

ROSHI: Here is a simple technique. When you feel yourself getting angry, breathe deeply and slowly from the bottom of your belly. Do this before the anger erupts and usually it will subside.

QUESTIONER: I have such a terrible temper that I find it impossible to control. Ever since I was a child I've had this problem. It must be in my blood.

ROSHI: Tell me, where is that hot temper of yours right now?

QUESTIONER: I don't know.

ROSHI: Were it in your blood it would always be with you, wouldn't it? Actually, it is something that you yourself create and therefore you can rid yourself of it.

SECOND QUESTIONER: Where does anger come from?

ROSHI: From ego, from the strong sense of I— "*I* am being put upon, *I* am being insulted, *I* am being abused, *I* am being frustrated"— I . . . I . . . I. . . . The angry person is never free of the oppressive and egotistic feeling, "The world is against me." He therefore lives a hellish existence in the midst of enemies: those opposing him, those antagonizing him, those taking advantage of him.

The only lasting remedy for this disease is realizing once and for all that the notion of self-and-other is the product of a dualistically oriented mind.

THIRD QUESTIONER: I've noticed that the persons assisting you—who I presume are your students—don't seem to show much emotion. They are friendly and helpful when you talk with them, but otherwise they seem so reserved. Why don't they laugh more or let go of themselves? Is that supposed to be good Zen?

ROSHI: Undisciplined persons lack stability and direction; they are forever scattering their energies, wasting them in useless pursuits and vain actions. They move like puppets on a string: jerkily, because they have no center, no well out of which their energies flow smoothly, spontaneously. When they see Zen students with poise and inner silence, it makes them nervous. Why? Because it accentuates their own lack of those qualities.

The individual who is centered in his *hara*, the region just below the navel, is neither slack nor euphoric in his responses and has a great reserve of energy. His zazen frees him from unhealthy repressions and he becomes open and responsive. In a hilarious situation he laughs uproariously; when grief-stricken he cries openly, unashamedly.

You say that my assistants are reserved, but what's wrong with that? The Buddha, it is said, rarely spoke unless spoken to.

Many years ago I witnessed an unusual courtroom scene. An attorney with an aggressive manner and a bellowing voice was haranguing the soft-spoken judge. With forbearance and dignity the judge withstood the lawyer's blustering, then gently said, "Counselor, haven't you heard the biblical saying, 'The meek shall inherit the earth'?"

"And that's the *only* way they'll ever get it, your honor!" shot back the lawyer.

The lawyer's remark typifies a prevalent ethic of our society, that aggression is not only accepted but even expected in advancing one's own interests. And if in doing so others' arms are twisted, heads bumped, or feelings fractured, the important thing is still to push, for it's the only way to get. Meekness translates as weakness.

The meek in the biblical sense, however, are those with forbearance and humility, not those who are spineless and obsequious. They are not proud, self-assertive, or grasping. At the deepest level meekness means self-surrender. With complete self-negation one awakens to the realization that the universe is no different from oneself. What, then, is there to grasp for?

28 / DO YOU HAVE TO GIVE UP SEX TO BECOME ENLIGHTENED? /

QUESTIONER: Don't you have to give up sex to become enlightened?

ROSHI: No, you don't. What is important is not to get hung up on sex.

QUESTIONER: Then why did the Buddha place so much emphasis on celibacy?

ROSHI: Not only the Buddha but every great spiritual master has made celibacy a primary condition of the monastic life. Why? Because the Buddha knew that sexual desire and gratification can easily lead to craving and clinging, thus binding men and women alike to the pleasures of the senses and the cycle of birth and death.

He also knew that if monastics were permitted to marry, their wives and children would have to be provided for by them. This in turn meant that the monks could not single-mindedly devote their time, energy, and concern to their quest for Self-realization, nor could they be similarly involved after they became teachers, for their families would have to come first. In the sutras and writings of the masters we find it stated that celibacy—when the body-mind is ripe for it—furnishes the ground for transforming sexual energy into the purer vibrations essential for the deepest states of samadhi and awakening.

Celibacy implies much more than abstention from sex. It is a transcendence of sex, a living through and going beyond. This "living through and going beyond" may take a short while or it may require many years. At its highest, celibacy is a rarefied state in which the coarser body-mind vibrations have been transformed into the subtlest and finest, producing an all-pervading calm and clarity.

SECOND QUESTIONER: But why repress sex—isn't it a natural function, like eating?

ROSHI: We can live without sex, but how long can we stay alive without eating? The point is that we are talking about transcendence, not repression, which is something else again.

Many regard sex as an open-ended experience indispensable to an intimate relationship. Yet there are many couples who eventually reach a point in their relationship in which they transcend sexuality in the narrow sense of intercourse and continue to have a rich life together. The highest love is grounded not in sexuality but in right knowledge of the interrelationship of all existence and the respect for life that it generates.

In speaking of celibacy and sex, however, we must not confuse the life situation of the householder with that of the celibate monk. For the householder a happy married life, and consequently an equable mind state for effective zazen, is often dependent upon a harmonious physical love relationship, especially in the early years of a couple's life together. For the monastic, of course, the very opposite is true. Thus a householder who tries to follow a monastic life, or a monastic a householder's, can only harm and not help his or her practice. In the end, though, the matter of celibacy is determined by one's karma.

THIRD QUESTIONER: But how do you know what your karma is with respect to sex?

ROSHI: There's a simple test. If the renunciation comes easily, almost inevitably—which is to say without compulsion and with little doubt or trepidation—it's fairly safe to assume that one's karma has matured in regard to sex and that one is ready for celibacy.

FOURTH QUESTIONER: But if you don't wish to be celibate— and most don't—can you indulge in sex, practice Zen, and become enlightened?

ROSHI: Yes, you can. There have been many householders in Buddhism who have come to deep enlightenment. The three most famous are Vimalakirti, in the time of the Buddha; Fu

Ta-shih, in the fifth century; and the Layman P'ang, in the ninth century. Vimalakirti, a married man with a family, was said to be second only to the Buddha in spiritual development, and many stories have been told of his wisdom and compassion.

Fu Ta-shih carried on his spiritual practice while living with his wife and two children, and still found time to work with great dedication toward relieving the sufferings of his countrymen.

The Layman P'ang also had a wife and two children. He is famous in Buddhist literature for having taken his considerable fortune of gold and thrown it into the sea, afterward earning his living as a maker of bamboo utensils.

All three carried out the responsibilities of family men and expressed in their lives the compassion and wisdom that grew out of their high spiritual state.

A slightly different case is that of Shinran, a master in the Pure Land sect. Shinran started as a celibate monk, but because he felt strongly that enlightenment could be realized by lay persons as well, he decided to get married and prove so. Before taking the step he consulted his teacher, Honen, a wise and saintly monk, many years his senior. Honen said, "If in order to carry on your spiritual practice best you need to marry, then marry. If you don't need to marry to do that, don't marry."

In Japan today most Buddhist priests, and a few Zen masters, are married men with families; celibacy is only required during training in the monasteries. In our Center we are, in effect, guided by Honen's dictum, for we have ordained celibate monks and ordained married men.

FIRST QUESTIONER: But doesn't sex become a problem for celibate monks when they must associate with laymen and women as they do at your Center?

ROSHI: Yes, it sometimes does. To help them and others learn how to deal with this emotion, commentaries are given on koans and stories that illustrate the wisdom of the Zen master in situations involving sex. Let me tell you such a koan.

A deeply enlightened old Zen woman allowed a young celibate monk to occupy a hut on her property and provided him with two meals a day and other necessities so that he could devote all his time to study and zazen. When he had lived there for three years, she felt it was time to find out how far he had progressed in Zen. Her young and attractive granddaughter came to visit shortly afterward and she told the girl, "I need your help to test the monk living in the hut."

"What can I do, Granny?" asked her granddaughter.

"Please take his midday meal to him today. After you set it down, put your arms around him, smile sweetly, and ask, 'How does this make you feel?' Then come back and tell me exactly what he says or does."

The girl was at first reluctant—this was a long time ago, remember—but her grandmother persisted, so she did as instructed.

The monk withdrew himself stiffly and replied, "I feel like a dead tree next to a cold rock in the middle of winter."

No sooner had the girl reported the monk's response than her grandmother exclaimed, "That worthless fellow! He hasn't learned a thing about Zen!" and she drove him from the hut and burned it down.

How would each of you have responded as a monk in that situation?

FIRST VOICE: I'd say, "I'm starved," and grab the food, not the girl.

SECOND VOICE: Not if I know you—you'd grab the girl and make passionate love to her.

[Laughter]

THIRD VOICE: I'd be suspicious that someone put her up to it, so I wouldn't touch her with a ten-foot pole.

FOURTH VOICE: If I were the monk I'd say, "What's a nice girl like you doing in a place like this?"

[Laughter]

ROSHI: Don't forget that the *Mahayana* teaches the middle way. If you grabbed the girl and made love to her, that would be one extreme, and if you acted disdainfully, as the monk did, that would be the other.

FIFTH QUESTIONER: Are you implying that the middle way would be to put your arms around her lightly, hold her hand, or kiss her on the cheek?

ROSHI: Would it be wise for a celibate monk to do even these things?

A VOICE: Well, what's the correct answer?

ROSHI: How can there be a single "correct" answer when the understanding of this problem may be demonstrated in more than one way? This koan, like every Zen koan, is thrusting truth at you, truth that cannot be taught but must be caught. You may see more clearly what is involved if I tell you a story my teacher told me when I was working on this koan many years ago.

In a Japanese monastery in the Middle Ages there lived a roshi who because of his exceptionally pure character and compassionate heart had been appointed by the abbot to be in charge of some five hundred monks. Close to the monastery was a *geisha* house noted for its beautiful women. . . .

FIFTH QUESTIONER: Is a geisha a prostitute?

ROSHI: No, traditionally a geisha would not be compared to a prostitute, although these days the distinction between them has become blurred. A geisha is talented in singing and dancing, and to become one a girl must at an early age begin training in these arts and in the social graces. First-class geisha live very comfortably in a geisha house, where for a high fee, they entertain businessmen, politicians, and others.

O-san, one of the geisha in the house near the monastery, was in need of a large sum of money to pay for a serious medical operation her aged mother required. Being a beautiful and talented geisha, she had well-to-do patrons. She approached each of them for a loan, but was refused again and again, as her debts to them were already high. She was in deep despair when a wealthy merchant entered the house—a man known as much for his miserliness as for his fondness for *saké*. Hoping that copious quantities of this elixir would loosen his heart and purse strings, she filled and refilled his cup, waiting for the right moment to make her plea. It came when he began to act giddy and sentimental.

"All I ask for is a loan," she pleaded after telling him of her mother's plight and the expensive operation. "Believe me, I will repay it."

He was silent for several moments, as if asleep. Then he raised his head and said, "I won't lend you the money, I'll *give* it to you—but only on one condition."

"I'll do anything you ask."

"Are you sure?"

"Yes! Yes!"

"All right. You know that roshi in the monastery nearby—the one who doesn't drink or smoke or have anything to do with women—I hate him and his righteousness."

"What does he have to do with me?"

"This: If you can seduce him I will give you the money you need for your mother's operation."

The girl's face darkened. "Everyone knows of his moral purity and strength of character. I could never succeed. And even if I could, I wouldn't want to—it wouldn't be right."

"Then you'll get no money from me."

O-san agonized over her plight. Already she had tried every other source for the money, to no avail. This was her last chance. The cost was frightfully high, but she reflected, "Without this operation mother will surely die. I have no choice. I must agree to his terms."

So the next day she made her way to the monastery. The cold drizzle that was falling fit in well with the plan she had formulated. At the far end of the monastery grounds she found the small house of the roshi. By now her clothes were dripping wet and her hair disheveled. When the roshi answered her knock she said, "Forgive me for disturbing you. I am lost and cold. Will you be kind enough to let me take a bath to warm up?" (Inviting a stranger in for a bath, by the way, was not uncommon in Japan at that time.)

"Come in," the roshi said and showed her to the bath. After bathing she returned dressed in a décolleté kimono. She now proceeded to employ all her feminine wiles in an attempt to seduce the roshi—but in vain.

At length she broke down and, weeping, told him the whole bitter story. "Believe me," she sobbed, "I didn't want to do this. I know you have a spotless reputation and are in charge of hundreds of young monks. But I was desperate. Please forgive me! I will go now." And she started to leave.

"Wait," he told her. "Since the only way for you to obtain the money for your mother's operation is for us to sleep together, you may stay all night."

Within a few days word had spread throughout the monastery that the beautiful geisha O-san had spent the night with the roshi in his quarters. Appalled, the abbot summoned the roshi and demanded to know whether the rumor was true.

"Yes, it is true."

"What!" exclaimed the abbot incredulously. "How could *you* of all people do such a thing? Don't you realize the effect this will have on the young monks under your charge? Your usefulness here is at an end. You must go."

"If those are your feelings I will leave." The roshi said no more and departed.

When the monks learned that the roshi had been dismissed, they went to the abbot and demanded that he be reinstated.

"But why?" asked the abbot. "Do you know what he did?"

"Yes."

"Not only was his conduct scandalous; even worse, he showed no remorse. Why should he be allowed back?"

"Because," repied the monks, "he taught us a valuable lesson in compassion. If you don't reinstate him we will all leave." So the abbot relented and recalled the roshi.

SIXTH QUESTIONER: Did the abbot know *why* the roshi had allowed the geisha to spend the night with him?

ROSHI: Evidently he wasn't interested in the reason. Uppermost in his mind was the roshi's moral transgression in sleeping with the geisha and the effect he thought it would have on the impressionable young monks. But if the roshi gave the monks a lesson in compassion, the monks taught the abbot another kind of lesson.

FIRST QUESTIONER: In helping this woman wasn't the roshi sacrificing his own moral integrity?

ROSHI: In one sense he was, and it must not be imagined that he did this lightly. But when it became necessary to decide between the upholding of his own virtue and the compassionate need to help the geisha and her mother, he naturally chose the latter—"naturally," because he was a Mahayana monk, and the Mahayana stresses the ideal of the bodhisattva, who out of his boundless compassion dedicates himself to helping others. A Zen master, when asked where he would go after he died, replied, "To hell, for that's where help is needed most."

29 / CAN YOU WORK ON A KOAN BY YOURSELF? /

QUESTIONER: You said this morning that one should not take a koan by himself, that it should be assigned by a teacher. Why is that?

ROSHI: Thank you for raising this subject; I had intended to speak about it earlier.

To work successfully on a koan your aspiration must be high and your ability to concentrate strong. Only your roshi is in a position to determine this. The nature of the koan is also important. Before assigning a particular koan a teacher usually will question the student closely to determine what koan is best for him. And when your practice is a koan you need to work closely with your roshi, especially in the beginning.

Normally a teacher prefers to assign a koan during sesshin, for with dokusan three times a day the student can get a solid start on his koan. Also during sesshin a commentary is given on a different koan each day, which is helpful to anyone working on a koan.

QUESTIONER: Relatively speaking, Roshi, is the koan *Mu* easy or hard to crack?

ROSHI: Both.

QUESTIONER: What do you mean by that?

ROSHI: Easy in this sense: When you resolve it you realize that the "answer" was there all the time. And hard because it takes longest to see what is closest to you.

30 / WHY REJECT THE WAY OF THE MASTERS TO FOLLOW THE EASY PATH? /

QUESTIONER: Won't you agree that we're living in an age with a higher level of consciousness? We know much more than the ancients did about the mind and the physical world through our discoveries in psychology, parapsychology, atomic physics, biochemistry, and other sciences.

ROSHI: In the deepest sense, do we really know more than the ancients did about man and the universe? What scientist can say why the sun rises in the east and sets in the west, why crows are black and herons white, why water boils at 100° C and freezes at 0° C, why dogs chase cats or cats play with mice? Can any psychologist or biologist explain the origin or nature of consciousness—even his own? For all their accomplishments scientists don't even know what man is. "All of today's philosophy," said Whitehead, "is but a footnote to Plato." Similarly, our knowledge of the human mind and the nature of the universe is merely a footnote to what the Buddha discovered twenty-five hundred years ago, a footnote to the wisdom within each of us. In the ninth century, a monk who later became a great Zen master declared upon his enlightenment: "The study and mastery of the profoundest philosophies is like a single hair in vast space. The farthest limit of human knowledge is a drop of water thrown into a deep ravine." [13]

SECOND QUESTIONER: Do *you* know what man is, Roshi?

ROSHI: What are you?

SECOND QUESTIONER: I'm my body and my mind: isn't that right?

ROSHI: Can you regulate the flow of your blood or prevent the aging and death of your body? Can you control your thoughts? If it were *your* body and *your* mind, you would be able to do that.

Tell me, what does this mind of "yours" look like?

SECOND QUESTIONER: I don't know. Can *you* tell me?

ROSHI: Do you see that towering pine outside the window? That's you bridging heaven and earth. Do you hear that bird warbling? That's the sound of your entry into the world. Look! Listen!

FIRST QUESTIONER: Could we get back to my first question? I hadn't really finished it.

ROSHI: Yes.

FIRST QUESTIONER: Why in Zen do you need to meditate for long hours in painful positions and take years to come to enlightenment? That may have been necessary in the past, but the tempo of human activity has speeded up tremendously and new therapies and techniques have shown us quicker and less painful ways to enlightenment.

ROSHI: Much the same question was asked in the late sixties when drugs were at the height of their popularity. It was commonly believed then that if you were tense, anxious, frustrated, or alienated, life could be made more bearable by smoking a joint, dropping acid, or taking some other drug. Problems were "dissolved" in chemical solutions. It was even thought that satori, the grand prize, could be had by the same lickety-split route.

While this madness for psychedelics was raging in our country I was living in Japan, totally unaware of the drug phenomenon. My first introduction to it came when a so-called "friend" sent me several Xeroxed pages from Aldous Huxley's book *Island*. I say "so-called" because this extract did anything but spur me on in my training. The gist of what he sent was that the aspiring mystic need no longer undergo the exertion and hardships of the masters of old who sought Self-realization. All he had to do was first consult his psychiatrist to have the knots in his psyche untangled, then go to a knowledgeable chemist who would give him the proper drug or chemical to awaken certain age-old brain cells and expand his consciousness, and presto! He was a mystic: enlightened, awakened, God-imbued!

Many in the counterculture went to psychiatrists, not to have their psyches straightened out, but because of their drug taking and what followed from it. And what became of those who loudly boasted of an "instant" chemical satori? Ironically, many of them are now in Zen and other spiritual/religious practices.

THIRD QUESTIONER: Have you ever tried acid or pot yourself, Roshi?

ROSHI: No. It has always seemed to me that taking drugs of any kind shows a lack of faith in the body-mind's inherent purity and its capacity to heal itself once the deluded notions and mistakes in living are removed. Drug-taking also betrays an unwillingness to take responsibility for one's own physical, mental, and spiritual health. Most drugs are agents of convenience, taken in the vain hope that they will accomplish easily what one refuses to take the time and energy to do himself.

As for the new therapies, how many of these have actually

brought about enlightenment? Individuals who claimed to have come to enlightenment through one psychophysical therapy or another have often asked me to test them. Of the dozens of people tested, not one had had even a tip-of-the-tongue taste of kensho.

Today the name of the game is meditation. People of all ages are being duped into believing that enlightenment can be had, not through the long uphill route of the Zen masters but in twenty days of meditation, give or take a few days. And pleasantly, too. Snooze, snore, slump—meditate as you like, live as you please, because for sure you're gonna get enlightened.

Then a medicine man comes along peddling another drug. "Three days to kensho!" he guarantees. Only a quack or a lunatic would make the brazenly preposterous claim that kensho—seeing into one's True-nature—can be realized by *everyone* in three days!

P. T. Barnum knew his suckers too. To keep them from lingering at the exhibits in his sideshow, he put up a sign reading, "This way to egress." Few knew the meaning of the word, but thinking that an egress must be an exotic animal, many flocked in the direction of the arrow and arrived outside the tent, exactly where Barnum wanted them.

"Three days to kensho," "This way to egress"—one lures them in, the other out; either way it's the same old con game.

Before concluding let me read you a relevant passage from John Wu's *The Golden Age of Zen:*

> "The Zen masters realize what a superlatively hard task it is to be a full-grown man, what heart-rending trials . . . what strangling doubts, what agonizing temptations one must go through before one can hope to arrive at the threshold of enlightenment. That's why they have approached it with all their might, and have never been willing to stop short of their ultimate goal."

PART TWO / THE SECLUDED TRAINING PERIOD (SESSHIN)

ENCOURAGEMENT TALKS AND COMMENTARIES / ENLIGHT-ENMENT ACCOUNTS / INTRODUC-TION /

Sesshin! Fifty-five men and women come together for seven days of climbing (zazen). Fifty-five intrepid individuals joining forces to scale the "silver mountain" of Mind. Fifty-five people with varying degrees of ardor, stamina, and determination. Some young, some older, some advanced in age. Many from distant points. All experienced to one degree or another, tested on smaller mountains.

They set off from the base, making their way over the foothills. Their leader and guide first climbed this mountain decades ago. He knows that during the first three days it is useless to push the group because they must find their climbing legs, acquire a feel for the terrain, and learn how to move quickly with their cumbersome packs (judgments, opinions, hopes, and other delusions) until they can discard them. Usually on the fourth day the ascent begins in earnest; until then the climbers must move at their own pace. They move steadily, finding their rhythm, building momentum.

As the leader looks at the climbers' eager, determined faces he wonders how each will respond to the pitfalls that lie ahead. How well will they stand up to the howling winds, the raging storms, the blinding snows (makyo)? He knows that as they approach the midway point they will be ambushed by the powerful and bedeviling ego spirits of the mountain, for no mountain is without them. Poised with every stratagem at their command, the ego spirits keep ceaseless watch on the expedition. Unwilling to relinquish their ancestral domain, they will labor energetically to drive the climbers back. During the day they will bewitch them with subtle calls to give up their effort. They will loose upon them falling rocks and sliding ice, and stir dissension into their ranks. If the group perseveres onto the upper slopes of the mountain, the spirits will grow desperate and throw all their malevolent might into discouraging them. As the climbers lie down to rest they will fill men's and women's minds alike with seductive visions, allowing the climbers no respite.

The guide knows that the climbers must have help in coping with these ordeals. Each day he will meet with them individually (dokusan) and review the trail they must follow, pointing out again and again the summit ahead and emphasizing the exertion necessary to attain it. Once a day, too, he will address them collectively (commentary), urging them on with the lore of the mountain, regaling them with anecdotes of his own efforts and trials as well as those of others, and inspiring them with accounts of the struggles and heroics of climbers who in the past succeeded in reaching the top of this loftiest of peaks. He will also emphasize that in truth the top and the bottom of the mountain are essentially no different.

The leader will not be alone in guiding; two experienced mountain climbers *(monjutors)* will give him able assistance. These deputies will encourage and coax so that none of the climbers falls behind. Twice a day the leader will meet with his aides to map plans and discuss strategy for the next day's advance. They will confer over the strengths and weaknesses of each member and how well he or she is sustaining the rigors of the climb.

The leader knows that no one can be carried to the top. He also knows what the others can only believe—that to reach the summit, conviction, determination, and exertion are vital. Above all, he is aware that the tautness of the collective effort must not be allowed to dissipate, for upon the climbers' cohesiveness as a group rests the success of the expedition.

But as the climbers pass the halfway point there are signs of weakening: for some in their legs, for others in spirit. Many of the stragglers have fallen under the spell of the wrathful spirits and are convinced that there is no use in climbing higher. Even some of the more steadfast start to fall back, thinking that they have surmounted the steepest ledges and that the peak, which appears so close, is within easy reach. Content, they look out over the cliffs below to admire the view. In privacy with the leader they ask, "Why climb farther? It can be no different on top than it is here. Why should we continue to exert ourselves?" The leader spurs them on, aware that unless checked this malaise will quickly spread to the others. No longer is it enough simply to encourage; the leader and his aides goad the weary climbers into redoubling their efforts.

Even climbers almost to the summit, not so much weary as bedeviled, begin to lose their ardor: "It is almost the seventh day—the worst terrain lies below us, so the rest is sure to be easy," they rationalize. And the leader sees that in their minds they are parading before friends and family, being congratulated and feted. Once more the leader exhorts the foremost climbers: "This is a silver mountain! There will be no footholds and nothing to grip onto from here to the summit. To attempt these last hundred yards will be grueling, exhausting. And the mountain spirits will unleash all their fury."

A handful of climbers has reached the upper ridge. Some three desperate climbers almost to the peak . . . a leap! . . . and then . . . they gaze around them with astonishment and joy . . . a deep primordial silence . . . a vast emptiness, yet how much they see! How much they know, have always known—yet never really knew!

Everything is as it needs to be; this and that, summit and base, self and other intersect, intermesh—nothing impinges . . . everywhere there is transparency and harmony.

Afterward the leader addresses the climbers as a group. He warns them that their descent from the mountain (integrating the experience into their lives) will be as difficult as the ascent, that they cannot speak of success until they have reached the bottom and returned to their homes and daily lives. He reminds them that mountain climbing is not pursued only for one's personal satisfaction, that the mountain is the Mind of man, and that what they have learned from the climb belongs to all who would set foot on such a mountain.

Clasped hands, tears, embraces . . . music . . . the slow movement from Beethoven's pastoral symphony . . . and a deep sigh of joy at the music that so fully expresses what could not even be attempted through words.

The preceding metaphorical account includes all the essential elements of the seven-day secluded training period known in Japanese as sesshin, for centuries the hallmark of the Zen sect. Zen masters have said that, awakening or not, a strong seven-day sesshin heals and strengthens one's mind, body, and emotions to a degree that would require between one and three years of sitting by oneself. Because sesshin calls for energetic all-day sitting, it is not for the weak or self-indulgent. On the contrary, it is geared to those with an unmistakable thirst for Self-realization, a strong determination, and a body-mind capable of sustained exertion. At the Rochester Center no one may attend a seven-day sesshin who has not first proven his ardor and stamina at a four-day sesshin.

Awakening, of course, is not confined to sesshin. But because in sesshin all the elements of Zen training are combined in a dynamic whole, with each participant receiving sustained support from the roshi, the monjutors, and fifty-five or so fellow participants, sesshin is unquestionably enlightenment's most potent incubator. This is true, however, only when the sesshin is led by a capable roshi and monjutors strong in spirit yet sensitive and compassionate.

For those too restless and impatient to undergo years of solitary zazen culminating in the natural fall of the ripe fruit of full enlightenment, the seven-day koan-based sesshin is a way to give the tree a shake that will quickly bring down the fruit. But fruit brought down this way is still green (corresponding to partial awakening), so it must be ripened through long work on subsequent koans both in and outside sesshin.

One of the essential elements of sesshin is the roshi's commentary. Given daily during sesshin, the commentary is more than a talk or lecture. Facing the altar while delivering it, the roshi is offering to the Buddha a live and concrete presentation of his Zen. In so doing he is not talking *about* Zen but thrusting truth itself at his listeners. Undiluted by philosophical explanations or psychological interpretations, the commentary can dash to bits annoying thoughts and fears and give a hefty boost to sagging spirits. It also gives direction and encouragement to beginners and advanced students alike.

Listening to the commentary is really a mode of zazen; the participants sit in formal zazen posture, eyes down, unmoving, concentrated. The roshi's words, springing deep from the gut, slice through to the listener's subconscious and plant there seeds of the buddha truth that must sooner or later flower into realization. It is during the commentary, more than any other time except dokusan, that the delusive mind can be broken through—if the time is ripe.

The commentaries that follow were given at a seven-day sesshin held at the Rochester Zen Center. They are presented here as delivered over the last four days of the sesshin. The first two are on koans taken from *The Blue Rock Record* [14] and the other two are on koans from *The Gateless Barrier:* these are the main books of koans used in Zen. Since the commentaries given during the first three days, when the sesshin was still coalescing, were on miscellaneous Zen texts rather than koans, they have been omitted.

Another vital part of sesshin is the encouragement talk. In a seven-day sesshin encouragement talks do not begin until the fourth day, for not until then, usually, does the collective energy of the sesshin reach the point at which encouragement is truly effective. Like a locomotive that must have its fires stoked before it can be opened up to full throttle, sesshin must coalesce into unified momentum before the participants are able to respond fully to exhortation.

Encouragement talks may be given by either the roshi or the monjutors at any time of day or night, but generally those that come just before dokusan, when participants are expected to bring before the roshi the results of their zazen work, are the most stirring. When preceded by ardent sitting and followed by dokusan, an encouragement talk can become the catalyst which inspires participants to propel themselves beyond their imagined limits. Not all encouragement talks are of the lightning-and-thunder type. Always they are keyed to the collective energy, which, like the alternating crescendos and diminuendos of a symphony, flows and ebbs but never loses its vital impulse.

The second half of this section is comprised of enlightenment accounts, all except the third of which are in the form of unsolicited letters. The third account also originated as a letter in which its author capsuled his post-sesshin awakening. Since he was a middle-aged executive and family man who had persevered in his zazen through years of difficulties common to those in business, he was asked to write in more detail about his experience and his life situation as it affected his Zen practice.

The enlightenment letters were each received soon after the sesshin at which the awakening took place except for the fifth account, which was received about a year after the kensho experience. The reader will note that this letter, unlike the others, includes a reply. Such a reply seemed necessary to dispel the misconceptions evidenced in the letter, misconceptions due in large part to the author's living far from Rochester with little opportunity to hear commentaries and other talks given at the Center. In all the letters fictitious names have been substituted for those of the actual writers.

These letters express, as no words of mine could, the frustration and despair which one must pass through, as in the mythological trials of the gods, to attain liberation, as well as the marvelous joy and freedom which follow.

I / ENCOURAGEMENT TALKS AND COMMENTARIES /1 / ENCOURAGEMENT TALK / FOURTH DAY / We have come now to the halfway point in this sesshin, and many of you have begun reporting makyo in dokusan. This is to be ex-

pected—the "storms" of makyo usually descend on the third or fourth day, when there is a greater mobilization of energy. In this sense makyo may be seen as positive, a sign that the energy of the sesshin is building. Makyo usually do not come either when one's concentration is lax or when one is in a sama-dhi-like state, so they mark a midway point in one's practice.

You've heard many times about the nature and cause of makyo, but somehow confusion and doubt concerning them still remain, so please listen carefully. Why do these fantasies and illusory sensations arise? When after three full days of sitting, the upper levels of the mind have been quieted and stilled, all manner of images and sensations, the residue of past experiences, bubble up into consciousness, not unlike dreams. For instance, it is common for people to see faces and animals on the wall in front of them. Many hear the neighborhood church bells tolling constantly, and others feel what seem to be insects crawling on them. You may even imagine that you are levitating, or that your body is melting away. Crying is one of the most frequent types of makyo. As long as you are not crying because you feel sorry for yourself, tears can have a purging effect, dissolving and washing away the encrustations of ego. Makyo may also appear when your mind and breath are out of kilter, resulting from a strained body and an overwrought mind.

Makyo also come disguised as psychological states: resent-ment, envy, or euphoria. Even depression and discouragement are nothing but makyo, a kind of deep black pit that most every sesshin participant falls into at least once.

Fantasies that you may slip into and out of for days are also makyo without your suspecting them. Pleasant and enticing makyo can be every bit as distracting as the frightening kind. Many years ago when I was in training, a head monk came to me a day or two after one sesshin and said, "During sesshin you were acting out a very strange makyo, one I've never seen before. In the middle of a round of sitting you would suddenly reach out with one arm as if to grab something and draw it toward you, and then do the same with the other arm. Soon both arms were going like this at once. Do you remember that makyo?"

"Yes, I do. I was going through the aisles of a large American supermarket, helping myself to steaks, eggs, cheese and other things not served here in the monastery.''

Makyo can also be persistent. One I had in the early days of my training involved the paintings of Paul Klee, which I had often admired in museums. In my makyo the whole universe was dyed with the magnificent colors of his paintings, colors richer and more vivid than even Klee himself had painted. For almost a month I wallowed in the pleasurable sensation of these cosmic colors, convinced that surely I was enlightened, and only after some stern warnings by the roshi did I finally let go of these visions, which were paralyzing my practice.

One of the commonest—and perhaps most treacherous—makyo is fear. Usually the worst fears rear up when one's practice has turned a corner and ego begins to feel menaced. In desperation it dredges up these fears in a last-ditch attempt to retain its dominance. There are specific fears: fear of doing with less sleep or food, fear of the encouragement stick, and even fear of kensho itself. And there are nameless fears, the vague anxiety that comes up to haunt one as concentration deepens. These fears stem from long-forgotten childhood experiences or even from past lifetimes. What is most essential is to fearlessly see them for what they are—unreal. True, they are real enough in that they are frightening, but they have no enduring substance, no abiding home. And if even our daily life is dreamlike, how much more so these fears? The point is that this sesshin, with the combined strength of the monjutors and the roshi, offers those of you beset by fears a tremendous opportunity. With all this concentrated energy working for you, never will you have a better chance to see through your fears and banish them once and for all.

There are also what might be called "high level" makyo: regressing to past lifetimes, speaking in tongues, deep psychological or philosophical insights. These may happen to you at this sesshin. Such makyo are nothing to feel elated about. If you cling to them in the mistaken belief that you have experienced something of rare or permanent value, they will become an obstacle to awakening. But they are beneficial in that they often free blocked areas in the body-mind and liberate energies normally not available to you. This freed energy, however, must be channeled in the hara region, where it becomes a wellspring from which you may draw to break through your koan. Allowing it to rise into your chest or head will only cause a painful heaviness or throbbing sensation in those areas.

The crucial thing to remember when faced with makyo of any kind is not to get involved with them. Makyo are the magic of the ego, and without an audience this wily conjurer will take his bag of tricks and be gone. Or they are like uninvited guests—if you don't make a fuss over them, they soon leave. Entertain them, though, and they linger on. What a pity to see sesshin participants leave their practice—their koan—to cultivate high-energy or blissful states, or out of some perverse fascination to wallow in the mud of dark, annoying, or frightening makyo.

Above all, don't make the fatal mistake of confusing these mind states with actual awakening. Just put your whole mind into your practice! This is not easy when the makyo are vivid and strong. To avoid falling prey to them, you need determination when they are pleasureable and courage when they are frightening. More than anything else you need faith—faith in yourself, in your practice, and in your teacher. If you are working on a koan, involve yourself in it so completely that "you" disappear and only the koan remains. Do this and the makyo will dissolve like ice under hot water.

COMMENTARY ON "THE THREE DISABILITIES" — CASE 88 OF THE BLUE ROCK RECORD / FOURTH DAY /

THE CASE: Attention! Gensha said to the assembly: Every master in the land speaks of guiding and aiding living beings. Suppose a man with three disabilities [blindness, deafness, and muteness] came to you; how would you deal with him? Holding up a mallet or waving a ceremonial whisk would be useless in the case of the blind. Talking would be of no avail to the deaf. And try as you might, you would not be able to make the mute speak. So how would you guide such a person? If you could not, how could the Buddha-dharma be of any help?

A monk took the problem to Master Ummon.

"Bow down!" said the Master. The monk did so. The master thrust his staff at him, and the monk drew back.

"You're not blind!" exclaimed the master. "Come closer!" The monk came closer.

"You're not deaf. Do you understand?"

The monk replied, "No, I don't understand."

The master said, "You're not mute."

With this the monk had an insight.

Here we have a fine example of how Zen masters work in subtle ways their wonders to perform. These two, Gensha and Ummon, had been brother monks under the same master, and their minds were so keenly attuned to each other and to their disciples that their methods meshed naturally without written or oral communication passing between them.

Of the life of Gensha we know only that he was born in the year 835 and died in 908, and that he had been a fisherman before becoming a monk.

Much more has been handed down of the life of Ummon. Although his birth date is unknown, the records show that he died in the year 949, just after the close of the T'ang era (618–907), when Zen Buddhism was at its zenith. It is recorded that he had a quick, brilliant mind, was eloquent in his speech, and vigorous and forthright in manner, qualities that in one degree or another have always distinguished the Zen masters. Even in his own day Ummon was renowned as a Zen master; except for the great Joshu no master figures in more koans than he.

Ummon's family, we are told, was extremely poor. Very likely this was one of the reasons for their placing him for his education, while he was still a young boy, in the hands of a master of the Vinaya—a sect of Buddhism that emphasizes the moral precepts and rules of conduct.

When the boy came of age he had his head shaved, symbolizing the severance of attachments to a worldly life, and received the precepts and vows of a novice monk—a homeless one.

But all this failed to satisfy his deeper aspirations or bring him to the realization of his Self, so he went to see a well-known

Zen master.[15] As Ummon was about to enter the master's quarters, the latter slammed the door in his face. When Ummon knocked, the master queried, "What do you want?" Ummon replied, "I'm not yet enlightened on the vital problem of my Self. I've come to beg for your instruction." The master opened the door a crack, took a quick look at him, then shut it quickly. For two days Ummon repeatedly knocked and met with the same response. On the third day, however, he squeezed into the room. Grabbing him, the master demanded, "Speak! Speak!" As Ummon fumbled for words the master pushed him out, exclaiming, "You good-for-nothing!" and shut the door so violently that it caught and broke Ummon's leg. With a cry of pain he came to awakening.

Commenting on this story a contemporary writer asked, "Was it necessary for the master to be so crude? Was satori worth a broken leg?" Let him ask the ghost of Ummon! Or let him ask a mother whether her child was worth the pain of childbirth! One can only smile at such naïveté. Zen dilettantes will never understand Ummon's persistence, much less the spirit of the fierce rebuffs he had to face.

Why did the master continue to slam the door in Ummon's face? It was an ironclad rule of his to give dokusan only to those with an unmistakable thirst for truth, for he knew, as all Zen masters know, that realization of the highest truth demands a sincere heart and unfaltering exertion, as well as pain and struggle. But was not Ummon such an individual? Would not one less determined than he have fled after the first rebuff? Why then did the master refuse to see him? You must see into this vital point.

You must also grasp the significance of "Speak! Speak!" What could Ummon have said that would have earned approval instead of such rough treatment? What would *you* have said in Ummon's position? You must respond at once!

In the literature of Zen, Ummon is also famous for his "no gap" responses. Savor these lightning replies of his:

"What is the one road of Ummon?"
"Personal experience!"

"What is the Way?"
"Go!"
"What is the road, where is the Way?"
"Begin walking it!"

The unhesitating response from the guts, not the head, is much admired in Zen.

Of the many anecdotes about Ummon the following is one of the most unusual in the history of Zen. In ancient China there was a Zen master who had been the abbot of a large monastery for some twenty years. During all that time he had not appointed a head monk. Whenever his monks questioned him about this he would reply cryptically, "My head monk has not yet become a novice." One day he announced to the assembly, "Today my head monk took the vows of a novice." Upon being asked when his head monk would arrive at the monastery, he simply said, "My head monk has not yet received the full monastic ordination."

Several years passed and the monks had all but forgotten the elusive head monk when the abbot announced, "My head monk was fully ordained today!" Again the assembly was mystified. Two more years passed and then one day the abbot said, "My head monk will arrive at the main gate at noon today. Strike the bell and send a delegation to welcome him." This sounded very strange, as had everything else the abbot had been saying about his head monk throughout the years, but at the appointed hour the monks nevertheless went to the main gate. There stood a monk who had just arrived, and he was none other than Ummon.

When Ummon came before the abbot to profer his greetings, he asked, "How could you have known that I would arrive today? I told no one I intended to come here." Smiling, the abbot said, "Many, many lifetimes ago—during the lifetime of the Buddha himself—you and I were brother monks. We both trained very hard and developed remarkable samadhi powers. But in a subsequent life you were reborn into royalty and led a self-indulgent, worldly life. Consequently you lost these powers. I, on the other hand, continued to train and discipline myself through many more lifetimes; therefore these powers were strengthened.

Thus I knew when you had become a novice monk, when you had been fully ordained, and when precisely you would arrive at this monastery."

Psychic abilities in one degree or another are natural by-products of persistent zazen and an awakened mind; as such they are not regarded in Zen as exceptional or wonderful. Zen masters never make a vain display of psychic powers, nor do they set out to cultivate them for their own sake. They are in fact looked upon as makyo—a subtle variety, but still makyo—which is to say, something other than enlightenment.

This background material on Ummon is essential to an understanding of his prominence in the history of Zen. Now back to the case.

This koan can be seen as a drama in two acts. In the first act Gensha creates the conflict, and in the second Ummon resolves it. Note how the first master puts the monks into a painful quandary: how to reconcile their bodhisattvic vows to liberate all beings with the seemingly impossible task of liberating one who couldn't hear what was being told him, who couldn't ask questions, and who couldn't see gestures. "If you cannot help such an individual," he implies, "are not your bodhisattvic vows exercises in futility?" How pitiless this Gensha! He casts his monks into a dungeon of doubt and then watches them squirm in desperate efforts to free themselves. But he is cruel only to be kind. Do you see why?

Zen deals with the concrete and the personal. What then is behind this master's seemingly speculative question? This is the first barrier you must surmount if you are to see into this unfolding drama. And why does the monk take the problem to Ummon rather than pursuing it with Gensha? Does he consider Ummon the greater master? If so, why isn't he training at his temple? Or is he trying to test Ummon? If so, in what way? And why doesn't Ummon, who was not one to suffer Zen fools gladly, dismiss the monk with "Go chase yourself!"?

Can it be that Ummon, with his sharp Zen eye, perceived at once that the question, though couched in speculative terms, was rooted in something deeper than mere curiosity, namely the monk's lack of faith in himself? Wasn't the monk desperately seeking reassurance, through the problem of the three disabilities, that he could, despite his own shortcomings, achieve awakening? Why else would he have dared face the lion Ummon in his den?

Sensing that the question springs from an anguished, self-doubting mind, Ummon meets the problem head on. Note that he does not engage the monk in a Socratic dialogue or paint a vivid word picture of the omnipotent Buddha-mind. He simply commands, "Bow down!" The monk obeys, believing no doubt that whatever the reason for this peremptory command his question will be answered. But no sooner does he raise his head than he spies the master's stick about to land on his shoulder, and he falls back. "Ah," exclaims Ummon, "so you are not blind! Now come forward." The monk, probably thinking to himself, "Yours not to reason why . . ." complies. "Oh, you are not deaf either!" observes Ummon. "Do you understand?" "Understand what?" asks the monk, his mind now totally devoid of thoughts as he responds no-mindedly. "And you can speak too! Well, well."

Take note of the "clean slate," one-pointed mind of the monk and its relation to his subsequent insight. This is vital.

Before considering what the monk perceived, let me ask you: What is true hearing? What is true seeing? What is true speaking?

There's an old story of three people at a party who are asked by a fourth, "What organ of your body do you consider most indispensable?" The first says, "My ears. I am a musician. What would my life be like if I couldn't hear the glorious music of Bach or Mozart or the laughter of children or the whisper of the wind through trees? Not worth living, really."

The second replies, "My eyes. I can think of no worse affliction than a life of perpetual darkness. Imagine being unable to view the Sphinx or the Taj Mahal or the Sistine Chapel, or to experience a magnificent sunrise or sunset!"

"For me," said the third, "nothing could be worse than to be without a tongue. I am a teacher. If I couldn't speak how could I carry on my profession? Besides, nothing gives me greater satisfaction than to engage in conversation with high-minded people about the latest trends in literature, art, and philosophy. To be without a tongue would actually make one lower than animals, for even they have tongues and can communicate by howls, squeaks, and chirps."

These three then turned to the fourth and asked, "What organ of your body do you treasure most?"

"My navel," he replied.

"Your navel!" exclaimed the other three in a chorus of astonishment. "Why is that so precious?"

"Because I love to eat celery in bed and that's where I keep my salt."

[Laughter]

No, they do not yet understand the true meaning of hearing, seeing, and speaking, for each is still attached to his sense organs and the discriminations arising from them.

With regard to hearing, tell me: Does the sound go to the ear or the ear to the sound? To grasp the source of sound, you must transcend ear, brain, and sound. In the Surangama sutra the Bodhisattva of Compassion tells how he attained perfect enlightenment through concentration on the true nature of sound. A Zen master of old advises, "Whenever you hear a sound inquire of yourself, 'What is it that is hearing this sound?'" But those of you working on the koan "the Sound of One Hand" [16] need only question single-mindedly, "What Is the Sound of One Hand?" Once you break through you will hear loudly and clearly the sound of no-sound—a ringing silence, a silent ringing.

True speech has nothing to do with beautiful or wise words. Listen! [Recites a verse.] Did I speak or didn't I? You don't have to be mute not to speak. Learn to speak without your tongue and lips and you will enter the womb of unfathomable silence; then you will understand what is meant by "All day long there is speaking, yet no word is ever spoken."

What is true seeing? For the truly awakened, who see with the eye of equality, nothing is higher or lower, better or worse, than anything else. Is this not the highest seeing? So it is said, "A buddha is deaf, dumb, and blind." He does not shut his eyes to see no evil, cover his ears to hear no evil, or close his mouth to speak no evil, like the three proverbial monkeys. On the contrary, he looks, listens, and talks, but his seeing is a no-seeing, his hearing a no-hearing, and his speaking a no-speaking. Do you understand? Do you really understand?

Returning to the monk, what is it that he suddenly perceived? That they see most who see without their eyes, that they hear all who hear without their ears, and that they speak best who speak without their tongues.

[Raising stick] Do you see?

[Striking stick] Do you hear?

Tell me, was anything said?

2 / ENCOURAGEMENT TALK / FIFTH DAY / Listen to these words of an ancient Zen master: "Zen work does not consist merely in reciting a koan. The main thing is to arouse the 'doubt-sensation.' But even this is not enough. You must break right through it. If you cannot seem to do so you must put forth all your strength, strain every nerve, and keep on trying."

What is this doubt-sensation? It is a burning perplexity, a fundamental question that gives you no rest. For example: If all beings are inherently flawless and endowed with virtue and compassion, as the Buddha declared, why is there so much hatred and selfishness, violence and suffering everywhere? This basic question can be pondered whenever you find yourself free to do so—at home, at work, anytime. But when you are sitting in the formal zazen posture and using the body-mind in a more focused manner, questioning a koan like "What is Mu?" or an inquiry like "Who am I?"—strictly speaking, "*What* am I?"—is a way of bringing to keener intensity this same basic doubt. The koan assigned you does not *replace* the underlying doubt-sensation; it simply sharpens it by raising it to consciousness. The basic doubt-sensation may be likened to a drill of which the bit is, "What is Mu?"

At first the Mu may seem artificial and outside you, but as you become more deeply involved with it, it will grow into your own most urgent life question, for Mu is but another name for Mind—this undefiled, all-embracing Mind common to everyone. You may wonder, "Why, if I already possess this pure Mind as a birthright, don't I know it?" The answer is, "Because your defilements, your deluded notions about yourself and your relation to what you conceive as the world outside you, obscure the light of this Mind." To raise the doubt-sensation, which grinds away these impurities, you must carry on your questioning at all times until the solution comes to you, for only then can you see into your fundamental nature, make real in yourself this Mind, and be reborn into a life that is truly alive.

Remind yourselves: Mu is my cushion, my mat, my body. And it is also what is *not* my cushion, what is *not* my mat, what is *not* my body. Mu seems to be a thing and a no-thing at the same time. Logically, this is a contradiction, so here, too, doubt arises. Or if you prefer, you may revert to the full koan, asking yourselves, "Why did Joshu answer 'Mu!' [literally, "no," or "has not"] when asked, 'Does even a dog possess the Buddha-nature?' " [17] Since the sutras say the Buddha-nature is intrinsic to all existence, Joshu's response is a contradiction, and doubt arises. How do you dispel this doubt? When you reach the point where there's not even a hair's-breadth separation between you and Mu, the "answer" will reveal itself and the contradiction be resolved, for the question and the answer are not two; they only appear so to your dualistically ensnared mind, which discriminates self from not-self, this from that.

In the beginning, working on Mu is like bobbing for apples. You try to bite into one and it slips away. You try again and the same thing happens. But just as you cannot begin chewing and eating the apple until you get your teeth into it, in the same way, before you can ask, "What is Mu?" you need to have the Mu firmly in your mind. After a while, having gone deeper into the question, you no longer need to ask the whole question; just concentrate fully on the word "Mu," or "who" if you are working on "Who am I?" The echo in your subconscious will be "What is Mu?" or "Who am I?" for the question has already been planted there. Remember, Mu is not a *mantra,* it is a penetrating probe, an intense questioning. But even at this point the question will only scratch the surface if the Mu or Who is merely repeated mechanically. Just "Mu," asked as a perplexing question, is enough if you really need to *know* what Mu is; this keeps the questioning alive, and it is the questioning, fueled by the doubt and the conviction that you can find out, that gives strength to the Mu.

Consider a man sitting in his office who suddenly notices that his watch is missing. He looks about, expecting to find it nearby, but it is nowhere in sight. If he had left his office momentarily, or was not certain he had been wearing the watch there, he would search lackadaisically or soon stop searching and assume the watch was elsewhere. But if he had not left the office and no one else had come in, and furthermore was certain he had been wearing the watch there, he would become more perplexed and begin searching the office thoroughly. Knowing the watch must be there, his determination to find it, and the energy he puts into the search, would grow stronger every moment until he had forgotten everything else. This is raising the doubt-sensation. This is how you must question Mu.

But to do this there must be the deepest conviction that you can see through the koan in this fashion. And there must be faith that by resolving the koan you will realize your True-mind. As one master put it, "Where there is great doubt there will be great awakening; small doubt, small awakening; no doubt, no awakening."

People often wonder when they hear "to strain every nerve" whether it means they are supposed to huff and puff and gnash their teeth and bellow "Mu." They may even try this, and soon find themselves tense and overwrought. But what it means to strain every nerve is that all of yourself is involved in the practice, whether it is Mu or something else. It means not to sit blankly, or "Mu" yourself to sleep. Look at a cat sitting absolutely still as it watches a mouse emerge from its hole. The cat looks frozen but actually is almost quivering with concentration. Here there is no wild or frantic activity—just intense, one-pointed attention. You also see this in a hungry dog that has a meat bone held up before it. At that moment the dog's whole world is the color and size of that bone. And there are also people who, while sitting completely motionless and silent in zazen, have broken out in a sweat during the dead of winter, so intense was their concentration. This same samadhi-like state each of you can experience yourself through single-minded absorption in your koan.

One final word: Remember that while these hints are meant to help you—the roshi and monjutors try in every way to stimulate and encourage, to pry and nudge—what works for one person may not work for another. If what is said applies to you, use it; if it does not, discard it. There is no one way, no should's or ought's. But do not resort to techniques; they are always from the outside. Techniques belong to the world of technology, not to spiritual practice. To apply yourselves fully some of you need to huff and puff, and this is all right for you because if you didn't work in this way you could never mobilize the energy necessary to break out of a certain level. The point is, you must find your own way.

COMMENTARY ON "BODHIDHARMA'S 'I DON'T KNOW'"¹—CASE 1 OF *THE BLUE ROCK RECORD* / FIFTH DAY / THE CASE: Attention!

The emperor asked the great master Bodhidharma, "What is the highest truth of the holy teachings?" Bodhidharma replied, "Emptiness and no holiness." The emperor asked, "Who [then] is standing before me?" Bodhidharma replied, "I don't know." The emperor did not understand. Thereupon Bodhidharma crossed the river and reached the land of Wei.

Later the emperor took the matter to Prince Chih [his spiritual mentor], who asked, "Does your majesty know who this man is?" The emperor said, "I don't know." The prince said, "He is the Bodhisattva of Compassion bringing to our land the seal of the Buddha-mind." The emperor was regretful and wanted to send an emissary to invite him back. "It is useless for your majesty to send an emissary to fetch him. Even if all the people of the land were to go after him, he would never return," the prince answered.

That is the end of the case.

The "Bodhi" of Bodhidharma refers to man's innate wisdom, and "dharma" to Truth, or the fundamental law that upholds and governs the universe.

Bodhidharma is the twenty-eighth patriarch in line from the Buddha and the first patriarch of Zen. He is said to have arrived in southern China from India in the year 520 at the age of 109. After an abortive attempt to establish his teaching in the South (which is the subject of this koan), he disappeared into the North, where he eventually settled in a small temple.

The emperor was a cultured ruler who lavishly patronized

In the paintings and sculptures of most Japanese artists Bodhidharma is less the wise and compassionate first patriarch of Zen than a caricature. When his jaw isn't jutting and his eyes protruding to show grim determination, he appears fierce and sinister, not unlike a pirate. In this brush drawing Hakuin, himself an outstanding master, shows us a clear-eyed, warmly human Bodhidharma with whom we can identify. The face is open and transparent, the eyes warm yet penetrating. The steady gaze is like that of an infant: in its depth it penetrates to the very essence of things.

Bodhidharma, founder of the Zen sect, drawn by Zen master Hakuin (1686–1769) at the age of eighty-three. The calligraphy reads: "Directly pointing to man's mind, seeing into one's essential nature, and attaining buddhahood."

Buddhism. A man of piety, he had many temples erected and decorated with outstanding Buddhist art, and had a number of Sanskrit sutras translated into Chinese. He is also said to have encouraged many men and women to enter the monastic life. In the light of orthodox Buddhist teaching of his day, it was natural for him to believe that he would derive spiritual merit from these good works and that this merit would facilitate his entry into nirvana.

When word reached the emperor of the arrival of this aged brahmin monk from the then fabled land of the Buddha, he lost no time inviting him to his palace. Evidently the subject of merit was uppermost in the emperor's mind, for he began his dialogue with Bodhidharma by telling him that since coming to the throne he had built innumerable temples, copied endless sutras, and supported countless monks. "What merit have I gained from these acts?" he asked. When Bodhidharma replied "None," the crestfallen emperor asked why. After Bodhidharma told him that such deeds were of limited worth, that they were basically unreal, and that their merit drains away in time, the emperor asked, "What, then, does true merit consist of?" Bodhidharma replied that it was to be gained only through the awakening of wisdom—seeing into one's own nature—and not through worldly pursuits. (Although this preliminary exchange does not appear in the present case, it is to be found in other versions of their dialogue.)

What a shock that reply must have been to the emperor! Believing he had earned his way to "the other shore," he could not but ask, perhaps with some sarcasm, "What, then, is the highest truth of the holy teachings?"

The holy teachings are the Buddha's dharma, and obviously the emperor was led to ask the question by Bodhidharma's statement that there was no merit whatever in all his good works. Savor Bodhidharma's forthright response: "Emptiness and no holiness!" How compassionate this Indian master; the emperor should have bowed down in gratitude. But he was too caught up in the dry orthodoxy of his day to grasp Bodhidharma's vibrant Zen.

What is this emptiness Bodhidharma speaks of? It's not a huge hole in the universe with Buddha's sign across it reading, "The Void. Not holy. Trespassing allowed." Nor is it an abstract void that stands against a concrete fullness. What can this emptiness be if not the substratum from which all phenomena emerge and to which they inevitably return? In the words of the Heart of Perfect Wisdom sutra: ". . . Form here is only emptiness, emptiness only form. . . ."

While I was in a Zen monastery in Japan an American schoolteacher familiar with Zen through wide reading came to stay for a short period. He was given a small room some distance from the common bathroom. When he had to urinate in the middle of the night he would do so in the garden rather than take the long walk to the bathroom. After he had done this for several nights, the roshi spoke to him about it one day when the three of us were standing in the garden:

"I was told you have been making water in this garden. Is this true?"

"Yes."

"The garden is a holy place. Use the toilet."

"Why is the garden holy? Didn't Bodhidharma say, 'Only vast emptiness and nothing holy'?"

With this the roshi struck him. "Don't make water in the garden—go to the bathroom!" he told him.

Why did the roshi hit him? Wasn't this garden also emptiness and nothing holy? From the perspective of absolute Mind nothing can be holy, nothing profane, true enough, but on the relative level of social ethics, you don't violate customs and standards of decency by urinating in the garden of a Zen monastery because you're too lazy to walk to the bathroom. Along with the absolute, or equality, aspect of our life there must be recognition of the relative. And, conversely, an awareness of relative differences must at the same time be balanced by equality.

In a democracy like ours equality is stressed and people tend to say or think, "I'm as good as everyone else"; consequently there is little respect for differences. Such a view is one-sided. It is proper, of course, to speak of equal consideration or equality of opportunity, but to imply that each person is born into this life with as much intelligence or talent or strength of will as every other reveals an ignorance of the workings of karma. Equally one-sided are the class distinctions made in stratified societies. Buddhism teaches that while in our essential nature we are all equal, we differ from one another by reason of individual karma. Equality and differentiation—these are two aspects of the one Buddha-nature. Did I say "one"? Drop it—and drop "Buddha-nature." So what do you have left? [Suddenly shoots up fist.]

What do you make of the emperor's question, "Who, then, is standing before me?" Is he genuinely puzzled or is he trying with this mild rebuke to salvage some of his wounded pride? Whatever the case, it implies, "How can you say there is nothing holy when you, a monk, are obviously a holy man?" And then Bodhidharma's baffling response, one of the most famous in Zen: "I don't know." Let me ask you: Is Bodhidharma actually answering the emperor's question or is he avoiding it? If he is answering, what does he mean by "I don't know"?

Ordinary knowing arises from a subject-object relationship. You think about an object or proposition—you examine and analyze it—and make an inference or come to a conclusion about it. But this method yields limited information. To completely understand anything you must experience the dimension where the discriminating intellect has not yet begun to function. Who can say anything about this realm? It cannot be taught or spoken of, it can only be experienced. Whatever you understand through your intellect can only be half the truth; what you *don't* know is true understanding.

"Holy," "profane"—aren't these arbitrary distinctions that tend to separate one from the thing named? True holiness—wholeness—is emptiness, no-thing-ness, no-self-ness, a condition in which one no longer stands apart from anything. My teacher once said, "If a person appears so holy that you would call him a saint, his spiritual development is incomplete. Were he fully evolved there would be nothing you could say about him; he would be beyond description or classification."

Do you see the subtlety of Bodhidharma's "I don't know"? Suppose he had said, "Yes, I am a holy man." He would be affirming a distinction that inherently does not exist, would he not? Further, wouldn't such immodesty be contrary to "holiness"? But if he had answered, "No, I am not a holy man" he would be denying the obvious. What then did Bodhidharma mean by "I don't know"? Surely he knew when he was cold or hot, sad or joyous, for he was not insensate. But most of all he knew that there is nothing to know because in the deepest sense nothing can be known; this knowledge is the highest wisdom. When the mind is free of such notions as holy and profane, emptiness and fullness, self and other, the truth stands revealed; here is the key to understanding another's mind. This was the condition of Bodhidharma's mind. Is this not true holiness?

Ah, that "I don't know"!—it resists every attempt of the intellect to pin it down. Truly to grasp it you must cast aside all notions and theories and plunge headlong into the depths of Bodhidharma's mind where the waves of "know" and "don't know" can't reach.

The koan resumes: "The emperor did not understand. Thereupon Bodhidharma crossed the river and reached the land of Wei." Here in a small mountain temple in North China Bodhidharma did zazen steadily for nine years, facing a rock wall. And it was here where his dramatic encounter with the man who later became his outstanding disciple—and the second patriarch of Zen—took place.

When the latter first came to Bodhidharma he was a well-known scholar, proud of his vast knowledge of Buddhism and the reputation it had earned him. Presenting himself to Bodhidharma, he stiffly asked for his teaching but was ignored. He persisted. Bodhidharma, sensing his conceit, offered no word of guidance or encouragement; he merely continued facing the wall in zazen. At last, after a night in which the buffeted scholar had waited outside unmoving through a violent snowstorm, Bodhidharma, seeing him standing in snow up to his waist, asked, "What do you seek?" "My only desire is that the Master, out of his infinite compassion, open the Treasure Gate. . . ." the future patriarch replied, his voice choked with tears.

"The incomparable dharma," replied Bodhidharma, "is realized only through long exertion at a practice difficult to practice, and long endurance of that which is difficult to endure. Why should you, with your shallow mind and conceited heart, beg me for the True Vehicle and suffer such hardships in vain?"

At these words, the aroused scholar drew out a sword, cut off his left arm at the elbow, and laid it before the master. Now at last Bodhidharma agreed to teach him. Do you find this hard to believe? Do you say it's a myth? All right, call it a myth.

But don't forget that a myth is not a story that is untrue but a story so profound, so majestic, that it can't be encompassed within mere fact. Without sacrifice, without cutting off your egotistical thoughts and your defiling passions can you ever attain the ultimate—awakening?

The next lines in the koan: "Later the emperor took the matter to Prince Chih, who asked, 'Does your majesty know who this man is?' The emperor answered, 'I don't know.' " Tell me, is the emperor's "I don't know" the same as Bodhidharma's "I don't know"? If not, what is the difference?

"The prince said, 'He is the Bodhisattva of Compassion bringing to our land the seal of the Buddha-mind.' " Iconographically the Bodhisattva of Compassion[18] is represented with innumerable helping arms.

The seal of the Buddha-mind is the transmission of the dharma from master to disciple—in other words, it is authentic Buddhism transmitted from the Buddha himself.

And the final lines: "The emperor was regretful and wanted to send an emissary to invite him back. The prince said, 'It is useless for your majesty to send an emissary to fetch him. Even if all the people of the land were to go after him, he would never return.' "

Why not? Because Bodhidharma knew that the people of southern China were not yet ready for his living Zen. That's one kind of answer. But there's a deeper one: Because he never left. And why didn't he ever leave? Because he never came!

Do you see Bodhidharma's overwhelming compassion? If not, you have yet to grasp the spirit of his hazardous journey from India to China—at an age when most men are lying in their graves—or the deep religious significance of his encounter with the emperor, or the vital meaning for all of us in his nine years of facing the wall—facing himself.

3 / ENCOURAGEMENT TALK / SIXTH DAY / At this stage of sesshin it is common to hear people in dokusan say, "No matter what I do, I just can't get beyond

a certain point. My concentration is strong but I feel as though I'm up against an iron wall. I try with all my might to push through this barrier but nothing happens—I just end up tight and exhausted. What more can I do?" These individuals may work hard, but are never quite able to go all the way. Their performance follows a pattern common to previous sesshins— "Always a runner but never a winner."

What can be done about this? It's as though they have dug a trench leading nowhere and can't move out of it, left or right. If you're one of those who have come to this impasse sesshin after sesshin, you must realize the need to break out of this familiar rut and find a new course. To be specific, if you are accustomed, say, to resting in the morning during the break after the work period, determine to yourself that you will sit then instead. Or if you regularly eat three meals a day during sesshin, try skipping one now and then and use that time for sitting. If you have never stayed up at night longer than an hour or two after the end of the formal sitting, make up your mind to sit until at least, say, midnight, and not give in to sleepiness. If during that time you usually sit in the zendo, take your cushion outside instead, or vice versa.

At a sesshin not long ago one person came to kensho when, after many sesshins of having sat up late at night and risen at the wake-up bell, he finally tried going to bed earlier and getting up in the middle of the night to sit. No matter how you manage to break out of your previous pattern, once you do, the energy begins to flow and you find yourself doing things you couldn't do at other sesshins. But the resolution must be made, followed by a dedicated and inspired effort. You've heard me say before: To a weak person a wall is an impenetrable cliff; to a strong one it is something to be climbed over. And ask yourselves: Would a weak person be able to go with as little sleep as you have? Would a weak person come warriorlike before the roshi in dokusan every day as you have?

One insidious pattern that should be mentioned in particular is what might be called the will to fail. Those of you who fall prey to this know that there comes a point in every sesshin when suddenly your mind is overcome with feelings that you will never do it. "I've failed at so many things," you tell yourself, "there's no chance kensho will be any different. What's the use?" Here again is the subtle work of the ego, which throws up every kind of roadblock to protect itself. The rationalizations for this defeatist attitude are many. "It just isn't worth it—what if I do come to kensho? So what?" Or if you have a lot of pain in your legs you tell yourself, "If I continue this exertion I might do myself permanent damage. So it's better to quit now." And usually in the life of such a person we find this same pattern, where he makes a strong start in one direction, reaches a certain plateau, and then the will to fail steps in, the rationalizations begin operating, and the enterprise ends up in what we call failure. This is really a copping out, an unwillingness to accept the responsibilities that you imagine success will bring. If you label yourself a misfit you can wash your hands of the task of awakening to your True-mind or of any other challenge.

You who are plagued by this life pattern have a supreme opportunity to uproot it once and for all at this sesshin, where you can draw from the pooled spiritual energy of fifty-four other people working strenuously day and night. Nor is there a better time than now, when the collective samadhi power has been building for some five and a half days. This is the time to try something new, to give a new burst of energy, to break the back of your old habitual patterns. Zen Master Bassui says, "If you push forward with your last ounce of strength at the very point where the path of your thinking has been blocked, and then, completely stymied, leap with hands high in the air into the tremendous abyss of fire confronting you, into the ever-burning flame of your own primordial nature, then all ego-consciousness, all delusive feelings and thoughts and perceptions, will perish with your ego-root, and the true source of your Self-nature will appear." This means you must become utterly naked, you must surrender everything. Do this and everything will be yours—you will be everything!

COMMENTARY ON "A MAN UP A TREE"—CASE 5 IN MUMON'S *THE GATELESS BARRIER* / SIXTH DAY /

THE CASE: Kyogen said, "It [i.e., Zen] is like a man up a tall tree hanging from a branch by his teeth. His hands can't grasp a bough, nor his feet reach one. Under the tree a man asks him the meaning of Bodhidharma's coming from the West. If he does not answer he fails the questioner. If he does answer he will lose his life. What should he do?"

MUMON'S COMMENT: Though your eloquence flows like a river, it is of no avail. Even if you can explain all the Buddhist sutras, that also is useless. If you can answer the problem properly, you can kill the living, bring the dead to life. But if you can't answer, you must ask Maitreya when he comes.

MUMON'S VERSE:

> Kyogen really spouts nonsense;
> he endlessly spreads poison.
> Stopping up the monks' mouths,
> he watches them writhe
> with the black piercing eyes
> of a devil.

You must not imagine that this koan is a teaser, having nothing to do with the realities of your life. On the contrary, it is intended to prove that your marvelous Mind, when you don't imprison it in all kinds of fanciful notions, is equal to every occasion.

Kyogen lived toward the end of the T'ang dynasty. Besides being well versed in the sutras, he had a quick wit and strong analytical powers. One day his teacher, Isan, told him, "You are a man of keen intelligence and wide learning. Now the matter of birth and death is the most fundamental of all. Don't tell me what you have learned from your reading of the sutras but give me an essential word about your Self before you came out of your mother's womb, before you knew east from west." Dazed, Kyogen was unable to utter a word.

Returning to his room still gripped by the question, he frantically searched through all his books, but every answer he presented to Isan was flatly rejected. At last, his intellectual resources exhausted, he implored the master to give him a clue. Despite his entreaties the master insisted, "Even if I should reveal it explicitly to you, it would be my experience and not yours."

In despair Kyogen burned all his books and notes, saying, "A picture of a cake doesn't satisfy hunger." Vowing to give up his study of Buddhism, he left Isan's monastery in tears to become a wandering monk. Eventually he came to the dilapidated temple of a famous Zen monk, long dead, and settled down as the self-appointed keeper of his grave. Undoubtedly what kept him here was the atmosphere and vibrations of the temple, which nurtured in him the yearning to resolve his teacher's nagging question and come to Self-liberation.

One day as he was sweeping the yard, Kyogen tossed aside a piece of broken tile, which happened to hit a bamboo tree with a sharp crack. Jolted by the unexpected sound, he suddenly awakened to his true Self and burst out laughing. He composed a verse at the time, which read:

> The sound of something struck,
> and I forgot everything I knew.

Returning to his hut he bathed, lit incense, and made obeisance in the direction of Isan's temple, saying, "Oh Venerable Master, how great is your compassion! I am grateful to you more than to my parents. Had you revealed the secret to me when I asked you, how could I have experienced this great joy?"

My first teacher, who had himself been a college professor for many years, used to say that because scholars and intellectuals are always trafficking in ideas, it is more difficult for them to awaken than for those not so burdened. He would also say that women usually come to enlightenment sooner than men, mainly because their minds do not ordinarily harbor and play with concepts to the extent that men's do. Then he would add, "But when the highly intellectual person does break through, it is usually a very thorough breakthrough." The point is that since the enlightened Mind is common to all, everyone has the potential of awakening to it.

Although this Wisdom-mind is closer than your own nose, it can't be brought into consciousness without search and struggle. When the tile hit the bamboo, Kyogen's mind had already been brought to ripeness by his agonizing search; that sound merely precipitated his awakening. It was like a lit match tossed onto the tinderbox of his parched notions and opinions, annihilating them all in the flames of his Self-transcendence.

To return to the case: ". . . Under the tree a man asks him, 'What is the meaning of Bodhidharma's coming from the West?' "—that is, from India to China. By common agreement of the masters this question is taken to mean, "What is the highest truth of Zen?"

The highest truth is not a lofty ideal or a system of morality. Nor is it the poet's "Beauty is truth, truth beauty." When Zen master Dogen was asked, "What truth did you find in China during your three years of training there?" he replied, "That my nose is vertical, my eyes horizontal." Another master when queried about the truth of Zen answered, "Excuse me, I must pass water. Just think—even a thing as trifling as that I must do in person." Still another replied, "When hungry I just eat, when tired I just sleep."

But if you are up a tree hanging by your teeth and someone below sincerely asks for the truth, how do you reply? What a dilemma! Look at that tree-hanger, teeth bared, trying to hold on! And yet . . . might he somehow be answering that momentous question? If so, in what way? The problem posed by this koan is a test of your Zen: how to respond fully to life's exigencies at every moment, in every circumstance.

Without awakening most are up a tree, hanging on by the skin of their teeth. They don't live—they simply exist. They don't grow—they merely dangle. They are forever opening their mouths to explain or complain and falling into a painful world of fear and suspicion, of loneliness and despair.

In life there is always "a man under the tree" asking disconcerting questions: Are you truly a loving husband or wife or parent or child? Are you acting as a responsible member of the human race?

Are we to remain silent to these questions? It is not speech or silence but the depth of understanding and egolessness behind them that is important. When you are being abused do you argue or retaliate, provoking anger in yourself and others, or do you stand humbly mute? When you see evil and violence being perpetrated, do you remain silent or do you speak out or act to prevent it? Silence may be golden but, as someone observed, it can also be yellow.

When Kyogen put this koan to his monks a senior disciple rose and said, "Never mind about the man while he was in the tree. How would he respond to that question after he has fallen from the tree?" At this Kyogen laughed heartily. Do you see why? What was your Buddha-nature before you were born, and what will it be after you die? Can there be a difference before and after?

What would you say if someone suddenly pressed you for the innermost truth of your life? Would you reply with a bit of philosophy? With poetry? With silence? Or would you slam your fist down? If you don't know what you're doing, it's just play-acting. Don't be a Zen phony! To make a true Zen response, your mind must be empty of notions of every sort—of self-concerns, of opinions, of ideals, and the like.

Sounds bleak, does it? Why no opinions? Aren't they the life-blood of the informed individual? Yes, and also a yoke into which he locks himself. Do you want to be free to make all manner of wonderful discoveries? Then shun opinion. As for ideals, be a real man, not an ideal one. And live life, don't judge or explain it away. Stop thinking and talking, start feeling and acting.

Some of you may have once seen the cartoon showing an elderly couple spending a quiet evening at home. She is sitting on one side of the room knitting and he is reading his paper on the other side. Without looking up she asks, "Do you love me, dear?" With eyes still glued to his newspaper, he mutters, "Of course I do." In the lower corner of the cartoon is a dog glaring at the husband as though saying, "For Pete's sake, don't just tell her, *show* her!"

Human beings are great seekers, great questioners. They are forever asking, "What is the meaning of life? What is truth?"

But tell me quickly, What is the meaning of the sun's shining? What is the meaning of rain or thunder? What is the meaning of a squirrel having a bushy tail, a mouse a straight one? What is the meaning of Bodhidharma's coming from the West?

The story is told of a famous concert pianist who once played a dissonant contemporary piece at a private gathering. After he had finished, an elderly person approached him and said, "I just don't understand that piece. What does it mean?" Without a word the pianist played it again. Then turning to the questioner, he said, *"That's* what it means!"

In the first two lines of his comment Mumon says, "Though your eloquence flows like a river, it is all of no avail. Even if you can explain all the Buddhist sutras, that also is useless."

In his "Affirming Faith in Mind," [19] the third Zen patriarch sings:

> When faith and Mind are not separate,
> this is where words all fail to reach,
> for here there is no yesterday,
> no tomorrow, no today.

The sutras are the entombed words of the Buddha. They point to truth but must not be mistaken for it. Zen does not denigrate the sutras; it simply warns that they are but a finger pointing to the moon and not the moon (Mind) itself. This is why Zen, alone among all the Buddhist sects, does not base itself on any sutra. Mind is the substance of Zen, and the sutras the mind of the Buddha. Were he alive today would he speak the same words recorded in the sutras?

The truth is more than anything that can be said about it. Explanatory words are dead words, devoid of the power to inspire. Explanations and descriptions are only peepholes on a limitless universe. So Zen master Hakuin [20] exclaims:

> The measure of words
> is like the seas and mountains—
> nothing but an overflow of delusions.

Mumon continues: "If you can answer the problem properly,

you can kill the living, bring the dead to life." Who are the living who need to be killed? They are the maddeningly active egos of those leading scattered, hustling lives, going round and round like stirring spoons, endlessly arguing and discriminating. Outwardly they may seem brimful of energy and purpose but inwardly they are confused, driven by corrosive fears and compulsions. Once they slay the cancerous ego-I—a product of ignorance and fear—and bring into consciousness their unblemished Mind, they experience a wondrous new world. Thus are the living killed and the dead brought to life. This is the miracle of awakening. This is liberation.

The comment resumes: "But if you can't answer, you must ask Maitreya when he comes." Maitreya is the bodhisattva who will become the buddha of the next world cycle, just as Shakyamuni is the buddha of the present one. It is said that Maitreya will appear 5,670,000,000 years [21] after Shakyamuni's death. Mumon's statement is not sarcastic. It is his inimitable way of warning that if you don't make a supreme effort to awaken, you face a great deal of pain for a long time to come.

And now Mumon's verse:

> Kyogen really spouts nonsense;
> he endlessly spreads poison.
> Stopping up the monks' mouths,
> he watches them writhe
> with the black piercing eyes of a devil.

"Spouts nonsense" refers to the dilemma the master is posing. This "poison" is the antidote for the monks' malady of intoxication with words and concepts. Mumon's praise-by-slander is characteristic of Zen. The masters have no use for what my teachers called "powder and rouge" expressions, endearing terms that can lead to bedeviling attachments. If we were habitually to speak of our True-mind as the "Treasure Gem of Freewill," idolize the Buddha as "Savior of the World," or eulogize Bodhidharma as "Our Glorious Founder," we would be gilding the lily—defiling our minds. Elsewhere Mumon says of Bodhidharma: "That broken-toothed old foreigner who self-importantly crossed the sea from a hundred thousand miles away. . . .

He had only one disciple and even he was a cripple.[22] Well, well!" Where but in Zen do you find such "respectful disrespect" and such "disrespectful respect"? Mumon is actually praising Kyogen for his compassion and wisdom, for his courage to dramatically cut from under his disciples their ego props of verbalization and discrimination, of clinging to names and forms and concepts.

Having done that, Kyogen, concerned master that he is, intently watches them "with the black piercing eyes of a devil" for the telltale signs of awakened Understanding.

4 / ENCOURAGEMENT TALK / SEVENTH DAY / Some six hours remain to this sesshin. Inevitably some of you will feel relieved to hear this. You may be telling yourself that after having put in so much hard work at this sesshin, there's nothing more to do now but coast through to the finish. You may also find yourself pursuing thoughts of what you are going to do after the sesshin.

To write off the sesshin in this way would be nothing short of tragic—tragic irony, really, for the greatest opportunity of the whole sesshin is at hand in these closing hours. Why is this so? Because this last half day becomes the distillation of 6½ days of continuous exertion. All the work up to now has gradually honed the mind into razorlike sharpness. Even if you are aware now of distracting thoughts, these are just surface ripples on the ocean. There is no one here whose mind has not been transformed through the sweat and tears of this sesshin into a state of far greater purity than it was a week ago. And to generate again the samadhi energy in this zendo now and reach this same state of clarity would take another 6½ days of sesshin, starting from the beginning.

Those of you who stayed up last night without sleep may not feel this energy and clarity at the moment. But it is there nontheless, and if you do not let up it will suddenly become available to you again. Remember too that when you are tired the ego is also tired. This means that fatigue can be made your ally if you do not give in to it. If you feel terribly tired, take a brief nap during the next break. If you did zazen all night, just fifteen minutes to half an hour's rest should be enough to revive you. You can then draw on the samadhi energy, and by no-mindedly absorbing yourself in your koan the answer will suddenly reveal itself to you.

Above all, remember that at this point in sesshin awakening can come at any time. Do not think that 6½ days are gone and behind you; they are not. They are all here now compressed into these last hours. No matter what condition you feel your mind is in now, in an instant it can change dramatically, Backed by the samadhi power that has built up in the zendo, any of you can with one mighty heave suddenly find your mind as empty as a white sheet of paper. And in this state all it takes is the right sound or word or touch to trigger awakening. There are members who have broken through their koan in the last ten minutes of sesshin, and some even after sesshin had ended.[23] A man in Japan who had attended sesshin with me was driving home after sesshin when he crossed a railroad track in front of an oncoming train. When the engineer blew his whistle the man came to awakening. But no one can anticipate kensho; as long as you are expecting something like this to happen, you can be sure nothing will.

It is not only for your own sake that you need to avoid thinking about the end of sesshin. In a very real sense anyone who lets up at this vital hour is undermining the efforts of everyone else. More than ever before, now when the sesshin has coalesced into a unified and sensitive whole, the unrestrained or negative thoughts of even one person are sure to be felt by others. The opposite is equally true—continue to exert yourself, and others will do likewise. This places the responsibility for the entire sesshin on the shoulders of each one of you.

There are at least half a dozen people here for whom it can truly be said, "Just one more step!" Some of you have been this close before, and after sesshin expressed regret that you had not worked just a little harder. Dostoevsky wrote in a letter to his brother: "To know that one single effort of the will would suffice to demolish that coarse veil and become one with all existence—to know all this, and still live on like the last and least of creatures—how terrible!" To know after sesshin ends that one final leap would have been enough to carry you through your koan—who here wants to walk out of sesshin with this on his mind?

COMMENTARY ON "THINK NEITHER GOOD NOR EVIL"—CASE 23 OF MUMON'S *THE GATELESS BARRIER* / SEVENTH DAY /

THE CASE: The Sixth Patriarch was pursued by a monk into the mountains. The Patriarch, seeing him coming, laid the robe and the bowl on a rock and said, "The robe and bowl symbolize the faith; are they to be fought for? I allow you to take them away." The monk tried to lift them, but they were as immovable as a mountain. Hesitating and trembling, he said, "I have come for the dharma, not for the robe. I beg you to teach your servant!" The Sixth Patriarch said, "When you were pursuing me and not thinking of good or evil but only of obtaining the treasure, where was your Original-self?" Hearing this, the monk at once became enlightened. His whole body was dripping with sweat. With tears flowing he made obeisance and asked, "Besides the secret words and meanings, is there anything deeper still?" The Patriarch replied, "What I have just told you is not secret. You have realized your Original-self, and what is secret is in you yourself." The monk said, "When I was training under the Fifth Patriarch with the other monks, I did not awaken to my Original-self. Thanks to your instruction, which is to the point, I am like one who has drunk water and actually experienced himself whether it is cold or warm. You are my master!" The Sixth Patriarch said, "We both have the same teacher; hold fast to what you have learned from him."

MUMON'S COMMENT: Of the Sixth Patriarch it has to be said that in an emergency he did something extraordinary. He has a grandmotherly kindness; it is as if he had peeled a fresh litchi, removed its seed, and then put it into your mouth so that you need only swallow it.

In the Zen sect the Sixth Patriarch is famed for having surmounted the handicaps of poverty and illiteracy to become an outstanding master. He is also beloved for his common touch, his simplicity and humility, his benevolence and wisdom. His strong sense of personal responsibility can be gauged from this widely quoted utterance of his: "When others are in the wrong I am in the wrong. When I have transgressed I alone am to blame."

The Sixth Patriarch's spiritual sensitivity and strong character can be seen in this unusual photograph of his embalmed body, remarkably preserved since his death in the eighth century.

The embalmed body of the Sixth Chinese Zen Patriarch (638–713).
The beads around his neck number one hundred eight, representing
the major defilements of man.

MUMON'S VERSE:

> You describe it in vain, you picture it to no avail;
> you can never praise it fully.
> Stop all your groping and maneuvering.
> There is nowhere to hide your True-self.
> When the universe is annihilated, "it" remains,
> indestructible.

The Sixth Patriarch is one of the most distinguished masters in the history of Zen. Almost single-handedly he stripped from Buddhism its Indian cloak of otherworldliness and emphasis on sutra reading and doctrinal study that had previously characterized it in China. In doing so, he laid the foundation for what we now know as Zen Buddhism. The episode of this koan is found in the Platform sutra, which is a record of his life and teachings and one of only two sutras that do not revolve around the life and words of the Buddha.

The Sixth Patriarch was born in the year 638 and was thus a product of the T'ang era, the golden age of Zen. It is recorded that his father died when the master was young and that the boy was brought up by his mother in extreme poverty. Since he went to work at an early age in order to support his mother, he did not attend school and so never learned to read or write. Many would consider such poverty and struggle tragic in a young life, but the introspection and self-reliance they fostered in the child undoubtedly hastened his enlightenment, which came under circumstances unique in the history of Zen.

One day a merchant bought some firewood from the youth and asked him to carry it to his shop. When he had delivered the wood and was about to leave the shop, he heard a monk reciting a sutra outside the door. Upon hearing the words spoken by the monk, the youth, who was now seventeen or eighteen and, as far as is known, had never sat in zazen, was suddenly awakened. He asked the monk what he had recited and was told it was the Diamond sutra.

At this point some of you may wonder, "If it is possible to gain enlightenment without strong exertion, why should I endure the discomforts of sesshin?" If this is what you are thinking, I can sympathize with you. Many years ago when I was feeling the pressure of Japanese friends in Kyoto to quit the austere rigors of the Zen monastery I put this same question to my teacher. And this is how he replied: "Rare indeed are those whose minds are so unstained that they can gain genuine enlightenment without zazen. The Sixth Patriarch was such a one. Undoubtedly he had so ardently disciplined himself in a previous lifetime that his mind, when he came into this existence, was uncommonly pure. This circumstance, and the fact that he had lost his father at an early age and had to struggle to support his mother, must have led him to question intensely the meaning of birth and death and brought about his awakening in such a manner. Most people, though, lacking his purity of mind and intense self-questioning, need to do zazen tirelessly to fully open their Mind's eye."

To continue with the Sixth Patriarch's life story: From the monk who had recited the sutra he learned about the Fifth Patriarch, who was teaching on a remote mountain. After thirty days of hard travel the youth reached the mountain temple of the Fifth Patriarch, who when he saw him asked, "Where do you come from and what do you seek?" Asking this question is like putting a stick in water to determine its depth. The future Sixth Patriarch replied, "I, one of the common people from the South, have come from far away to pay my respects to the venerable master in order to become a buddha." To this the master retorted, "How can you, a bumpkin from the South, possibly become a buddha?" Savor the young man's outspoken reply: "Although there are Northerners and Southerners, the Buddha-nature knows of no South or North. The appearance of a bumpkin may be different from that of a monk, but from the standpoint of Buddha-nature can there be a difference?"

In other words, Buddha-nature is our common birthright. Confirmation of this comes from the highest source, the Buddha himself. On the occasion of his supreme enlightenment he exclaimed, "Wonder of wonders! All living beings are inherently buddhas, endowed with wisdom and virtue."

Let me ask each of you: Do you truly believe the Buddha was not mistaken when he said this? Do you have the firm conviction that regardless of whether you are physically strong or weak, mentally keen or dull, well-educated or illiterate, you have the all-embracing, nothing-lacking Buddha-nature and can, with pure aspiration and strong determination, awaken to it at this very sesshin? Have you struggled to resolve the "doubt-sensation"—the seeming contradiction between the Buddha's pronouncement that all are innately flawless and the evidence of your senses that there is only imperfection, in yourself and others?

Unless your responses to these questions are in the affirmative, you won't open your Mind's eye no matter how often you do zazen or how many sesshins you attend. All you will gain is a certain calmness of body and clarity of mind, and while these qualities are not inconsequential, they are as different from enlightenment as chalk is from cheese. The ultimate aim of Zen training is full awakening, not serenity or high-energy states, which are only by-products of zazen. To awaken, what is most essential is a questioning mind growing out of a fundamental perplexity, or "ball of doubt." Zen masters have repeatedly said, "Where there is great questioning there is great enlightenment; where there is little questioning there is little enlightenment; no questioning, no enlightenment."

There is more to the Fifth Patriarch's response: "For a bumpkin you're very clever with words," said the master. "Say no more now but go to work with the other monks." The novice was then assigned to pound rice in the granary for eight months.

How many of you could go to a Zen center for training, be put down by the master in your first encounter, then be ignored by him and not even allowed into the zendo for eight months? If the master had not thought highly of the brilliant novice, you can be sure he would not have treated him this way. That the latter remained in spite of this treatment shows his strong faith in both his teacher and his own Buddha-nature.

When the Fifth Patriarch felt the time had come to transmit the dharma, he summoned all his disciples and asked that each compose a verse expressing his own understanding. He told them that the one who revealed the deepest truth would inherit the robe and become the Sixth Patriarch. The head monk submitted the following:

Body is the tree of bodhi,
the mind is the stand of a mirror bright.
Wipe it constantly, and with ever watchful diligence
keep it uncontaminated by worldly dust.

When the rice-pounder heard these words repeated by a young monk in the granary area, he realized that the author had not yet perceived his Self-nature, so later he composed his own verse and asked this same monk to write it down for him:

Fundamentally no bodhi tree exists
nor the stand of a mirror bright.
Since all is voidness from the beginning,
where can the dust alight?

The Fifth Patriarch, upon reading this verse and learning who had composed it, went to the granary and told the young granary worker to come to his quarters at night so that he would not be seen by the others. That night the Fifth Patriarch transmitted to him the robe and bowl, saying, "Now you are the Sixth Patriarch." The Fifth Patriarch knew that the monks would never tolerate this novice as the master's successor, so he urged the Sixth Patriarch to return to his native place in secrecy, telling him to live incognito while maturing his enlightenment and only after doing so to begin his formal teaching. He also told him that because the transmission of the robe might easily become a source of contention in the future, there were to be no further transmissions of the robe after him and that hereafter it was to be a transmission strictly fróm mind to mind. Then the Fifth Patriarch ferried with the new patriarch to the other shore of the river, where they parted, never again to see each other.

The present koan revolves around the incident of the Sixth Patriarch's departure from the monastery carrying with him the robe and bowl. Now even though the old patriarch had made the transmission in great secrecy, it soon became known that his heir was departing with the robe and bowl as the Sixth Patriarch. The succeeding events are related in the koan:

"The Sixth Patriarch was pursued by a monk into the mountains." This monk, it seems, was a rough and impulsive man who had been a general before he became a monk. But it would be a mistake to think of him as a villainous person. He should rather be looked upon as a zealous defender of the dharma, to which he was overly attached. To this middle-aged, simple-minded monk, and the others as well, it was inconceivable that the precious dharma, symbolized by the robe and bowl, be en-trusted to the care of a young layman with practically no formal training. Such concern, misguided though it was, shows in itself that this general-turned-monk was a sincere and ardent follower of the Buddha's Way.

"The Patriarch, seeing him coming, laid the robe and the bowl on a rock and said, 'This robe and bowl symbolize the faith; are they to be fought for? I allow you to take them away.'" To get a handle on this koan you must first see why this statement by the Sixth Patriarch was not simply an attempt to avoid violence but was made as a challenge. Why the challenge? This is the first barrier of the koan.

"The monk tried to lift them, but they were as immovable as a mountain." If you believe that the reason for his inability to move them is that, suddenly realizing the enormity of the act he was about to perpetrate, he was paralyzed by feelings of remorse, then you are underrating the power of the dharma and that of the Sixth Patriarch who embodied it! If faith can move mountains, why can't it immobilize a robe and bowl?

"Hesitating and trembling, he said, 'I have come for the dharma, not for the robe. I beg you to teach your servant!'" Unless you sense his desperate mind state behind these words, the koan may seem to you no more than a charming fable about the would-be larceny of some insignificant religious objects, and the circumstances of the monk's enlightenment may appear a great mystery. The key to understanding his mind state is the supplication, "I beg you to teach your servant!" for it reveals his complete and sudden change of heart. Without the egoless-ness expressed by this cry for help, the monk's awakening could not have taken place. "All religion," said William James, "begins with the cry 'Help!'" One of the enlightenment accounts in *The Three Pillars of Zen* contains this passage: "'I am dying,' I sobbed. 'I have killed all my gods. I have no key to resurrection.

I am totally alone.' Stark fear and utter despair possessed me and I lay on the floor for I don't know how long until from the pit of my abdomen a cry came forth, 'If there is any being in the entire earth who cares whether I live or die, *help* me, oh *help*.me!' " This mind state is the precondition of awakening.

The koan resumes: "The Sixth Patriarch said, 'When you were pursuing me and not thinking of good or evil but only of obtaining the treasure, where was your Original-self?' " Here we come to the core of the koan. If you are to *demonstrate* in dokusan your understanding of this passage and not simply verbalize about it, you must put yourself into the mind and being of the agonized monk.

"Not thinking of good and evil" means not making the kind of gratuitous evaluations and judgments that erect a wall between you and others and divide the world into the familiar "here with me" and the alien "out there with you." Zen teaches that things are not good *or* bad but good *and* bad, or rather, *beyond* good and evil. "Original-self" is your fundamental aspect before your mother gave birth to you. In the words of an ancient Zen master, "It is the True-nature of all sentient beings, that which existed before our own birth, and which presently exists, unchangeable and eternal. . . . When we are born it is not newly created and when we die it does not pass away. It has no distinction of male or female nor has it any coloration of good or bad. . . ."

Young though he was, the Sixth Patriarch must have perceived that his pursuer was a desperate man, driven by frustration and anxiety as well as by a deep hunger for Self-realization. Why otherwise would this general-turned-monk have persevered in a chase of, according to some accounts, one hundred miles? Picture him during the chase, arms and legs pumping vigorously, eyes staring intently, panting and sweating as he pursues the Patriarch, first excitedly, then doggedly, and finally no-mindedly until he catches up with him. Unless you have yourself experienced that "dark night of the soul" in which you passionately struggle with a koan or other spiritual problem as the sweat and the tears flow, you won't be able to enter deeply into the heart of the tormented monk. This heart-mind, purged now of greed and self-seeking, had become a clean slate. Unhesitatingly the master delivered the *coup de grâce* with his timely words, which must have struck like a bolt of lightning.

Now tell me: Where was the monk's Original-self at that moment?

"Hearing this, the monk at once became enlightened. His whole body was dripping with sweat. With tears flowing he made obeisance and asked, 'Besides the secret words and meanings, is there anything deeper still?'" These tears were tears of relief and gratitude, and the spontaneous prostration before the master a gesture of profound thanksgiving. Genuine though the enlightenment was, it fell short of total liberation, and so the monk asked, "Is there anything further still?" This question is understandable. Awakening, and the realization that one does not acquire anything one did not already have, is so simple and obvious that it is only natural to feel there must be something further still. "Secret words and meanings" here connote an intimate understanding. Enlightenment evokes the strongest feelings of intimacy. If you have ever been estranged from your spouse or child, from a family member or old friend, you know the joy of reunion. Realization of Buddha-nature is realization of the kinship of all forms of life. These feelings are beyond words. If there is a secret involved it is an open secret, known by everyone in his heart of hearts but forgotten or lost sight of in the hurly-burly of ego-dominated thinking and feeling.

"Thanks to your instruction . . . I am like one who has drunk water and actually experienced himself whether it is cold or warm." Zen emphasizes experience, tasting. If one picture is worth a thousand words, one taste is better than a thousand pictures. To know how honey tastes one must eat some; to know what enlightenment is one must awaken.

Observe the master's loyalty to the Fifth Patriarch: "We both have the same teacher; hold fast to what you have learned from him." He is really saying, "Be grateful for his having taught you that there is nothing to learn—wisdom is inherently yours—and therefore there is nothing to strive for."

Now Mumon's comment: "Of the Sixth Patriarch it has to be said that in an emergency he did something extraordinary." This seems to imply that the Patriarch, confronted suddenly with his pursuer's threatening presence and then with his quick change of heart, was at a loss and struck out blindly with the words, "When you were pursuing me and not thinking of good or evil . . . where was your Original-self?" Mumon appears to be criticizing the Patriarch, but actually he is praising him, although he does so in his usual tongue-in-cheek manner.

In the Platform sutra, previously quoted, there is a somewhat different version of the events of this koan: "The Sixth Patriarch said to his pursuer, 'Allow no thoughts to arise in your mind and I will instruct you.' So the monk did zazen for a long time, after which the Patriarch began, 'Do not think this is good,'" etc. Note the words "After the monk had done zazen for a long time . . ." Whether his predisposing mind state was induced by sitting zazen, as in the second version, or brought about by running zazen, as implied in the koan proper, the precondition of awakening, a "clean slate" mind, was present.

To continue: "He has a grandmotherly kindness; it is as if he had peeled a fresh litchi, removed its seed, and then put it into your mouth so that you need only swallow it." "Grandmotherly kindness" is unnecessary or excessive kindness. Mumon appears to be putting down the Sixth Patriarch for his gentle manner and for doing more than needed to be done. Actually he is praising by condemning. After all, the monk did come to enlightenment through the Patriarch's words and actions. At the same time Mumon is admonishing us, "The Sixth Patriarch's words and manner were effective in this instance, true, but don't assume that full awakening is attained easily; it demands years of dedicated zazen, of sustained effort." Mumon's own enlightenment with the koan Mu came after six years of persistent zazen.

Finally Mumon's verse: "You describe it in vain, you picture it to no avail." While it is true that when the spoken word comes directly from the guts it has the power to move us in a way impossible for the devitalized written word, still all words, concepts, and imaginings are at best only sketches of the infinitely extensible "it." Makyo—that is, hallucinations and fantasies—are also only pictures, so don't cling to them even though they afford you relief from the tedium of concentrated, objectless zazen. And don't attach yourself to names and forms. "Original-self," "Buddha-nature," "Mind"—these are but tentative designations for what cannot be named or measured, for what is formless yet informs everything.

"You can never praise it fully: Stop all your groping and maneuvering." Mumon is saying that nothing equals this formless self, so why look for anything else? Stop flirting with the seductress Astrology or the sorcerer I Ching, stop chasing after other vain pleasures. This fumbling and searching will never bring you to realization of your True-self.

"There is nowhere to hide your True-self." It stands revealed everywhere, right under your nose—no, it *is* your nose. To hide, your True-self would have to stand outside every conceivable universe, would it not?

"When the universe is annihilated, 'it' remains, indestructible." Your True-self cannot be destroyed for the very reason that it is destruction itself. Never having been born, it can never die. Yet it is the creative force behind every single thing.

II / ENLIGHTENMENT ACCOUNTS / 1 / "SUCH HAPPINESS MAKES YOU REALIZE HOW UNHAPPY YOU HAD BEEN BEFORE" /

DEAR ROSHI, this is written in the hope of encouraging others, especially those who live far away from the Zen Center and have had to practice in solitude, those who are older and physically hampered, and those who feel they lack faith. In the five years that have passed since I first came to the Center at the age of forty-nine, I have been able to attend only three seven-day sesshin (chiefly because of an injured back and stiff legs)—but that third sesshin was the dynamic miracle-worker of October '75. And now distance, delays, pain, age, crises of despair, even solitary practice—all are seen as a shower of blessings.

Although right from the opening ceremonies that sesshin catapulted me into an urgency and intensity of practice I had not known before, there certainly was no intimation that it was to be "my sesshin." I had orginally given Zen five years, which were now ending, so a new inner agreement had been reached: "Well, we'll give it three more years. And then we'll see." For how could there be any immediate hope for someone whose practice was so distracted, carried away by thoughts? someone who read incessantly? someone who scarely could sit still on the mat? The only thing to be said for my practice is that it was *dogged,* doggedly faithful and persistent, no matter what the problems. Several times, after crises, I vowed to give up, to stop "wasting all this time," tried to, and found I could not. Zen had picked me up and was shaking me like a terrier with a rat. I could struggle and try to escape, but the process was inexorable.

But now we were in sesshin and ancient history was irrelevant and forgotten.

The first two days. My practice launches itself with a rush, thanks in part to hard preparation at home. Pain in the back, distracting thoughts, but I am able to come back, and come back, and come back again. Roshi's commentary on the second day takes deadly aim at those who depend on words. They are lost, he says. As a lifelong word-person and former writer, I feel those arrows cut into my heart, and weep bitterly. I remember the notebooks and journals dating back thirty years that I am so proud of, gathering dust but not thrown away—bondage to the past, bondage to the ego. "I will burn them," I promise. "I will be born afresh each instant." My practice is heating up. I am helped by everyone around me—unbelievably given *specific individual help* by at least four sesshin neighbors.

Third day. Black Tuesday. Everything crashes, collapses. I plunge into the blackest depression of my life. Can't practice. Never could. Can't hold Mu more than thirty seconds. I will leave sesshin, leave Zen forever. What is there to live for? I dwell on suicide. Why not? Suicide. Why live? Won't go to dokusan. Haven't the heart. What would be the use? What could I say? I'm already burned out, a two-day fizzled-out rocket . . . great, great. Sodden, sniffling misery. At last I drag myself to dokusan, the last one in the line. Roshi braces me, encourages me. It is not true the sesshin is lost to me. I can pull out. Can I? Yes, I can, and I will, I will. Slowly the black cloud lifts, and as it does, practice resurges on a deeper level. Energy flows again.

Fourth and fifth days. Things are happening. Always the observer-reporter, I note them with mild surprise. *But here's the luminous sky I've read about!* Thoughts float across like clouds, innocent, free. Ah wonderful, unbelievable. Time passes, I analyze and observe my new state, clinging to it. Of course it fades, flickers, vanishes. Gloom again, distractions, self-pity, paranoia. Back to square one. Mu . . . Mu . . . Mu . . . The young man to my right is practicing with the solidity and strength of a mountain. I absorb his strength, I even tune in on his breathing. It works! Energy and strength well up. Suddenly the observer notes: *The silver mountain . . . the iron wall!* The silver mountain is as slippery as ice; the iron wall has a solid gate but it is bolted and barred. I dash myself against it again and again. I plaster myself against it. Mu and Mu and Mu . . . And it too vanishes and won't come back.

I don't know what to do. I'm at a dead end, in a box, a room with no doors or windows. I must break out, but *how, how, how?* Right through the walls, scratching and clawing. Desperate, I must try anything, do *anything.* Feverishly, I review all the instructions I have heard and read. I will be a child, a simpleton. I must believe? I *will* believe. I *do* believe. They say I am Mu? Then I *am* Mu. If I am Mu, I know Mu. Therefore I do know Mu. I am Mu, I know Mu. I am nothing but Mu. I am a simpleton child who is Mu, and sees Mu everywhere . . . and on, and on, and on. My desperation comes and goes in waves. Still no sense whatsoever of any resolution impending. Only struggle, struggle for its own urgent sake. I must break through and yet I do not expect to break through or think what it would be like to break through. And still my effort is riddled with distractions. . . . In bed, I struggle to take Mu along into sleep. Again and again I pull myself back from sleep. You want to sleep? Very well, you may . . . but only when Mu goes with you. Not sure if this succeeds as hoped, but it does appear to open pathways for Mu to penetrate deeper levels of the mind. Now in and out of the zendo, the distractions matter less and less. I don't fight them anymore. Mu returns readily; it is always there just under the surface froth.

Sixth and seventh days. The belly's laughter. Taking a sponge bath, I must have been standing in an odd way, for a strange ridiculous belly is looking up at me with its one eye. It seems twice as big as I remember and has a droll personality all its own. We salute each other and fall down laughing. And I had imagined it was "mine." How presumptuous, how ridiculous! What I had thought was me was a bunch of funny entities. After work Friday morning I am lying in bed resting when Joshu himself suddenly stands there in the shape of a great brass steam whistle. The pressure inside is building, building. The valve opens—it is his mouth—steam rises and

M U !

issues forth in a world-shaking blast. Then I am Joshu and the blast is coming out of me, is me, is everyone, everything! Barriers begin to fall; the mind is working feverishly; mysterious sayings become clear. Of course, of course! How wonderful, how *right*. . . . An enormous happiness came over me. Doubt remained—wasn't this understanding still too intellectual? But the doubt could not dampen the happiness nor the sense of gratitude that began flowing so strongly that it was very nearly beyond bearing. That day and the next, the last of sesshin, were spent in a daze of happiness, enjoying each moment as it came. Skipping in the *kinhin* line, then crying to think how much I owed the roshi, the *sangha,* the patriarchs, the mysterious benevolent force that moves our lives.

Perhaps the powerful emotional impact of this experience, which was only shallow and partial, was due to the very hopelessness of my condition before it happened: almost completely without faith, dry as a bone, sterile, dull, dead, locked into the vise of skepticism, unable to break free. And yearning always—the hungriest of hungry ghosts.[24]

Such extraordinary happiness makes you realize (among so many other things) how truly unhappy you had been before. Not in the life circumstances but in your *self,* your miserable, restless, eternally dissatisfied self. This joy is the joy of dropping burdens, burdens you didn't even know you had—so deeply had they entered you—dragging you down, grinding you down, making you weigh heavy as lead, move as sluggishly as thick cold molasses.

Now for the first time I experienced the joy that comes with an overpowering sense of faith. Before, my faith was limited to the rock-bottom minimum: *Englightenment exists.* The rituals at the Center embarrassed me. I was embarrassed and uneasy when anyone spoke of faith, even Roshi, and would turn my thoughts elsewhere. "Don't make a problem of it," I would tell myself. Now, with a great leap, faith extended far and wide. It did not seem like faith at all but surest, clearest knowledge. The inexorable workings of karma (which of course I had never accepted), the extraordinary, intricate cunning of the way things work themselves out, the intermeshing relationships, all became clear to me and left me breathless with amazement and gratitude.

The lines written by a Christian mystic appeared in my head:

> All shall be well
> and all shall be well
> and all manner of things
> shall be well. . . .

Yes! I thought. And not only *shall* all be well, all is well *right now!* And always had been well, only I had been too blind to see it. The incredible combination of fortunate circumstances that had led me to this moment, including all those I had considered blackest misfortune: the injured back, the writer's block, the spells of depression, family difficulties, delays in being accepted as a member of the Center, lost letters, knees that swelled and refused to bend, the move to far-off Mexico—all formed an intricate and loving pattern leading me to Zen, to this moment, preventing a headlong impetuosity that this middle-aged frame could not have supported, teaching me patience, feeding me disappointments and humiliations at a pace I could absorb, carrying me forward exactly in the right way, for me. And I knew the same miracles were unfolding for everyone.

This way of thinking may be usual among many sangha members; to me it was a 180-degree turn; it was a revolution as well as a revelation. Now if the writer's block stays with me— fine! I trust it, respect it, revere it even, am joyous in it. A benevolent wisdom is at work here I cannot hope to fathom. Amazing, amazing!

As sesshin moved toward its close there seemed to be a gaping hole in the crown of my head and another in my chest, as if a bomb crater had been left there. As if a huge tumor—the ego-tumor—had been successfully removed, leaving me for the first time in my life *free*. Free! Wailing "Mu" with everyone on Friday night, I became aware that the pain of longing was completely gone. For what did I lack?

My particular experience was limited and shallow. The tyrant, I suspect, is not defeated once and for all. I felt impacted, blasted, tilted far over—but not fallen completely. This understanding— well, it is what it is. Whatever it is, it brought with it the purest joy, the greatest fulfillment of my life.

Walking in the kinhin line, a verse kept singing itself:

> Five years of misery
> have ended in a song!

> With hands palm to palm,
>
> Christine

2 / "I TOOK ONE STEP AND THE UNIVERSE TURNED INSIDE OUT" /

DEAR ROSHI, it is now a week since the October sesshin, and the daily routines of job and family have re-established themselves. Yet that sesshin changed the whole world! As you said in the closing talk, it was an unusually powerful sesshin. People here in Wisconsin have commented they were very aware of the sesshin even during the midst of everyday activities; one young woman said she found herself just *having* to get up at night and do zazen and that the hours simply flew.

For me, the first half of the sesshin was extremely difficult. What a state I was in! It seems now that I must have spent half my time in utter despair, confronting as I had never done before the fact that in the deepest sense we own nothing, control nothing, not even our own bodies and minds. The other half was spent despising Zen: "I never used to fear death," I told myself. "I never used to feel such helplessness in the face of this impermanent world. I have Zen to thank for all this damn misery! Well, when this is over I'll return to home and family and live a *normal* life, like *normal* people who aren't practicing Zen!"

Underneath all this indulgence the *joriki* was building, and through all the negative mind states I was able to keep asking, *Who* is afraid? *Who* is helpless? *Who, who, WHO* is going through all this? Then the last night came, with all that extra help given by the monjutors, and suddenly, twenty minutes before the last dokusan, I *knew!* It was as though I had taken one small step and the whole universe turned inside out.

I must have literally squirmed in my seat waiting for dokusan. I wasn't waiting to be tested, but to express my utter astonishment, this state of joyful Surprise. It seems strange now that Surprise was the overriding feeling at that time. But I know now why it was, and it's really this point that needs focusing on. I realize now that throughout all the years of practice there always remained, even in what seemed moments of deepest faith, a residual kind of skepticism about the possibility of really *freeing* oneself. Deep down there was always the feeling that "life is gonna get you," and if life didn't, well, death would. There wasn't *really* a way out. There were even times when I intellectually convinced myself there was a way out; but without the *experience* that there was, this was little more than a crutch that could, and did, fall out from under again and again. What joy to taste, to really experience, this marvelous Freedom. How much more "space" there is in this great Universe!

There was another kind of skepticism that was also present during these past years. I had started practicing Zen after a period of real disillusionment with political and social activity and I had the hope that Zen would be a way to help alleviate, in at least a small way, the suffering I saw in the world. But through these years I was often troubled by thoughts that sitting and staring at a wall hardly seemed to be a reasonable way to do anything for anybody. In time, of course, the awareness grew that zazen made one more responsive, more able to help in small ways, less likely to cause pain. But this still seemed like so little in the face of such a dark, suffering world. So imagine my surprise when it was glimpsed at last that indeed there is no greater aid we can give than to awaken to our True-nature and dedicate ourselves to the awakening of all beings. "All Beings, without number, I vow to liberate." What a vow!! Before there is even the intention to speak such a vow, all beings are complete and perfect, totally Free.

Yet without all buddhas and bodhisattvas, without the sangha, without you, Roshi, you old lip-flapper, how could we ever know this? Thank you for my very Life!

> With palms raised in the ten directions,

> Don

3 / "LIMITLESS, JOYFUL PEACE" /

In a way the *rohatsu* sesshin [in December, commemorating the Buddha's enlightenment] started in October. At that sesshin a new hope was generated. This hope, with the abiding faith that had stayed with me, gave me the conviction that success would be mine. Between October and December my wife and I spent our time preparing for this sesshin. We sat through several weekends, attended *jukai* [receiving of the precepts] at the Toronto Zen Centre, and had a "word fast" in which we read and wrote as little as possible. When the rohatsu came around we were both well prepared.

The first two days proceeded without too much incident. The normal settling-in was done. On the third day the roshi probed with a few test questions and I was aware of the spontaneity of the responses and of his evident pleasure. I yelled at the top of my voice, "This is my sesshin!" Returning to the zendo I flung myself totally into the koan.

The next few days were lived in unmitigated fury. Urged on by the *kyosaku*, the shouts of the monjutors, the urging of the roshi, I tried to get deeper into my koan, but thoughts always persisted. Try as I might during the work period and mealtimes to stay focused on the koan, my mind wandered.

The hope that had been nurtured by the two months between sesshins slipped away. The old doubts crept in: I can never do this; those who have passed their first koan are on the staff; they are all young and can take it. Look at so-and-so, how hard he has worked and he is not through his koan; what chance is there for me?" The tautness of the mind slackened. It was hopeless, and with that, despair rose up.

For a brief moment I let go of the koan and speculated thus: The reason I feel such hoplessness is because I yearn for Mu so much. If there was not such a tremendous need for Mu, there would not be this discouragement or despair. In fact, then, despair is my ally, the measure and expression of my need. This despair is really the voice of my True-nature! This all passed through the mind in a flash. But having seen this, my heart opened up and a great yearning for Mu took possession of me. I yearned for Mu so much that my own body was not enough for the task, and I borrowed, as it were, the bodies of all the sesshin participants, of the monjutors, of the roshi. I yearned their yearning and they yearned mine. I became the sesshin. When someone cried out he cried out my pain. When another rushed to dokusan he announced my eagerness. When the monjutors wielded their sticks and breathed so mightily with their exertions, they breathed Mu for me. The roshi's efforts were my efforts. An awful responsibility became mine. I could not let the sesshin down. The force of the entire sesshin seemed to become focused in my hara. The shoulders, chest, arms, and stomach were all relaxed but there was this mighty concentrating force at work.

The struggle took on titanic proportions. Dry periods came, but my impatience was too much for them. It was just as though one were smashing through a wall. On the fifth day I rose at 2 A.M. and sat until four without moving, totally absorbed in Mu. The pain in the legs was intense and yet easily transformed into the questioning of Mu. I rushed to dokusan but came back bewildered. Roshi had questioned me, had helped me, but when I came back a doubt about him arose. "He is going to pass me too easily. He is not deeply enlightened and doesn't want anyone else to be." The monjutor struck me. It hurt. "This whole Zen business is a hoax! Harada-roshi admitted that all he did was sell water by the river. He even admitted that he was a sham. There is nothing in it!" I struggled with a sinking feeling of being all alone, utterly forsaken.

The roshi's commentary that morning cleared up my doubts completely. Roshi talked about the intellect, about how it is the servant, yet claims to be the master. I began to cry. He seemed to be talking to me alone, sawing, sawing, sawing away at my depths. I do not remember what he said, but it was very painful. It was surely this experience that made way for what was to come.

At dokusan on the last night the roshi was about to repeat to me his oft-time warning of the importance of the last day and the need for great effort. I interrupted him and said vigorously, "Yes, I know, I promise you I will, I'll do it!" And on leaving the dokusan room, I turned and flung out a final "I will." I had resolved to myself to sit up all night and pour myself simply into Mu.

After the closing bell had rung and that evening's closing ceremony performed, I resumed zazen in the zendo but found that my attention was scattered. I was sitting for twenty-minute periods and moving constantly. At midnight I felt it would be best to go to bed, but, remembering my vow to the roshi and myself, could not do so. Although it seemed that the sitting I was doing was pointless and having no effect, I nevertheless struggled on. Finally at 2:30 A.M. I gave up and, full of shame, went to bed.

Strangely, the next morning, when the waking bell rang, I slipped out of my sleeping bag with a feeling of cool assurance. On getting to the mat I found that the sitting that had been so earnestly sought the night before came with great ease. Having at last got a grasp on Mu, I decided not to go to dokusan but instead to continue working at my practice.

A monjutor tapped me on the shoulder and whispered, "Go to dokusan." I went reluctantly and with a feeling of misgiving about his having interrupted such good sitting. But, sitting before the roshi, I found that answers could now be given that had not been available before. The dokusan was a great success and charged me with the resolve to work harder. I had grasped my practice and was working furiously. But at the last dokusan, the roshi, on testing me, pointed out that my answers were still too intellectual and were no advance on what had been given in the morning. Returning to the zendo I was totally discouraged and felt I had to give up. I had no energy and, it seemed, no will. The young man on my right, however, was sitting straight and evidently working extremely hard. I thought, "He has not given up, so why should I?" And by a total effort of will alone I concentrated on searching into Mu in the hara; my spine straightened of itself and remained straight until the end of the sesshin.

Upon awakening at 2 A.M. the morning following the sesshin, my attention turned to my inner state. This turning inward revealed that there was a closing, a tensing, that arose from a lack of faith, and a resolve was made to have greater faith at future sesshins. Then it was decided to express this faith immediately by allowing the closing to open. This opening was accompanied by a feeling of falling and of fear.

At one time roshi had urged on sesshin participants by saying that they could not fall out of the universe, and recalling this gave me the courage necessary to allow the opening to continue. The feeling of falling went on and was accentuated by probing an ancient fear. A realization came that liberation was the freedom to suffer, and not freedom from suffering, and this insight speeded up the process (the word "process" is used for want of a better one, although the word gives the appearance of something happening; all that was happening was a "knowing"). The feeling of dying arose with a fear of death.

I said to myself, "I am dying and if this is the case then let me observe what happens." The fear and alarm increased until it was noticed that my heart was beating, and the realization dawned that if the heart was beating then the process was not one of dying. I then found myself in a vast, empty space, lit as it were by moonlight, with a feeling of just being at home. I then realized with complete but nevertheless unconcerned certainty that I could not possibly die.

Yet a new fear arose, and that was that if I could not die,

then I would suffer a form of cosmic insomnia. Along with this was the concern, "Is this then all there is?" And the answer came, "No, there is walking, talking, eating, and sleeping." It was seen that Joshu's "When I am hungry I eat, and when I am tired I sleep" had a new reality. (Ordinary man looks at his life of walking and sleeping and eating and asks, "Is this all there is?" and answers, "No, there is 'higher life,' a life beyond this world." I was asking, "Is this all there is?" and answering, "No, there is the life of everyday existence.") The concern left me, and I remained alone in vast empty space.

There is no way in which the condition can be described other than terming it "natural." It was not an "experience." There was nothing that was outside to "cause" the experience, nor was there an inside, just a wholeness and completeness. There was no feeling of needing to control anything, nor was there a feeling of being in any way out of control. Perfect but natural liberation.

The process came slowly to an end through what seemed to be going to sleep, but that turned out to be waking up. The clock registered 4 A.M. The whole process had lasted two hours.

My wife awakened about 4:30 A.M. I described in detail to her what had happened. Already the "reality" of the world was supplanting the reality of the process, and doubts were arising about whether in fact I had been dreaming. My wife and I discussed at some length what we should do.

I felt increasingly concerned that what had happened was simply a dream, or makyo. There was no feeling of any greater insight or understanding of the koan Mu. There was a sense of trepidation at displaying another experience to the roshi, who has without doubt been bombarded by thousands of such experiences. There was the nagging temptation to say, "Let's leave it; let's just go home." The question, however, remained: "What was this?" and deep in my hara was an intuition. My wife urged me to stay and see the roshi.

At 7 A.M. I went and knocked on his door. He called out, "Who is there?" I replied and gave my name. I felt sick. He opened the door and overcame my fumbled apologies with a compassionate welcome.

Feeling foolish, I sat down and stuttered that I had had some sort of experience and felt that it needed validation or rejection. After I had given a broad outline he slowly probed and sharply questioned until the story given above had been fully told. He was obviously interested and rejected my suggestion that it might be makyo.

He asked some questions about the koan Mu. I thought about the first question he asked and felt it didn't make sense. He tried again and asked another question. And again the only answer that I could give was an intellectual one. He tried a third time and I felt a restlessness stir in me. I stood up and walked away from him. The question suddenly went deep and an eruption, a volcano, roared up from the hara. I shouted "This is Mu! Mu! Mu! Mu!" I was yelling and laughing, "Lovely Mu! By God, this is Mu! This is Mu! Mu! Mu!" The paroxysm spent itself at last, and my teacher, watching me with the greatest intensity and as compassionate as ever, said, "Yes, you have seen Mu, but now you must take hold of it. You must widen and deepen what you have merely glimpsed." Then he proceeded to point out certain things to me about future practice.

Afterword

Eight or nine hours after leaving the roshi we arrived home. That night was passed sleeplessly. Limitless, joyful peace. I was exhausted but could not sleep, so great was my joy.

Throughout the rest of the week and beyond there has persisted the feeling of being unobstructed, of walking on my own feet, of seeing with my own eyes. Except for periods of profound gratitude toward roshi and the sesshin members and my wife, it has all been natural, easy. The joy left, the peace left, leaving just a natural, open feeling.

A veritable explosion had occurred, but debris remains. Old habits, mind states, reactions--they are still there. But they have lost their grip. Old enemies rise up, crumble and turn to dust, and that tyrant the old dead king is broken, he need be fed no longer. Like a boil that has been lanced—still a bit painful but so easy.

My sitting has also changed—it has become deep and smooth, it is no longer something apart.

Perhaps the foregoing account will be of greater value if it includes something of my personal background, for so often people worry about whether they can possibly carry on Zen practice and live in the world at the same time. It is unlikely that anyone would consider me exceptional, and it should be taken as a great consolation that if one person can carry on Zen practice, a full business career, and family life, anyone can do it.

My marriage has been a great success and has produced three fine children.

I work in the personnel department of a large company, and it could be said that I am moderately successful and probably in line for promotion to a vice-presidential position in the not too distant future.

Real Zen practice started for me in 1966 when I attended an all-day sitting in Canada conducted by Yasutani-roshi. Before this encounter my spiritual life had been one flounder after another until in 1964, exhausted and depressed, I started sitting on my own.

After the sitting with Yasutani-roshi I made enquiries about further Zen training. Can anyone imagine my joy and gratitude upon hearing that there was a sesshin about to take place in Rochester, at which an American Zen teacher, Philip Kapleau, was to be installed? But the joy also had a most devastating effect on me in that it awakened in some way a fear of death, which was to haunt me almost without respite for the next two years. I was saturated by terrible anxiety and psychological numbness. I was terrified of being alone. On one occasion I was so sure that I was going to die that I stopped the car and got out so that I would not die unattended. As it happened, the shock of the cold air when getting out of the car braced me and brought me back to my senses.

The doctor recommended tranquilizers, but I knew that to yield to his persuasion would probably be the end of zazen. In any case, there was the constant and abiding faith that zazen would of itself, in due time, bring about a cure. During this period my teacher, Roshi Kapleau, gave constant encouragement and pointed out that, in effect, to have such a fear was good fortune in that it would drive me deeper into my practice, as indeed it turned out to do. The force and power of the anxiety aroused great energy, and the sitting that was done during those anxious times was deep.

My work was also a great help, and although there was a constant temptation to withdraw in some way from the work situation, I hung on. The very mundaneness, the inconsequential problems, the battles and disagreements were spurs to continue my practice. The constant humiliations that were suffered through my trying to introduce new ideas were very powerful ego abrasives. Although the struggle was wearing, in a deep way a profound reconciliation developed between my life of Zen and my business life. At the same time I acquired a vigor and energy that enabled me to carry through several large and somewhat difficult programs that would probably not have been accomplished had there not been the resources available from Zen training.

My wife and I have practiced zazen now for eight years from five o'clock until seven-twenty each morning and for an hour each evening. Once a month the two of us have a one- or two-day sitting over a weekend. We have also found it helpful to read inspirational books, so, in effect, much of our time is spent in Buddhism.

During one hot summer I developed insomnia accompanied by excruciating tensions, and this was to plague me for eighteen months. My teacher urged me to go on with zazen. "Go to work exhausted if you have to, but don't give up your sitting."

Very soon in our practice my wife and I gave up eating meat, which created something of a problem at work. It made me seem faddish and difficult, but in time our friends came to accept this "quirk." Worse, however, is the fact of not drinking alcohol. On almost any occasion bottles are got out and drinks passed around when in the business world. Sometimes I would simply take plain ginger ale, and when people repeatedly pressed liquor on me I would say that I was a reformed alcoholic. Often I just stayed away from the affairs.

Despite these difficulties, the sense of being one with the work situation has grown, and the very challenge that the life imposed by Zen has created has been instrumental in providing the energy necessary to overcome the problems thrown up by that challenge.

The general feeling that is in me at the moment is of having been a privileged member of some great work of creation. "I" was often an unwilling participant in this great work. The measure of "my" unwillingness is the gratitude I now feel toward the roshi for his imposition of rigid discipline and the respect I feel toward others for complying with this discipline. This account is written to give expression to this gratitude, but with the feeling of the clumsiness and dreariness of words. A clean and clear *gassho,* on the other hand, is a relief.

With deepest gratitude,

Roger

4 / "SO GRATEFUL TO BE A HUMAN BEING" /

DEAR ROSHI, How incredible! *Just* to wake up in the morning— what joy! Instead of waking up to that awful, tense, hungry, aching loneliness and isolation that have been there ever since I can remember, to wake up to just this solid Mu. Just this Mu, just this Mu. At the very thought of Mu, gratitude arises, such gratitude—for practice, for you, for all the painful, frustrating, seemingly negative things that have happened to me. How true that verse about its taking a cold winter to enjoy the plum blossoms in the spring. One feels *exactly* as though one has just been let out of prison—first Mu takes you and shows you how utterly imprisoned you are, and then it sets you free!

It is difficult for me even now to believe the point of tension this body-mind had reached before the October sesshin. For six months before I could scarcely eat anything—I lost more than twenty pounds. I was *miserable,* and for no apparent reason, as my daily life was more harmonious than it had ever been. It literally felt as though Mu were eating me up, and sometimes I just hated zazen. A resistance to zazen arose, so strong that often I had to practically nail myself to the mat in order not to run out of the zendo. At the same time it was so painful to have this resistance so strongly that it made me want to do more zazen in order to overcome it. The week before sesshin I was so sick and full of resistance it seemed almost impossible even to go. Yet for just one clear moment the thought flashed in my mind: The only reason this is coming up so strongly is because you are *absolutely* determined to get through.

As soon as sesshin began, though, that determination was there, overriding everything, grinding away all those body-mind states that had held me back so often before. Now I see that every fear, every pain, every doubt was truly bodhisattvic—once one is completely determined not to give in to these things, they become a great spur, pushing one on in order to overcome them.

Telling you during that first dokusan that I didn't care anymore what you thought of me—this little me—was also important. It was a declaration of independence that had to be made before I could do for myself what I had to do. After that—just Mu and Mu and Mu. So little do I remember about the week—just Mu. Toward the middle of the sesshin, body in a state of total exhaustion, thoughts of giving in and giving up arise; familiar suicidal, running-out-of-the-zendo thoughts. *But not this time.* There was no way, Roshi, just no way, I could go back to that life of tension I had created. Something had to give, I had to do something. On the sixth day I realized I had never really tried to go through Mu. Over it, under it, around it, away from it—but never really facing it, right through it. Right then this huge Mu rose up in front of me and there was just nowhere else to go.

When you told me I could now work on subsequent koans, everything was so simple, so clear, so natural, so matter-of-fact that it hardly seemed anything had happened. Racing down the stairs, I didn't know I was running into a whole new world—a world where that resistance to zazen is utterly gone, and I find myself wanting to do zazen just as one drinks when one is thirsty, wanting to do more and more zazen, not for any reason, not for this goal that hung in my mind for so long but just *because*. A world where everything that has ever been said to me about practice is *true*. If only people would just believe you when you say things, Roshi—not to mention the Buddhas and Patriarchs. And yet, even though everything you say is true, there's no way to tell anyone—everyone has to find out for themselves. How wonderful that we can! This world—who would ever have believed that everything could be so RIGHT? Ever since I can remember I have felt so threatened by things that I saw as being outside "me"—causing an anxiety so deep, so constant. Now everything is *different* in a way impossible to describe. A feeling arises of wanting to take everything in my arms, embrace the world—but there's no need to. It's already done, it can't be otherwise!

Recently a friend who used to practice told me she felt that five years ago the focus of her life had been zazen, but now it was emotional health. It made me sad to hear this—Mu is the best psychiatrist anyone could ask for! In working on Mu you see everything about your small psychological self you could ever need to see—but it also offers you the way to see through this self to your True-self. Who would ever trade the joy, the *solidity*, that the slightest glimpse of this Mu provides for some ghost called emotional health?

One already sees habit patterns that were momentarily blasted away creeping back. One realizes the need to work in a whole new way. I'm so used to pushing against myself that even though there's nothing to push against, the pushing goes on. Feeling deeply the need for dokusan, often, I wish I could go to sesshin again tomorrow. I feel like I don't know quite how to walk in this whole new world.

And as for you, Roshi, I remember hearing something somewhere about peeled litchi nuts. You just fed me and fed me, every step of the way—just by being yourself and speaking the truth. Gassho, gassho, gassho. There's nothing to do but to keep going and going. Now at last I can really begin to work. So grateful, for the first time in my life, grateful and glad to be a human being alive in this world.

I bow down to you,

Pamela

5 / "SOMETIMES I THINK THE SEX-UAL EXPERIENCE WAS MORE REAL THAN THE KENSHO"—WITH ROSHI'S REPLY /

DEAR ROSHI, it's been so long since I've seen you that I thought I'd write to you. It suddenly struck me that though I have been a student of yours for some time, you really don't know too much about me, so let me tell you something of myself.

I was born in Chicago in 1949. I have one brother, one year older than me, but we were never very close. I graduated from university with a B.A. in education, and currently am employed as an elementary school teacher.

I feel that I have suffered a great deal in life and this suffering is what led me to Zen. I had many misconceptions as to what it would be like to be enlightened and I sought enlightenment as a means of alleviating this pain. I only worked on the koan Mu for about two months before coming to awakening. For the first six months I was ecstatic, and at the four-day sesshin I attended it reached a peak. Since that time I have slowly begun to realize that this shallow awakening is not the answer to life's pain. I will always do zazen, but I must know what lies beyond from one who has experienced greater depths of enlightenment. I realize that koan study is valuable, but I can also see that a person who does not study koans can be just as free from life's pain as one who does.

I still have many desires, many hopes and emotions. Your commentary on the koan "Jumping from the Top of a Hundred-foot Pole" [25] was very helpful to me, for in it you mentioned that a highly enlightened person has no desires, hopes, or ambitions, for he is completely satisfied with his life, be it good or bad, and takes the joys and pains of life with peace and calm. I realized then that if only I could accept my life for what it was and cease harboring all these hopes, desires, etc., my life would be calmer. After the *teisho,* I consciously tried to employ this notion in my daily life. It was like a koan that I had solved. It helped so much and I was surprised that I could make it work by consciously thinking about it. Previously I had thought that subsequent koan work was useless because one had to consciously think of the koans and their lessons in order to derive benefit from them and that this was totally unnatural. Now I see that this is not unnatural at all.

I wanted enlightenment because I wanted to know the meaning of life. I must confess that I still don't know. Sometimes this life seems endless. Even though I have gained a measure of freedom from my body, I cannot stand the thought of growing old.

Only one experience has had as profound an effect on me as kensho, and that was my first sexual experience, at the age of twenty-two. Sometimes I become confused because I start to think that the sexual experience was more real to me and more important than the kensho experience. I know that eventually I will discover that this is not true, and yet the desire of the flesh still has such a hold on me that I cannot but compare the sexual experience to enlightenment and think that the former revealed a truth greater than enlightenment. You must think that I am losing faith in the dharma and that I shall become lost in the pursuit of worldly pleasures. I am full of questions that must be answered even though I know that in time I will find the answers.

How can I express my gratitude? Anything I say would fall short of what I feel. I know that you ask nothing of your students except that they reach full enlightenment and I shall continue to sit every day of my life.

Please take care of yourself, Roshi, during these long winter months.

Deepest thanks,

Joan

A Reply /

DEAR JOAN, thank you for writing. I'm always glad to hear from my students, especially those from' out of town who have less opportunity to come to the Center.

You speak of pain, Joan. The Buddha was once approached by a woman half mad with grief over the death of her newborn child. Laying the baby at his feet, she pleaded with him to restore it to life. After listening patiently the Buddha told her to go into town and bring back a mustard seed from a house in which there had never been a death. The woman went from door to door throughout the entire city but found not a house untouched by death. Realizing that death comes to all, she finally accepted the fate of her child.

Is there anyone who has not suffered? And is it not that very pain and the wish to overcome it that brings people to Zen and other spiritual traditions?

Although my students have heard me say repeatedly that a shallow awakening is merely a glimpse into the true nature of things, they nonetheless find this hard to accept. A first kensho experience may be compared to lighting a single candle in a vast underground cavern; total darkness no longer prevails, but visibility is still slight. Deepening one's enlightenment is analogous to lighting more and more candles, thereby illuminating the cave in detail.

Your present state is not unlike that of a kitten that has just opened its eyes on the world; it is no longer immersed in darkness but it cannot yet fend for itself. In the same way that it still needs its mother, you need further contact with your teacher. But at least you now know from your own experience that enlightenment does not sweep one into permanent bliss, and your practice can be free of this common misunderstanding. Do not fail to recognize, though, that your kensho, modest though it was, has been liberating for you in a fundamental way. Do you recall how you, previously so shy and timid, suddenly came before me like a warrior? It is true that certain types of makyo can also release untapped stores of energy, but what happened to you was not makyo. Do you remember how quickly and surely you answered my testing questions? You say that the ecstasy and high energy lasted six months—an unusually long period of time. What you say reveals that you had a deeper kensho than you realize, and that your aspiration is deep, for otherwise you would not be so dissatisfied with this initial breakthrough.

Be assured that there is before you a breadth and clarity of enlightenment that you can now hardly imagine. This you can make your own, however, only if you persist with courage and determination. In some respects your letter reminds me of Yaeko's in *The Three Pillars of Zen*. Do you recall how she described her joy and excitement as a "mad state"? The deeper realization she went on to experience is one that you too can attain.

The many desires and hopes that you say persist are nothing but illusions. One day you will realize this. While it is true that a supremely enlightened, fully evolved buddha is free of all desire, we lesser mortals have desires to contend with. But bear in mind that there are low-level desires and worthy desires. The desire to transform one's life and character, the desire to fully awaken so as to help relieve the anguish of humanity—these are desires of the highest order. My teachers used to say that what distinguishes a bodhisattva from a buddha is that a bodhisattva is still attached to the compassionate desire to free all beings from suffering, whereas a buddha no longer thinks in terms of freeing or not freeing; he helps people as naturally as he breathes.

Emotions, you add, also linger with you. And why not? You needn't apologize for them. Haven't you heard me say that while regular zazen dissolves in its path such abstract concepts as hopes, regrets, and expectations, there is no attempt in Zen practice to suppress emotions? When a Zen master was weeping openly at the funeral of his favorite disciple, a young monk who saw this took him to task, saying, "I would have thought that you were beyond such things, Master." "If I did not cry at the funeral of my closest disciple," replied the master, "when would I cry?" Genuine feelings are real enough; to hope or desire is to "poison the real with the ideal."

Your comments on my teisho "Jumping from the Top of a Hundred-foot Pole" show that you have misunderstood a vital point. In regard to the awakened person having no hopes, desires, or ambitions, it is not a matter of his being "completely satisfied with his life, be it good or bad." Satisfied, dissatisfied— thinking in those terms is putting yourself in a mental vise. Just flow with the karmic current of your Buddha-nature and life will flow with and through you. Reflect deeply on this.

The enlightened person neither opposes nor evades what lies before him. Everything depends on the occasion and the timing. When he needs to act he acts. When one's action is decisive and one responds with nothing left over, it is as though he hasn't acted at all.

You say, "Sometimes this life seems endless. Even though I have gained a measure of freedom from my body, I cannot stand the thought of growing old." This life seems endless only because you postulate an end, a goal. You must free yourself from the bind of time. You yourself are time—your body, your mind, the objects around you. Plunge into the river of time and swim, instead of standing on the bank and noting the course of the currents. The thought of growing old arises from a narcissistic preoccupation with the body. What have you learned from Zen training that you speak in dualistic terms of "old" and "young"?

My own age, conventionally speaking, is sixty-five. I do not think of myself as old. Only an individual who thinks of himself as young could say, "He's an old man," and to make such a judgment he must stand apart from me. That way he can never know the true age of my heart. But if we embrace warmly, at that moment of no-minded oneness where is the "old" person and where the "young"? Who remains to say, "He is old, I am young"?

You write that only one experience has had as profound an effect on you as kensho, and that was your first sexual experience. Yes, sex. Zen enlightenment, you know, has been described as a cosmic orgasm. Yet only in a narrow sense can enlightenment be compared with physical orgasm. To experience soaring oneness and joy with a person you love in the sexual embrace is soul-shaking, to be sure, but it is still limited to and induced by a particular person. Universal or cosmic love, on the other hand, is a natural outpouring toward all creatures, great or small, and is fueled not by sexual love but by direct awareness of the indivisibility of all life. When one loves in this way there is no attachment and no expectation of something in return. Such oceanic love is realized not by standing apart, alone with the beloved, but by relinquishing one's self and in so doing embracing all selves.

At this point in your training the sexual experience may well seem more real to you than your kensho, which by its very nature offers nothing to hold onto. It is this "no-thingness" of awakening that flies in the face of all attempts to nail it down as another, albeit extraordinary, experience. As you know, enlightenment is not an experience not one kind of happening standing against others. The sexual experience, though real in the sense that it is so strongly felt, is transitory like every experience. In meeting someone with whom you feel a strong mutual attraction and understanding, it is easy to be deceived by the emotional upsurge that follows and to confuse it with your ultimate destination and home. If you stop with the enjoyment of sex or art or music, for example, then your progress toward full enlightenment will be impeded and the better will interfere with the best.

It is the discriminating mind that nurtures such residual notions as "wanting to know the meaning of life." If you are fully absorbed in what you are doing at each moment, where is there room for wondering about its meaning? The mystery of life is revealed through living it, not pondering over it.

How gratifying that you realize the importance of zazen after kensho and are continuing to sit regularly. For as Zen Master Dogen says, "There is no beginning to practice or end to enlightenment, and there is no beginning to enlightenment or end to practice."

As far as other questions you might have, the answers, as you say, will come.

With an embrace,

P. K.

6 / "EVERY DAY THE TREASURE OF LIFE GAINS IN LUSTER AND BEAUTY" /

1

DEAREST ROSHI, there has been a prima ballerina dancing in the streets of Rochester since the sesshin. I still cannot believe that what has happened is real and not just a passing fantasy or dream. Why is it that when we come upon what we have been earnestly striving to find for so many years or so many lifetimes, we are shocked, are so joyously surprised? It is so difficult to accept that the answers to all one's questions about life, death, and reality are not to be found in obscure places or obscure practices but are to be found *in* life, *in* death, and *in* reality. The questioning and the answers are not two. Although I do not know how my experiences relate to kensho, my awakening is as real as getting up in the morning from a meaningless dream and splashing cold water on my face. You laugh to recall the antics you had just been going through in your dream, then take a deep, wonderful breath and go about your business.

What other way can you say it to yourself than BELIEVE—*believe that it is real?* How could you question life if you were not really alive? Your doubting, confused, bumbling mind is none other than your Buddha-nature. If you cannot have faith—the kind of faith that knows your nose is below your eyes—you will never find the life for which you are looking. You will be like a spoiled child who with his mouth full of oatmeal cries that he is hungry. The life for which I was looking was none other than the one I already possessed. My life *is* my life. How queer, how amazing to realize this!

As I walked down the street yesterday the whole universe was suddenly born. My rational mind was left a devilish, whimpering fool, like Iago at the end of *Othello.* How can it be that *I am the universe*—that I have the power of life and death over life and death itself? I was shocked.

All the people and things that had been such a puzzlement

to me were suddenly all my long-lost children.

Tears of joy and amazement well up at every sight and sound—
the ring of a teacup as the spoon lightly touches its side while
I stir the sugar, my hands as they collate papers to be stapled
together, a red tomato. . . .

Am I mad to think that I alone have created heaven and earth?

My feelings are inexpressible. For this one, who has always
abhorred the routine and the mundane, to find that her everyday
life is the key to the universe and the suffering of all sentient
beings is surely the most mind-blowing, wonderful thing that
has come to pass. I have just been born and yet there is no
birth . . . there is nothing. As I write, not a trace of myself or
what I have said remains. How can this one help but be joyful
when this very notion that has perplexed her for months is dissolved; now surely to see in the round that . . .

> there is absolutely nothing!

Roshi, I cannot comprehend the implications of what has been
happening. I cannot even say I know what *has* happened. What
I am sure of is only what is felt, and nothing else. How can
such experiences come to one as simple-minded as myself?

I sit now amazed, humbled, and mute. Barely to have opened
the gates of dharma and seen the precious jewel inside is more
than I had ever really thought possible. How can anyone treat
lightly the body and the mind, knowing that even in the most
defiled creatures is found the very key to existence, to life and
death?

And to think that I may live for many more years—how wonderful! Just to be alive—I can hardly believe my good fortune.
What gratitude I feel toward my body!

There are many more things I should like to say. Perhaps
sometime soon I will find myself in a mind state to say them.

Please do not think me a fool. If what I have spoken of seems
the product of deceptive thought, it is obviously because delusions still cling to this ignorant girl.

I promise to work as hard as I am able to fully realize my
Bodhi-nature, and to strive to be worthy of the great blessing

of having been born to undertake this most wonderful of all tasks.

Yours most gratefully,

Margaret

2

DEAR ROSHI, the respect and reverence and intimacy I feel toward everyone at the Center the past few months I have been working there—and indeed toward all human beings—seems a kind of natural miracle. In my heart of hearts I know that my living in accordance with the wondrous way of the dharma helps every sentient being come closer to the truth, just as the loving actions of a mother positively influence her children.

Every day the most mysterious treasure of life gains in luster and beauty. I shall continue to try to live and work in truth. The feeling is so strong that my karma at this time lies at the Center—or I should say that the karma of everyone here, and elsewhere in the universe, is my karma—and mine theirs.

Very gratefully yours,

Margaret

3

DEAR ROSHI, can life continue to flow on as surely as it has now that winter is upon us?

Today at last have I come to understand the words of Dogen that have echoed in my heart since I first heard them: "I have returned home with empty hands. I retain no trace of Buddhism. I say only this: My eyes are horizontal, my nose is vertical."

How natural, how utterly natural is my life now!

Roshi, I gassho to you again and again, for now at last I can move swiftly and unhindered. Even my deep-rooted attachment to you and everything that relates to the immaculate and perfect way of the dharma is melting as quickly as the snowfall we had last week. That *this* should be the most natural and inevitable outcome of persistent zazen is astounding. The most mysterious secrets of the dharma have been revealed as surely as the fact of my turning from a silly girl into a young woman, without my knowing how or why.

Roshi, rejoice with me that I have been so thoroughly blessed with the will and good health to follow in the true way of Buddha in this lifetime and all future lifetimes.

As you can see from the nonsense I write, a thousand, no, a million defilements yet remain. But they are pebbles in the path of a surging river. And yet there are neither pebbles nor water. No longer are there choices to be made or sentient beings to be saved. I know only this: In the morning the sun rises and in the evening the moon shines brightly.

Roshi, please do not overwork yourself and do watch your health.

Gratefully, gratefully,

Margaret

7 / " 'O MAN'S MOST WONDERFUL WORK—JUST TO WALK UPON THE EARTH' " /

DEAR ROSHI, it is irrelevant to speak of what might seem to be the history of the true miracle that has so freed my life and reached such culmination during this past sesshin. I have awakened to the inescapable dharma and know directly and unmistakably the truth of the words of all the masters I have ever studied. All the more now I know my need to study them. The Buddha's precepts are all clear, unnecessary to voice or reason about, and are seen to be so necessary for the life leading to awakening (which is the life beginning with awakening) and they all follow from—are identical with—the perfection and interpenetration of everything in the universe. *That* I have, beyond all possibility of doubt, absolutely perceived—no—entered—no—nothing, nothing, nothing. There is no word but the one wordless absolutely meaningless and absolutely meaningful word that thunders in the timeless all-comprehending silence. For me, this word, thanks to your kyosaku and your strong and gentle hands, was Mu. As you insisted, finally driving me through all walls—*only Mu, only Mu.*

So—in short now—from the ever present, fading, and irrelevant past I was gripped by this *Mu.* And I saw all the follies and barriers of my life to be based upon ego and that the smashing of this real illusion was necessary. And then within me wrestled all the furies and demons of every Pilgrim's Progress and every Tibet and I vowed that I could/would *never* stop until it was *all* gone and even then I would not stop. And Mu gripped me by the throat one night and would not let me sleep. I heard voices and things crawled upon me, but Mu and Mu and Mu. I knew tearfully next day I did not and could not know *anything* about Mu—that *I do not know* was the answer to every conceivable question. And I went out into the fields at noon among the warm and peaceful birds and insects and grass and I cried bitterly as I saw that *there was not anything to hold to*—nothing, and that I had no choice but to submit. And I came back and sat in the zendo and Mu welled up further in me. And I have no idea of time at all now—only the experience of this bell and that clapper that drove or smashed or awakened something further, and I had already from the evanescence of past "great experiences," and from this week particularly, learned not to cling to "experiences," no matter how joyful—and so Mu continued. Mu. MU. The kyosaku whacked me whenever it whacked anyone in the zendo and the bells and wind and cicadas were all in my own mind and Mu and Mu and I would not stop. One final whack in some part of my mind across the room on someone else's shoulders brought finality and I was wrenched into a black, black ego-shattering paroxysm by Mu, Mu, Mu. And it happened a second time and I did not yield to the temptation to rest in anything called "glorious" or "I am there." And thank that THAT

that has held me forever and now has taken me fully into its currents of joyful work that I did not hold but released, and that nothing could distract me, and I saw that nothing in the universe existed that could separate me from the totality of deathless being with which I now knew mySelf to be one! But more was to come. Time had no existence those days, those aeons, and then my body and mind disappeared and I was solid as all mountains and without fear. And nothing could be done anywhere that was not done here and now. And I came down from my seat in the zendo because the bell sounded the turning of the dharma's wheel, in such joy, such joy, and you were there and I reached through the tears for your hand and I said to you it was so easy, so easy. I was so thankful and you embraced me and I you and nothing existed or does now exist and there is no beginning or end.

Sometime that day I placed a stick of incense on the altar. I felt such quiet, easy authority to do so. And sometime in kinhin my naked foot touched floor, and words came to me:

> o man's most wonderful work—
> just to walk upon the earth.

I obeyed and wrote them and left the slip of paper at your place in the zendo. And in dokusan there was no doubt, but foolishly, out of the waves of my dimensionless new being, I asked you what to do now and you said, looking at me as at the Buddha, "You know what to do—just go on." And I know that Mu and zazen and you and I and the great wheel of dharma, to turn with which is the Great Liberation, will go on and will go on in the perfect freedom of no-choice forever, for the gateless gate of dharma has been torn asunder and I walk freely between heaven and earth.

And now having said all that necessary stuff I'll try to throw it away. It's just one more thing. The only reason I wrote it was that I had nothing to do with it anyway and it got written without restraint, so maybe it will be useful somewhere sometime as anything else I or anyone else has ever written is mysteriously used.

I know you now as a deep friend and teacher and I thank you so much for your channeling touching role in my life and in the buddha-work, and now I must learn to find my way, with your help, in the new old world, and obey the dharma-voice, and get rid of all traces of ego and enlightenment and any other garbage and clutter, and go on, and go on, and try to live this most profound of truths, to go on and not to try to dwell anywhere.

I salute you gratefully, my dharma-brother. . . .

Carl

PART THREE / DEVOTIONS

CHANTS / A LETTER AND A REPLY / DIALOGUES / INTRODUCTION / There are many who, having been exposed to Zen only through academia, find themselves after entering a Zen center gaping in confusion at the buddha and bodhisattva figures, the chanting and the rituals. Zazen, yes, they tell themselves, that is to be expected—but this? Yet the twenty-five-hundred-year-old living and growing discipline called Zen Buddhism is a full-bodied spiritual tradition in which such devotions play a vital role. Indeed, it is artificial to speak of Zen devotions as separate from zazen. Bowing with hands in gassho upon entering and leaving the zendo, doing prostrations before buddhas and bodhisattvas [26] and making offerings to them, taking part in regular confession and repentance ceremonies—these acts when performed no-mindedly refine the emotions and purify the mind, gradually softening the sharp corners and rigid outlines of the personality. And because they all serve to "prune" the ego-I, they hasten awakening. Sincere devotional practices also help to liberate our inherent compassion so that it may work freely in everyday life.

Ceremonies performed for centuries in traditional Buddhist

The large standing drum (above) is played as sitters file into the main zendo for chanting. The *keisu*, or bowl-shaped gong (opposite, top), is used to introduce each chant. The wooden-fish drum (opposite, bottom) sets the cadence of each chant.

countries have now taken root on American soil. At the Zen Center these observances have been adapted to our Western culture through a process of natural evolution. In addition to rites of passage—funerals, weddings, and ordinations—the calendar of ceremonies includes the Buddha's birthday, death day, and day of enlightenment; Bodhidharma's death day; Founder's Day; New Year's, and, each month, a confession-repentance ceremony and a ceremony dedicated to the aid of starving people throughout the world. Equally significant are the celebrations held each year at Thanksgiving—celebrations that, because they are a deep expression of gratitude, fit ideally into Zen devotions and add substance to a home-grown American Buddhist holiday.

At a time when many followers of traditional Western religions appear to have no significant understanding of or relationship to rites and ceremonies, it is well to remember that formality need not be an empty shell. For where gratitude, reverence, and other genuine spiritual feelings are present they can be deepened and made more significant when expressed through a formal pattern, just as movement can be made more meaningful when turned into dance, or sound into music.

No element of Zen devotions occupies a more central role than chanting. There is hardly a Zen temple or center where men and women do not assemble in the main hall at least once a day and chant sutras and the words of the masters who have realized the highest truth. Chanting forms the vocal ground on which every ritual, ceremony, and rite of passage is performed, setting a tone through which participants acquire a heightened awareness of and receptivity to what is being enacted.

Each day at dawn the thunderous beat of the large standing drum breaks the zazen silence to signal sitters to file into the main zendo for chanting. After this initial, booming call, the drum player sweeps his wooden sticks over the brass beads along the drum's rim, producing a deep, rushing sound. Then the sharp strikes to the wooden rim itself—"clackety clack, clackety clack"—building in tempo before leading into a final rhythm on the face of the drum.

After the drum ends, with no gap the large *keisu* (pronounced "kay-su"), or bowl-shaped gong, is struck, its deep resonance filling the zendo. The keisu player sits poised before it, deftly holding a large padded cylindrical striker in both hands to intone the introductions to the different chants and to punctuate the chanting after all have joined in. He "drops" the heavy striker onto the rim of the gong, aware that contact which is either too hard or too soft, or aimed at either the incorrect angle or the wrong point on the keisu, will fail to release the full and rich body of tones coiled within the instrument. In Zen it is said, "Don't strike the instrument; let it be struck."

After each chant has been introduced, the wooden-fish drum comes in. It begins slowly, "thump . . . thump . . . thump," gradually building in speed, like a departing train, as the individual voices blend into a single sonorous drone. As with the keisu, the drum player with his padded stick does not "beat" the instrument but rather, by handling the striker lightly, simply guides it, with the effect that the instrument in a sense "plays itself." The sound of this fish-shaped, hollowed-out drum is deep enough to ride underneath the vocal chanting, thus setting a cadence that can be followed by all.

A chanting service blends a wide range of diverse elements. The strong, clear voice of the lead chanter is heard alone to introduce the chants, evoking a response in the full "chorus" of between fifty and three hundred chanters. The pulselike throb of the wooden drum offers counterpoint to the vibrant ring of the bowl-gong even as they mesh to contrast and harmonize with the drone of chanting.

During chanting the whole body is relaxed. The energy for the chanting comes from the lower belly with the sound resonating in the head cavities. In Zen there is no swaying or rocking during the chanting; it is carried on in an erect and stable posture with the hands in the lap.

Each chanter takes his or her own lowest natural pitch—a note in the lowest part of one's range that can be maintained easily without strain—while at the same time blending in with the dominant pitch to form a harmonious unity. The particular words of the chants emerge from one's basic pitch; thus the words flow together into a drone issuing from the hara. The pitch does not rise and fall in a singsongy way. Zen chanting is a unique way of engaging the deepest level of mind. It circumvents the intellect to awaken Understanding and energetically expresses feeling without emotionality.

Broadly speaking, there are two types of chants: sutras and *dharani.* In the category of sutras, which are the purported words of the Buddha, may be included the words of the masters. The advantage of chanting these in one's own language is that when repeated regularly the truth of the words is hammered home to the subconscious mind, thereby instilling greater understanding and faith. No conscious effort need be made to grasp the meaning, for it is absorbed spontaneously, unchecked by the rational mind. The mind state created by the chanting—involvement to the point of self-transcendence—is of primary importance.

A dharani is an extended mantra, a rhythmic sequence of sounds that expresses, through its unique spiritual vibrations, the essential truth transcending all duality. The power of such a formula to evoke unseen forces when chanted wholeheartedly depends to an extent on the sound itself, but even more on the mind state of the chanter. Thus a dharani will carry greater potency when uttered by one pure in faith, concentrated in mind, and responsive in heart. The structure of a dharani is not insignificant; it must be rhythmic, melodious, and the outgrowth of genuine religious experience. Since no one yet has managed the difficult task of making suitable English chanting versions of them, no mantra or dharani are presented here except for the mantra at the end of the Heart of Perfect Wisdom sutra.

Chanting must be distinguished from reciting. The latter may be nothing more than repetition of an account or passage. Chanting, however, is generated deep in the belly, and when performed egolessly has the power to penetrate visible and invisible worlds. Mind is unlimited; energetic chanting done with a pure mind, with single-minded involvement, is another form of zazen, another mode of learning the buddha-truth in a direct, nonconceptual way. Performed in this manner, chanting is also a means of strengthening samadhi power and of helping to bring about awakening.

At the Rochester Zen Center most of the chants are in English; the most well-known are The Four Bodhisattvic Vows, Heart of Perfect Wisdom, Chant in Praise of Zazen, and Affirming Faith in Mind. These chants are set forth to open this section on devotions. While there are other English translations of these works, what distinguishes those that appear here is that they were adapted specifically for chanting, rendered with an ear for euphony and cadence.

Following the chants are a letter and several dialogues, which more than any others reveal the most frequent and persistent difficulties in the area of Zen devotions. Helpful though these selections may be, readers will still need to take part in the devotions themselves in order to fully appreciate their significance.

I / CHANTS / 1 / THE FOUR BODHI-SATTVIC VOWS / The Four Great Vows of a bodhisattva comprise the most widely recited chant in Mahayana Buddhism:

> "All beings, without number, I vow to liberate.
> Endless blind passions I vow to uproot.
> Dharma gates, beyond measure, I vow to penetrate.
> The Great Way of Buddha I vow to attain."

The content of these chanted vows commonly poses difficulties for Western students, who over the years have expressed two main objections. Students of Christian background complain that, having left Christianity and its missionary spirit, the last thing they want in Zen is more of what they misconstrue in the first of the Four Vows as "saving." Others ask, "How can I vow to liberate all beings when I haven't yet liberated myself? And if I do liberate myself, how would it be possible to liberate *all other* beings?" One serious aspirant put it this way in a letter:

"What troubles me about the Four Vows is that I cannot *honestly* commit myself to them. To myself I have to add, 'as far as the limitations and weaknesses within me permit,' which destroys the value of saying the Four Vows. I would like to be able to affirm these vows, but in all sincerity I cannot."

The problem behind both of these objections is that of seeing the Four Vows as an external formula that must be learned and somehow, against all odds and reason, lived up to. In the first of the Four Vows, that which is traditionally translated "to save" is chanted as "to liberate" at the Rochester Center. This difference of expression avoids the moralistic and un-Buddhistic implication of redemption from sin, and more truly reflects the spirit of the original. Understood correctly, this vow is a statement of the purpose and scope of one's practice, an affirmation that one's zazen is not for oneself alone but also for all humanity. The remaining three vows outline the mind state by which one is empowered to aid the numberless beings throughout countless realms.

The expression "all beings" is not hyperbole. Zen awakening reveals unmistakably that all is one—oneself—and that oneself is all. Whatever happens to any one being inevitably affects every other being. Thus when one awakens, everything is charged with the same awakening. This was affirmed by Zen master Dogen when he said: "Without enlightening others there is no self-enlightenment."

In Zen a bodhisattva is anyone who has vowed, out of his great compassion, not to enter nirvana until all beings have entered—that is to say, he naturally puts the welfare of others before his own. He does continue to develop himself, however, for no one who needs help himself can truly help another. The vow stresses that having dedicated himself to those in need, he will not turn back.

The bodhisattvic vows, then, are far more than mere positive thinking. In the same sense that the peach stone vows to become a peach, the acorn an oak, the infant a man, the man a buddha, the Four Vows are a reaffirmation of our innate vow to become what we intrinsically are—whole and complete. Seen in this light they are nothing less than a call to Self-awakening, to Self-liberation.

2 / HEART OF PERFECT WISDOM[27]

The Heart of Perfect Wisdom, chanted daily in Buddhist monasteries and centers throughout the world, is considered the most potent formulation for piercing the delusive mind. It is the kernel, or core, of the Buddha's teaching, the condensed message of the wisdom sutras he gave over the course of twenty-two years. Also referred to as the Heart sutra, it is to be grasped not through the intellect but with the heart—that is, through one's own deepest intuitive experience. Thus "perfect wisdom" here means transcendental wisdom, as well as the path leading to the attainment of this wisdom and the text of the teaching conducive to its realization.

In the Heart sutra the Buddha is speaking to Sariputra, a chief disciple noted for his wisdom. The Buddha recounts how the Bodhisattva of Compassion realized through deep samadhi that the human personality is merely the product of five *skandhas* (literally "aggregates")—form, feeling, perception, tendencies, and consciousness—that are fundamentally empty of real substance. The Buddha then discloses the illusory nature of the eighteen realms of sense, made up of the six sense organs, the corresponding six types of sense data, and the six acts of sensing; the twelve links in the chain of causation; the Four Noble Truths; and even the dualistic conception of nirvana and *samsara*.

The Sanskrit mantra at the end of the sutra may be rendered into English as follows:

> Gone, gone
> gone beyond,
> fully beyond.
> Awake: rejoice!

It is difficult to translate the word *svaha* exactly; it is a word of exultation, meaning "hail."

The Sanskrit mantra at the end is pronounced:

> Gə-tay, gə-tay
> Pah-rah gə-tay
> Pah-rah som gə-tay
> Bod-hi sva-ha

[An upside-down *e*, ə, is pronounced like the *u* in fun.]

HEART OF PERFECT WISDOM

The Bodhisattva of Compassion
from the depths of prajna wisdom
saw the emptiness of all five
skandhas and sundered the bonds
that caused him suffering.

Know then:

Form here [28] is only emptiness,
emptiness only form.
Form is no other than emptiness,
emptiness no other than form.

Feeling, thought,[29] and choice,[30]
consciousness itself,
are the same as this.

Dharmas here are empty,
all are the primal void.
None are born or die.
Nor are they stained or pure,
nor do they wax or wane.

So in emptiness no form,
no feeling, thought, or choice
nor is there consciousness.

No eye, ear, nose,
tongue, body, mind;
no color, sound, smell,
taste, touch, or what
the mind takes hold of,
nor even act of sensing.

No ignorance or end of it
nor all that comes of ignorance:
no withering, no death,
no end of them.

Nor is there pain or cause of pain
or cease in pain or noble path
to lead from pain,

not even wisdom to attain,
attainment too is emptiness.

So know that the bodhisattva
holding to nothing whatever
but dwelling in prajna wisdom
is freed of delusive hindrance,
rid of the fear bred by it,
and reaches clearest nirvana.

All buddhas of past and present,
buddhas of future time
through faith in prajna wisdom
come to full enlightenment.

Know, then, the great dharani
the radiant, peerless mantra,
the supreme, unfailing mantra,
the Prajna Paramita,
whose words allay all pain.
This is highest wisdom
true beyond all doubt,
know and proclaim its truth:

> Gate, gate
> para gate
> para sam gate
> bodhi, *svaha!*

Heart of perfect wisdom.

3 / MASTER HAKUIN'S CHANT IN PRAISE OF ZAZEN /

One of the great lights of Japanese Buddhism is Zen master Hakuin (1686–1769). Although his teaching stands in the tradition of the old masters of China, he effectively adapted it to Japanese culture, creating a living Zen that was accessible to laymen even while it was rooted in the pure heritage of his own monastic orientation. Hakuin is perhaps best known for his revitalization of the koan system and for the koan he himself devised, still widely used in training:

"What Is the Sound of One Hand?"

Even in his own day Hakuin was widely respected and beloved, especially by the common people, whose lot in the feudal society of his day was a bitter one. They came to him in great numbers seeking relief from their heavy burdens of poverty and oppression.

High government officials also received his teaching, and in his bold and colorful replies to letters from them we find him inveighing against proponents of an adulterated mass-appeal Zen [31] and "dead sitting and silent illumination."

Hakuin's chief concern, naturally, was the training of his monks and disciples and the development of qualified successors. He himself says in one of his letters that he seldom had less than five hundred monks and laymen training under him.

A man of extraordinary versatility and inexhaustible energy, Hakuin was not only a vivid and powerful writer, he was also a respected painter and calligrapher and an accomplished poet and sculptor. Brilliant Zen master, Renaissance man—this is the author of the "Chant in Praise of Zazen," still regularly intoned in Zen temples in Japan, at the Zen Center in Rochester, and elsewhere. Perhaps nowhere else is there to be found so spirited and eloquent a testimony to the power of zazen.

ZEN MASTER HAKUIN'S CHANT IN PRAISE OF ZAZEN

From the beginning all beings are buddha.
Like water and ice,
without water no ice,
outside us no buddhas.
How near the truth
yet how far we seek,
like one in water crying "I thirst!"
Like the son of a rich man wand'ring poor on this earth,
we endlessly circle the six worlds.
The cause of our sorrow is ego delusion.
From dark path to dark path we've wandered in darkness—
how can we be free from the wheel of samsara?
The gateway to freedom is zazen samadhi;

beyond exaltation, beyond all our praises,
the pure Mahayana.
Observing the precepts, repentance, and giving,
the countless good deeds, and the way of right living
all come from zazen.
Thus one true samadhi extinguishes evils;
it purifies karma, dissolving obstructions.
Then where are the dark paths to lead us astray?
The pure lotus land is not far away.
Hearing this truth, heart humble and grateful,
to praise and embrace it, to practice its wisdom,
brings unending blessings, brings mountains of merit.
And if we turn inward and prove our True-nature—
that True-self is no-self,
our own Self is no-self—
we go beyond ego and past clever words.
Then the gate to the oneness of cause-and-effect
is thrown open.
Not two and not three, straight ahead runs the Way.
Our form now being no-form,
in going and returning we never leave home.
Our thought now being no-thought,
our dancing and songs are the voice of the dharma.
How vast is the heaven of boundless samadhi!
How bright and transparent the moonlight of wisdom!
What is there outside us,
what is there we lack?
Nirvana is openly shown to our eyes.
This earth where we stand is the Pure Lotus Land,
and this very body the body of buddha.

4 / AFFIRMING FAITH IN MIND [32]

The third Zen patriarch, Seng Tsan, is one of the many out-standing masters of whose lives we know little. Beyond the fact that he is recognized as author of Affirming Faith in Mind, history provides only the barest biographical sketch. That he was of the sixth century is certain, although the place and year of his birth are unknown. As part of his spiritual discipline he entered a life of religious mendicancy, traveling throughout the country—a not uncommon practice in ancient China. He is said to have been notably kind and gentle, and to have come to the dropping away of all bondage and illusion. When a persecution of Buddhism began, he, with thousands of others of the Zen sect, fled to the mountains. There, leading a simple and disciplined life, they were able to subsist on very little, and it was this adaptability that helped Zen recover from the persecution more quickly than any of the other Buddhist sects. Before his death, in A.D. 606, Seng Tsan passed on the robe and bowl to the Fourth Patriarch. One man's life . . . the teaching goes on. . . .

Affirming Faith in Mind is believed by many to have been the first Chinese Zen document. It is one of the most widely admired of Zen writings, and since ancient times the masters have quoted liberally from it; its opening lines alone are the bases of several koans in the *Blue Rock Record.* The work has already acquired similar popularity in this country since its appearance in *Zen Bow,* the Rochester Zen Center's publication.

Comprised originally of 584 characters, each of the 146 unrhymed lines that make up Affirming Faith in Mind is of four characters rather than the usual five or seven of Chinese verse, giving it a Zen-like brevity that prevents any literary or rhetorical flourishes. The title's first character, *hsin,* means faith or trust. Far more than even strong belief, faith is conviction growing out of the intuitive awareness—if only for fleeting moments—of the indivisibility of all existences. The second *hsin* signifies Mind, the substratum of all phenomena, that which *knows,* the birthright of each of us.

AFFIRMING FAITH IN MIND

The Great Way is not difficult
for those who do not pick and choose.

When love and hate both disappear
the Way stands clear and undisguised.

But even slight distinctions made
set earth and heaven far apart.

If you would clearly see the truth,
discard opinions pro and con.

To founder in dislike and like
is nothing but the mind's disease.

And not to see the Way's deep truth
disturbs the mind's essential peace.

The Way is perfect like vast space,
where there's no lack and no excess.

Our choice to choose and to reject
prevents our see'ng this simple truth.

Both striving for the outer world
as well as for the inner void
condemn us to entangled lives.

Just calmly see all unity,
and false views vanish by themselves.

Attempts to stop activity
will fill you with activity.

Remaining in duality,
you'll never know of unity.

And not to know this single Way
lets conflict lead you far astray.

When you deny that things are real
you miss their true reality.

And to declare that things are void
also denies reality.

The more you talk and think on this
the further from the truth you'll be.

Cut off all useless thoughts and words
And there's nowhere you cannot go.

Returning to the root itself,
you'll find the meaning of all things.

If you pursue appearances
you overlook the primal source.

Awak'ning is to go beyond
all emptiness as well as form.

All changes in this empty world
seem real because of ignorance.

Do not go searching for the truth,
just let those fond opinions go.

Remain not in duality,
abstain from it with every care.

If there's a trace of right and wrong,
True-mind is lost, confused, distraught.

From One-mind comes duality,
but cling not even to this One.

When mind in *Tao* rests undisturbed,
then nothing in the world offends.

And when no thing can give offense,
all things at once cease to exist.

If all thought-objects disappear,
the thinking-subject disappears.

For things are things because of mind,
as mind is mind because of things.

These two are really just the same,
and rooted in one Emptiness.

In Emptiness these are not two,
and in each are all worlds contained.

Once coarse and fine are seen no more,
then how can there be taking sides?

The Great Way is without limit,
beyond the easy and the hard.

But those who hold to narrow views
are fearful and irresolute;
their frantic haste just slows them down.

If you're attached to anything,
you surely will go far astray.

Just let go now of clinging mind,
and all things are just as they are.
In essence nothing goes or stays.

Be one with the nature of things,
and you're in step with the Great Way,
thus walking freely, undisturbed.

But live in bondage to your thoughts,
and you will be confused, unclear.

This heavy burden weighs you down—
O why keep judging good and bad?

If you would walk the Single Way,
do not reject the sense domain.

Accepting the world of senses
conforms with true enlightenment.

The wise do not strive after goals,
but fools themselves in bondage put.

The One Way knows no diff'rences,
the foolish cling to this and that.

To seek Great Mind with thinking mind
is certainly a grave mistake.

From small mind come rest and unrest,
but mind awakened transcends both.

Delusion spawns dualities—
these dreams are nought but flow'rs of air—
why work so hard at grasping them?

Both gain and loss, and right and wrong—
once and for all get rid of them.

When you are no longer asleep,
all dreams will vanish by themselves.

If mind goes not discriminate,
all things are as they are, as One.

To go to this myster'ous Source
frees us from all entanglements.

When all is seen with "equal mind,"
to our Self-nature we return.

This single mind goes right beyond
all reasons and comparisons.

Stop movement and there's no movement,
stop rest and no-rest comes instead.

When rest and no-rest cease to be,
then even oneness disappears.

This ultimate finality's
beyond all laws, can't be described.

With single mind one with the Way,
all ego-centered strivings cease.

Doubts and confusion disappear,
and so true faith pervades our life.

There is no thing that clings to us,
and nothing that is left behind.

All's self-revealing, void and clear,
without exerting pow'r of mind.

Thought cannot reach this state of truth,
here feelings are of no avail.

In this true world of Emptiness
both self and other are no more.

To enter this true empty world,
immed'ately affirm "not-two."

In this "not-two" all is the same,
with nothing sep'rate or outside.

The wise in all times and places
awaken to this primal truth.

The Way's beyond all space, all time,
one instant is ten thousand years.

Not only here, not only there,
truth's right before your very eyes.

The smallest and the largest fuse,
for length and breadth do not pertain.

The largest is the smallest too—
here limitations have no place.

What is is not, what is not is—
if this is not yet clear to you,
you're still far from the inner truth.

One thing is all, all things are one—
if this is only realized,
perfection will not worry you.

When faith and Mind are not sep'rate,
and not sep'rate are Mind and faith,
this is where words all fail to reach.

For here there is no yesterday,
              no tomorrow,
              no today.

II / A LETTER AND A REPLY / RELIGIOUS ZEN—"IT TURNS ME OFF!" /

DEAR ROSHI, this letter is the result of months of stewing about a problem that I had assumed would disappear on its own or that I could resolve somehow. But nothing seems to be happening, so I'm writing in hopes that you can shed some light on the subject.

Basically, my problem is this: The whole "religious" aspect of Zen turns me off. I don't see what buddhas and bodhisattvas, the heavens and hells of Buddhist cosmology, the six realms of existence, and all the other flowery conceptions of the sutras have to do with the pure and simple task of finding out who I am.

Zen appealed to me in the first place because it is so simple and direct, cutting through abstractions and fantasy for a clear view of the Truth. No baloney, just zazen. But since I've been at the Center there have been more and more ceremonies and chants and I just can't get used to them.

The whole time I am participating in a ceremony or chanting it is very difficult to continue doing zazen. I feel as if I am in a movie about some exotic religious cult. I think a lot of other people feel this way too, and this gives our ceremonies a kind of stilted, self-conscious feeling.

Perhaps my problems stem from a childhood faith in fundamentalist Christianity. I was a devout and emotional believer for years before skeptical adolescence laid bare the hypocrisy and basic emptiness of our Church. I must admit that sometimes the Heart of Perfect Wisdom sutra moves me to the point of tears, and this makes me angry because my emotions have betrayed me before. What does getting all choked up about a bygone buddha have to do with becoming a buddha right now?

Bowing and prostrating before the buddha in the zendo also throws me. It is meaningful for me to bow to you, my teacher, for whom I feel a deep respect and gratitude. It is also wonderful to be able to bow after each round of sitting to fellow members of the sangha whose zazen helps sustain mine. But I feel no direct, immediate relationship with the gilded statue on the altar, no sense of oneness like I feel with you and the sangha. The plate of cakes and fruit in front of the buddha always makes me want to burst out laughing. Who eats them, anyway? If we're all buddhas, why not just pass them around the zendo? If everything is buddha, why not simply bow to each other or to a beautiful flower instead of a statue that inevitably arouses feelings of idol worship?

Please don't think that these feelings are frivolous or fleeting. They run deep and seem to constitute my major problem in practicing here at the Center. A friend of mine once remarked that the appealing thing about Zen Buddhism is that "you can just take the Zen without the Buddhism." Here at the Center at least this isn't so. Why is "religious Zen" necessary? How can I stop viewing it as a distraction and a nuisance and use it to find out who I am?

Love,

Carol

A Reply /

DEAR CAROL, your sincere and forthright letter caused me to sit up and actually think about what is behind the devotional aspects of Zen, and about the reasons I used to give myself for doing what now comes as naturally as eating when hungry and resting when tired. The sentiments you express about "religious Zen" might also have been written by me some twenty-five years ago, so I can sympathize with you.

Before I went to Japan and began training in Zen I had read and studied the philosophical approach to Zen of D. T. Suzuki and other scholars. I was shocked and dumfounded, then, after landing in a real Zen monastery, to find myself surrounded by figures of buddhas and bodhisattvas and in the midst of chanting and other ceremonies that struck me as weird and un-Zen-like. Like yourself, I wondered, "What do these rituals have to do with the truth of my being? What is the need for flowers and fruit on the altar when you have zazen?"

How well, too, I remember the first time I came before my teacher in dokusan. As you know, it is customary to prostrate oneself before the roshi as a sign of respect and humility. But how that went against my grain, and how I resisted it! "Why should I bow down before another human being? Are we not all supposed to be equally endowed with the Buddha-nature? Why doesn't he bow down before me? Anyway, what does all this have to do with Zen?"

My teacher, well aware of these thoughts within me, said nothing, viewing my frustrated maneuvers at each dokusan with an amused smile. Then one day, when I was having a more awkward time than usual trying to prostrate, he suddenly shot at me, "Kapleau-san, when you make prostrations in dokusan you are not bowing down before me but before your own Buddha-nature."

"Aha! So I'm not bowing down to him, I'm bowing down to myself! That's different." Thereafter bowing came more easily, but many more years had to elapse—years of prostrating and bowing before buddha—before the last barriers of self-and-buddha disappeared.

Not long after this revelation in dokusan I met a wise monk

with whom I could converse in a way not possible with my formal teacher, and I took up the matter with him.

"What is the point of offerings and prostrations to buddha? From everything I've read and studied in Zen, none of the great Chinese masters did anything like this."

"Are you not familiar with Zen master Huang Po?"

"Yes, of course."

"After making offerings to buddha he would do prostrations with such fervor, pressing his head to the floor, that he acquired a permanent red mark on his forehead. This may not appear in English translations of Zen texts, but go to any Zen monastery and raise doubts about prostrations and you will be told this story."

You ask, Carol, what the devotional aspects of Zen have to do with "the pure and simple task of finding out who I am." Actually Huang Po, in his wholehearted prostrations, was declaring with great eloquence who he was, affirming that his own essential nature and that of the Buddha are indivisible. At the same time, in bowing down he was offering to buddhas the fruits of his zazen out of gratitude for their beneficence, which made it possible. Were he to have seen the buddha figure as merely an aesthetically fashioned sculpture, his obeisance to it could rightly be called an act of idolatry, since he would have been reverencing only one fragment—the form—at the expense of the whole. Furthermore, in bowing down no-mindedly he was breathing life into the buddha image. What was previously only a statue now became a living reality with the singular power to obliterate in himself awareness of self and buddha at the moment of prostration. As long as one is aware that the true buddha is the self-buddha, that the one who prostrates and that which is prostrated before are not two, the act is not an idolatrous one.

Huang Po's devotions were done with the deep awareness that came from his enlightenment. But prostrations, when entered into sincerely, are a source of spiritual nourishment that everyone, awakened or not, can tap. As your practice deepens, feelings of respect, of gratitude, and of humility toward the Buddha, his teachings, and those who practice it will grow stronger and naturally seek expression. It is this yearning and need that make possible a true "horizontalizing of the mast of ego" in the unself-conscious act of bowing or prostrating.

Yes, a flower is buddha, Carol, but have you ever tried bowing down regularly before a bowl of flowers? Very soon the act degenerates into a mere calisthenic and, paradoxically, has the effect of making you more self-conscious instead of less. Furthermore, bowing and prostrating selflessly before buddha figures help open us up to an intuitive understanding and appreciation of the exalted mind of all buddhas. In this way an intimate rapport is formed with them, a karmic bond that acts as a powerful impetus to practice.

Your bewilderment and discomfort at the idea of making food and other offerings at the altar is shared by many beginners, especially those whose minds adhere fast to the logical and literal. But isn't it in the *idea* of it that the problem lies? After all, what could be more natural when feeling grateful than to express your gratitude? Not just with thoughts or words, but with flowers, fruit, candles, incense—concrete expressions of such feelings—all of which have significance. Rites and ceremonies that have substance behind them permit us gracefully to express such feelings; otherwise we become frustrated.

Your asking, "Who eats them, anyway?" brings to mind the story of two men, one Chinese and one Caucasian, who found themselves at adjacent graves in a cemetery, paying respect to their deceased relatives. As the Caucasian laid his bouquet of flowers on the grave at which he stood, he looked over to see the Chinese offering at the next, not flowers but rice and cakes. The Caucasian turned to him and with a wry smile asked, "When are your ancestors going to come up to eat that food?" To which the Chinese replied, "When your ancestors come up to smell those flowers."

This is not to overlook the importance of the buddha figure itself; it is far more than a metal or wood symbol. Every original buddha image stands as a vivid manifestation of our True-mind, radiating the poise and equanimity, the sensitivity and compassion, the strength and unity that are within each of us. Count Keyserling, in his book *The Travel Diary of a Philosopher*, observes,

"I know nothing more grand in this world than the figure of the buddha; it is an absolutely perfect embodiment of spirituality in the visible domain."

An original buddha figure is a work of prayer and meditation. The task of one who would create it is to give dynamic expression to the attributes of a giant among men. To have any hope to succeed in this, a sculptor had to adhere strictly to a religious life, at least during the period of his work. Only through profound meditation could he attain the purity of mind required for the task. A figure created by such a person inevitably absorbs his rare vibrations and in turn imparts them to those who with believing heart make obeisance before it.

The quality of a buddha is not primarily a matter of aesthetics but of reverence. An original figure might receive careless handling by an art dealer, thus sapping its power. Nor does it fare much better in a museum, where, though it may be cared for respectfully, it is not revered spiritually. But when a figure has "lived" for some time in a Buddhist monastery or center, nourished by the actual zazen done there, it acquires a deep silence and, regardless of its aesthetic qualities, a radiance. Endowed with great power to inspire those receptive to it, it will speak to them directly, powerfully. It may not be a treasure artistically, but if it is treasured—that is, consecrated as a religious object— its value is immeasureable.

Besides the buddha figure, the whole altar on which it stands, with its arrangement of bodhisattvas and offerings, is a tangible and vivid expression of the Buddha's basic teachings. Emptiness, impermanence, oneness, compassion—these qualities are all there.

It is true that in an ultimate sense every buddha image is so much "baloney," for it purports to depict that which is beyond all shapes. Then why all the figures, prints, paintings, murals, and carvings of buddhas? Zen master Hakuin once said, "Buddhas and bodhisattvas in reality have no form, and as they have no form they are unknown to those who dwell on the materialistic level. They have been given form out of our necessity." In order to identify with buddhas we humans need to do so through concrete forms. Without such representations our Buddha-mind would, for many, be something remote, cold, abstract—and utterly ungraspable.

I wish you could have been at Temple Night last Thanksgiving, Carol. As in years past, it was an occasion for which all of our buddha and bodhisattva figures were assembled in the Buddha Hall, where members could come and express devotions as they wished, in an unstructured setting. What a convocation it was! On the main altar was the All-encompassing One, Vairochana Buddha. Like a beacon of light, sitting in vibrant composure, he looked down with a radiance beyond joy and bliss, beyond knowing and not knowing. Not far away sat Bodhidharma like a mountain, glaring in awesome, wide-eyed determination. Surely he, too, must have smelled the fragrance of incense being offered. And of course there was ancient Kannon, in his tender, merciful strength, reaching out to the parents and children who prostrated and offered flowers and fruit before him.

An air of dynamic calm permeated the hall, which at the same time seemed to expand with light. This light became somehow interwoven with the deep, melodic chanting to create a single charged fabric of light-sound-people. All at once the solemn and sonorous urgings of the Four Vows rang out as if from the walls and ceiling: "All beings, without number, I vow to liberate . . . ," slowly gathering force and momentum. Next followed the Heart sutra, with its stirring coda: "Gate, gate, para gate. . . ." Then in unison, as if directed by some unseen force, people rose and began circumambulating, winding from corner to corner of the Buddha Hall like so many vertebrae of a single spine. "OM-MUNI-MUNI-MAHA-MUNI-SHAKYA-MUNI-SVAHA! OM-MUNI-MUNI . . ." over and over—chanting that seemed to issue forth from the earth itself—a soundless sound that rather than breaking the silence enriched it. "OM-MUNI-MUNI . . ."—it united the chanters in a wave of awareness beyond thought and emotion. It plumbed the mind, drawing it deeper, back to itself. Afterward, one man described how moved he had been by it, how he realized for the first time the power of Zen chanting to transport one beyond all thoughts and imaginings into a realm of no-mindedness. Similar words came from others.

There is much more that could be said, Carol, about buddhas and bodhisattvas, the six realms of existence and the sutras, but perhaps this is enough. I have written at such length because you are a long-standing and valuable member. If this letter succeeds in dissolving your doubts, then the time it took to write was well spent.

With an embrace in thought,

P. K.

III / DIALOGUES / 1 / ISN'T IT BROWN-NOSING TO MAKE OFFERINGS TO BUDDHAS? /

QUESTIONER: You have said several times that Zen is a religion, although one without dogmas and creeds. But you haven't said a word about prayer. A religion without prayer seems like a fish without water.

ROSHI: The reason you haven't heard anything about prayer is that so few people ask about it. You are right, though. Prayer is the lifeblood of religion. Since prayer requires concentration of mind, it can be said that all religions have in them an element of Zen.

There are three general categories of prayer: petitionary, in which you ask for something; prayer of assistance, in which you ask for help to do something yourself; and absolute prayer, in which you ask for nothing but instead merely become *one* with a deity or buddha or bodhisattva.

The difference between the first and second categories is illustrated by an old story about three tramps who were wondering how they were going to get a turkey for a Christmas dinner. The first asked his companions, "Why don't we pray to God to send us one?" The second demurred, saying, "When I pray to God for something, I never get it." The third said, "The trouble is, you don't know how to pray. God always sends me what I pray for." The other two turned to him in surprise. "He does? Tell us how you pray." "Well, I don't ask God to *send* me something, but pray to him to send me *after* it. That way I always get it."

Beginners in Zen often call on buddhas for strength to rid themselves of greed and delusion so they may persevere in their spiritual training. One can't, however, pray to buddhas to be granted enlightenment. Nor can one pray to be saved from the karmic consequences of his follies, although through prayer one can gain the determination to persist in zazen and thereby change the karmic pattern of one's life.

Prostrating before buddhas and bodhisattvas and offering up incense or flowers to them is another type of "prayer" in Zen.

QUESTIONER: Isn't it "brown-nosing," pardon the expression, to make offerings of incense and flowers to buddhas?

ROSHI: Such devotions are expressions of gratitude to buddhas; at the same time they provide a means of venerating and exalting them. Devotions help create a rapport with buddhas—a karmic, link, if you will—which increases one's faith in the truth of their teachings and thus strengthens one's practice of these teachings.

SECOND QUESTIONER: Are you going to say something more about absolute prayer?

ROSHI: Yes. In absolute prayer there is no element of petitioning because in the deepest sense there is no one who asks and no one who responds. In times of frustration or despair, sitting before a buddha figure radiating compassion and wisdom can open you up to buddhic forces, which interact with your own Buddha-nature to inspire and strengthen you.

SECOND QUESTIONER: You said that petitionary prayer is not practiced in Zen. Why not?

ROSHI: Because this type of prayer can easily degenerate into a selfish bargaining with buddhas—"Grant me this favor and I promise you I'll be a good person." Such prayer enlarges the sense of self instead of diminishing it and encourages dependence on an external power rather than on one's own efforts. It's like running to your parents whenever you need money instead of earning it yourself.

Still fresh in my mind, after twenty-five years, is the time I stayed up all night in the monastery, prostrating before a figure of the buddha and praying desperately, "O God, O Buddha, please grant me satori and I'll be humble, even bowing willingly before you. . . ." When still unenlightened the next morning, my faith in buddhas—never strong—was shattered. The only gainer was my ego, engorged by my disappointment, chagrin, and resentment toward the roshi for having urged me to stay up all night (though not to pray). And several years elapsed before that faith was resurrected.

THIRD QUESTIONER: But we can't be strong all the time, can we? Don't we need help from others?

ROSHI: Yes, we do. For example, a person who breaks a leg needs a doctor, usually his family's help, and crutches. But if he continues to use the crutches beyond the time that they are necessary, he will become progressively weaker instead of stronger. The point is that while help is at times essential it cannot serve as a substitute for personal effort.

FOURTH QUESTIONER: I read somewhere this "prayer" of an agnostic: "Dear God—if there is a God—save my soul—if I have a soul." What does Zen say about God?

[Roshi remains silent.]

2 / COMPASSION, LIKE LOVE, ISN'T SOMETHING ONE TALKS ABOUT /

QUESTIONER: Where does compassion fit into Zen?

ROSHI: Where *doesn't* it fit into Zen?

QUESTIONER: Then why hasn't compassion been mentioned in this workshop?

ROSHI: Compassion, like love, isn't something one talks about.

QUESTIONER: Why not? I don't understand.

ROSHI: Reflect on this anecdote: Once the governor of a province in ancient China spent several days in the mountains with his Zen teacher, a famous master. As the governor was preparing to depart, the master asked him, "When you return to the capital, how will you govern the people?"

"With compassion and wisdom," replied the governor.

"In that case," commented the master, "every last one of them will suffer."

QUESTIONER: What does that mean?

ROSHI: A truly generous person doesn't boast of his generosity nor an honest man of his integrity; these qualities are so deeply entrenched as to be second nature.

One who, for example, constantly says to his partner, "I love you, believe me I do," is confessing his inability to love. Reiteration of "I love you" becomes for him a mantram, which he hopes will magically bridge his separation from the other person. True love lays no claim to loving. It loves silently, spontaneously, like a plant turning to the sun.

We Americans glorify love, even to the extent of making it the tenth word in a telegram and the last in a letter. Is it because, as a people, we shrink from the responsibilities of loving? In India the ideal of *ahimsa* (nonviolence) is stressed. Can it be that the Indians extol nonviolence because they wish to restrain the violence they sense within themselves? The Japanese exalt politeness to the level of a national ideal. Without a disciplined consideration for others, given their drive and abrasive proximity to one another, the orderly society they prize might become chaotic.

QUESTIONER: To get back to the story, I still don't see why the master said what he did to the governor.

ROSHI: To say anything more would destroy the story's value as a koan by depriving you of the chance to reflect on it and come to your own realization of its deeper meaning.

QUESTIONER: Oh, that's a koan?

ROSHI: Yes. Do you understand now why you asked your original question?

[No answer.]

3 / DOES KANNON, THE BODHI-SATTVA OF COMPASSION, REALLY EXIST? /

QUESTIONER: Last year I gave an introductory course in Buddhism and one of the texts was the Lotus sutra, in which the Buddha says that if anyone in the world who is about to be destroyed by fire or flood invokes the name of Avalokitesvara, he will be saved. Frankly, I find this impossible to accept. But if you say he exists, tell me fast where I can find him!

ROSHI: To meet him face to face, all you need do is perform a selfless deed. Avalokitesvara, or Kannon (to call him by his Japanese name), is the embodiment of your own compassionate heart. This statement, however, expresses only half the truth. The other half is that Kannon is a living reality who never fails to respond to impassioned cries for help from those who believe in him. So Kannon is not a mythological being, but is a prototype of the highest compassion realized by human beings. Of him it must be said what Voltaire said of God, that if he did not exist he would have to be invented.

QUESTIONER: Kannon lived ages ago, so when you say he is a living reality, you're just speaking symbolically, aren't you?

ROSHI: Kannon was one of the Buddha's highly evolved disciples. Since he had a strong compassionate nature and was deeply sensitive to suffering, the Buddha gave him the name which means "regarder of the cries of the world." He has dedicated himself to helping those in distress, and by reason of his transcendental wisdom and psychic powers can do so in subtle and often mysterious ways. In Buddhist iconography he is represented with innumerable embracing arms and all-seeing eyes, expressions of his limitless activity.

SECOND QUESTIONER: But every living being dies—why do you speak of Kannon as though he is still alive?

ROSHI: The law of conservation of energy says that no energy disappears; [33] why, then, do you speak of Kannon as though he were *dead?*

Before I entered a monastery a Zen friend told me, "Once you enter upon the Buddha's way with sincerity and zeal, bodhisattvas will spring up everywhere to help you." That's exactly the way it happened, and my gratitude to those bodhisattvas is too great for words. I met them in Japan, in India, in Burma, and in our own country. When they were nowhere to be seen I knew that my sincerity had waned and my zeal slackened.

Remember, the strength of Kannon's response is in direct proportion to your openness to him—that is, your humility and egolessness. If you selflessly call upon Kannon, trusting in his wisdom and compassion, a response is assured, for in essence his compassionate heart and yours are the same. In fact, the calling of his name is possible only because he is already moving toward you in a dynamic invocation-evocation process.

SECOND QUESTIONER: I noticed that in your Kannon room there are three sitting cushions arranged in front of the figure. Why would people sit there instead of in the zendo?

ROSHI: Since in the popular mind compassion and sympathy are associated more directly with Kannon than with the Buddha, those in distress feel more intimate with Kannon. In Asian Buddhist countries believers think of this bodhisattva as a woman; compassion and tenderness evidently are considered attributes more common to women than to men. As a devotional figure Kannon outshines even the Buddha.

QUESTIONER: Let's say that just before the Allied forces closed in on him, Hitler appealed to Kannon to save him from his impending doom. Would Kannon have helped him in spite of the suffering Hitler had inflicted on so many millions of people? And if Kannon did rescue him, thus enabling Hitler to escape karmic retribution, wouldn't that be a supreme travesty of justice and a mockery of the doctrine of karma?

ROSHI: Yes, it would be a mockery of the doctrine of karma. But it couldn't happen. Ask me why.

QUESTIONER: Okay, why?

ROSHI: Because the Lotus sutra promises protection only to those who call on Kannon with a *believing heart.* Could an egomaniac like Hitler do that?

The Lotus sutra says nothing about wiping clean the slate of past karma, and you can be sure that Hitler will have to pay his karmic debts like everyone else. He has already paid a portion with his violent death, and one can only shudder at the thought of the hellish existences facing him.

THIRD QUESTIONER: In what way does Kannon help those who appeal to him?

ROSHI: Kannon responds in ways that often seem strange and mysterious. Let us say that one who has just committed a burglary goes before Kannon and prays, "O Compassionate One, protect me from getting caught. If I am captured I will be imprisoned and my family will suffer." At the same time his victim may sit in front of Kannon and implore, "With your all-seeing powers, O Kannon, help the police catch that dirty thief who stole my hard-earned savings and see that he gets his just desserts." A policeman assigned to the case may appeal to Kannon by saying, "O Kannon, help me capture that burglar so that I may get the promotion I deserve."

How will Kannon respond to each of these pleas? No matter how long or how hard the burglar implores Kannon to save him from the consequences of his act, he will have to pay his karmic debt in the form of future suffering. But his sufferings will be eased and his burden lightened if he makes restitution, sincerely repents of his wrongdoing, and resolves to be law-abiding in the future. Thus the burglar may suddenly find himself determined to go straight in the future. This would be Kannon's response to the burglar's appeal. The victim, upon reflection, may suddenly realize that the burglary was karmic retribution for his own past evil deeds and that therefore he was partly responsible for what happened. This would produce in him a change of heart, softening his vindictiveness. Here would be Kannon's answer to the victim's prayer. The policeman may see that his appeal to Kannon to help him catch the burglar for his own glory is an impure one, and he may now exert himself out of a sense of duty. This, too, would be Kannon's reply.

As you see, the difference between egotistically soliciting favors from Kannon and humbly opening oneself up to the workings of his compassion is a subtle one.

THIRD QUESTIONER: Is there a point in Zen training when you can dispense with the figures of both Buddha and Kannon and just do zazen?

ROSHI: Buddha, Kannon—they can be thought of as rafts, necessary to reach another shore but not to be clung to after crossing.

FOURTH QUESTIONER: A Christian is commanded to love his neighbor as himself. Is there a Buddhist commandment to be compassionate?

ROSHI: No, there is not. True compassion is grounded in the realization that "when Martha stubs her toe in Rochester, Mike feels pain in Denver." How then can compassion be enjoined as a moral duty?

FIFTH QUESTIONER: What does that mean—"When Martha," etc.?

ROSHI: All right, let's be philosophical. The interrelatedness of all life is illustrated in one of the sutras in the image of a great web extending through all universes. Its vertical lines represent time, its horizontal lines space. Imagine that wherever the fibers of this limitless net intersect there is a crystal bead symbolizing a solitary existence. On the bright surface of each of these crystal beads is reflected every other bead in this vast network as well as every reflection and the reflections of reflections. These endless reflections are in one respect independent of each other, but at the same time they are bound together as one whole.

It is from the realization of this fundamental interdependence that true Buddhist compassion flows, like a river fed by a spring. When this awareness is absent, loneliness and fear arise. The embrace of Kannon gently washes away these obstructions, allowing the waters of wisdom and compassion to flow freely. This is the miracle of Kannon.

SIXTH QUESTIONER: I thought that Zen Buddhists didn't believe in miracles.

ROSHI: This is a miracle that does not require suspension of natural law—only the suspension of disbelief.

4 / CONFESS YOUR WRONGDOINGS AND HIDE YOUR GOOD DEEDS /

QUESTIONER: I have heard that there is confession in Zen Buddhism. What is the purpose of it?

ROSHI: To help clear away the obstructive effects of guilt and other emotions that often follow pain-producing behavior. But it is not enough merely to confess wrongdoing. To be meaningful, confession must be followed by repentance and a determination not to repeat such thoughts, speech, and actions. For these reasons confession and repentance are essential elements of Zen training.

Most people hide their bad deeds and boast of their good ones. In Buddhism the opposite is encouraged: Confess your wrongdoings and say nothing of your good actions. A practice cultivated in Zen is "secret virtue," which consists of doing things for others without taking credit for it.

SECOND QUESTIONER: Do confession and repentance get rid of your bad karma?

ROSHI: No, you still have to pay your karmic debts. By willingly paying them, however, and not incurring new ones, you ease the burden of repayment. The situation can be likened to the case of a man sentenced to prison. If instead of becoming bitter and resentful he concurs in his sentence and confinement, even feeling grateful for the chance to repay his debt to society, then his adjustment to prison life is less painful and his prospect of an early release greater.

THIRD QUESTIONER: Could you tell us more about confession and repentance? Is there some kind of formal ceremony, and if so, how often do you have it?

ROSHI: At our Center we have a ceremony each month for the staff.

FOURTH QUESTIONER: Is confession required?

ROSHI: Attendance at the ceremony is mandatory, but confession itself is not. Is there anyone, though, who has nothing to confess and repent? An individual who considered his behavior faultless would need to confess and repent of his very smugness, for of all faults surely the worst is to be aware of none.

The substance of the ceremony is as follows: After the participants have seated themselves on cushions in half circles there are two or three minutes of silence. Then the leader lights a stick of incense and places it in an incense pot, which he hands to the first person. If this person wishes to confess something he now does so, perhaps saying something such as:

"The other day when a dharma sister asked me a serious question I gave her a curt, flippant reply instead of responding fully and courteously. This has happened before with this person; I must hold some resentment toward her. I deeply repent of my behavior and resolve to work through my negative feelings so that I can respond to her helpfully in the future."

When the speaker has finished, the leader asks, "Does anyone wish to address this dharma brother (or sister)?" At this point anyone present may point out something he feels should be acknowledged, such as, "Yesterday at lunchtime you left your tools on the floor. Later a dharma brother stepped on one of them and cut himself. You have done this before, and need to make a strong effort to overcome such carelessness."

The one confessing remains silent, his only response being a slight bow. Then he passes the incense pot. If the next person does not wish to confess anything, he simply bows after taking the pot, waits to see if anyone addresses him, and then passes the pot.

FOURTH QUESTIONER: What is the purpose in having each person confess in front of everyone else? Wouldn't people be more inclined to confess serious offenses in private?

ROSHI: To confess and repent aloud in front of one's dharma brothers and sisters reinforces the strength of one's resolve not to repeat the offense. But confession can be done in privacy or with a friend or partner, and no set routine need be followed. Some of our members go through repentance alone, sitting before a buddha or Kannon either in the form of a figure or picture.

You have heard the first part of the ceremony. It concludes with the leader introducing the repentance verse. Then all in unison chant the heart of this verse three times:

> All evil actions committed by me since time immemorial,
> stemming from greed, anger, and ignorance,
> arising from body, speech, and mind,
> I now repent having committed.

FOURTH QUESTIONER: Why isn't once enough?

ROSHI: The repentance impresses itself deeper with each repetition.

What is important in confession and repentance is that it be sincere. To confess and repent what weighs heavily on one's mind is cathartic and revivifying. To regret deeply, states Thoreau, is to live afresh.

PART FOUR / MORALITY AND SOCIAL RESPONSIBILITY

LETTERS AND REPLIES / DIA-
LOGUES / A DHARMA TALK /

INTRODUCTION / "To think of good and evil is to be in heaven and hell"—this warning comes from a Zen master. But how can anyone walking the tightrope of spiritual practice afford to ignore distinctions between right and wrong? If the quality of one's conduct and of one's relationship to others is not a fundamental concern in Zen, what is the point of zazen and long training?

In the fifties and sixties, during the "intellectual" phase of Zen in the West, many came to Zen attracted by such statements as that above. Having read that Zen offered a way out of the underbrush of moral rules common to most religions, they imagined that in the name of Zen they could act as they pleased, without needing to question their responsibilities to their fellow man. This distorted notion of Zen cannot stand up to the fact of authentic Zen training, in which the emphasis is not on doing what you like nor even on liking what you do but on just doing no-mindedly what needs to be done. In Zen the essence of moral and social responsibility is *responsiveness:* wholeheartedly responding to the demands of circumstances and to the legitimate needs of others. To develop this responsiveness has always been a central aim of Zen training.

The opening letter of this section is from a college teacher of religion. His questions, which probe the relation of the precepts to Buddhist morality and to human freedom and compassion, reveal some common stumbling blocks to the understanding of Buddhist morality as well as the common reaction to Zen of persons, especially college instructors, who approach it on a philosophical level. In fact, many of the questions raised in this letter reflect the dilemma created when Zen is taught academically. The academic instructor with the best of intentions, even if armed with practical knowledge, finds himself thrown back on theory and abstract conceptualization. And if he has been brought up in the Judeo-Christian tradition, his difficulty in understanding the nondualistic ethics of Buddhism is compounded.

The second and third letters in this section are from members of the Center, people who are no longer struggling with Buddhist theory but practicing Zen itself. Their questions grow out of the strongly felt need to understand their true relationship to family and society and how it bears upon their spiritual practice. The problems expressed in these letters are typical of those faced by many men and women who in the early stages of Zen training have yet to disabuse themselves of two fundamental misconceptions: that the practice of Zen precludes societal involvement and that awakening aids only oneself and not others.

The subject of moral problems as they are seen after awakening and as they relate to the precepts is also addressed in this section in three dialogues.

Following the dialogues is a transcribed dharma talk given by me on the first of the ten precepts of Buddhism: not to kill but to cherish all life. The word "dharma" distinguishes it from a talk on social, health, public, or other general topics. Although dharma has many meanings in Buddhism, for most purposes it refers to the Buddha's teaching—the law of the universe. Unlike a commentary, which is less a talk than a demonstration of Zen offered directly to the Buddha, a dharma talk is delivered somewhat informally, with the roshi facing his listeners. Also unlike a commentary, a dharma talk may include questions, although in this particular case, since the talk itself was lengthy, no question period followed.

I / LETTERS AND REPLIES / 1 / " WHAT DOES LIVING IN THE WORLD AS A ZEN BUDDHIST MEAN?" /

DEAR ROSHI, in the course on Zen that I offer as a college teacher the question frequently arises in class discussions as to just what living in the world as a Zen Buddhist means in concrete terms. In books on Zen available in English the reader often encounters general references to the great significance of compassion, but usually little more is written about the moral ideals that guide a Zen Buddhist in his daily life outside the meditation hall. Therefore, I have been much interested to hear you speak in workshops on Zen of the importance of the ten precepts of Mahayana Buddhism; it would be very helpful to me both as a teacher and as one personally interested in Zen if you would send to me any essays or extended comments you may have prepared on the way in which you as a Zen roshi understand the nature and purpose of these ten precepts.

Perhaps I should be more specific about the kind of moral and religious issues with which I am especially concerned. If I understand you correctly, Zen teaches that all men and women should endeavor to follow the ten precepts. What reasons are given for this? Would it be correct to say that from the Zen point of view there is a moral order governing human life and the precepts are a formulation of this moral order? What is the relation of the ten precepts to human nature? Do they constitute a law that has been arbitrarily imposed on human nature by an external, omnipotent, divine will, or is there an intimate and natural interrelationship between the precepts and human nature? For example, what continuity is there between the specific prohibitions and demands of the precepts and the deeper human desires for self-knowlege, self-determination, and self-realization?

What is the nature of the obligation a Zen Buddhist feels in relation to the precepts? Are the precepts moral absolutes for the Zen Buddhist as the Ten Commandments are for those Jews and Christians who believe that mankind has an unconditional obligation to obey the Ten Commandments and that they must strictly observe the letter of the law at all times regardless of the endless variety of circumstances surrounding different situations? How does Zen understand the consequences of not observing the precepts? How does Zen deal with the problem of guilt feelings that may arise from failure to fulfill the law of the precepts?

Is outward conformity to the law in itself that important to Zen, or is the critical issue an inner conformity, purity of heart? Is this possible short of deep enlightenment? If it is not possible, does the hard task of striving to fulfill the ten precepts inwardly and outwardly help a person toward enlightenment?

If there is real human wisdom in the precepts, do all men and women have at least the potential to apprehend this wisdom for themselves through their own experience, reason, and insight? Or must they be content to accept the precepts as wisdom on blind faith, trusting in the authority of the founders of the Buddhist tradition?

This letter has raised many questions but they are closely interrelated and I hope they provide you with an idea of the kind of clarification being sought. Also, in addition to the general issues raised above, I am, of course, interested in your interpretations of the specific meaning of the individual precepts.

Thank you very much.

Sincerely,

Bob

A Reply /

DEAR BOB, although the questions raised in your letter are really best answered through your doing zazen, obviously your intellect is not yet satisfied that what you are about to do has value and relevance. For this reason, and because you teach Zen academically and what you do or say to your students is bound to influence them to some degree, I am going to depart from my usual practice and reply in some detail to your questions, which, though theoretical, in reality mask deep spiritual concerns.

You ask about the nature and purpose of the ten precepts of Mahayana Buddhism. They comprise one of the three legs on which Buddhist teaching and practice stand; the other two are zazen and enlightenment-wisdom. These three are intimately related. The strongest effort to keep the precepts can be only partially successful if it is divorced from zazen; and a zazen apart from the precepts is weak and uncertain. It is through zazen, buttressed by the precepts, that awareness of our True-nature is raised to consciousness (awakening), and in this True-nature the precepts, zazen, and enlightened wisdom are grounded.

While it is common enough upon first seeing the ten cardinal precepts of Buddhism to think of the Ten Commandments in Christianity, to compare them is to distort both the precepts and the Ten Commandments, for each can only be comprehended in its own religious context. Understand that the precepts are not a moral manifesto handed down from "above." Neither are they contrary to nor do they make constraints upon your fundamental nature. Rather, they are an expression of the self-actualized, awakened Buddha-mind, a description of the way in which a highly evolved being, with no sense of self-and-other, acts.

To take an analogy: To live by the precepts is to travel the Way of unity and harmony in which the road is smooth, the obstructions few, and the scenery strikingly beautiful. To transgress the precepts is to take a side road that appears interesting but which soon turns bumpy, becomes monotonous, and ends in the dead end of regret and apprehension.

Zen master Dogen said, "To gain a certain objective you must first become a certain kind of man; but once you have become such a man, attaining that objective will no longer be a concern to you." Interpreted in the light of your letter, Bob, this means that in order to see into the unreality of the ego-I and grasp the identity of self and other, you cannot continue to think and act in response to the demands of your dualistically-oriented ego; you must heed the deeper call of the precepts. And yet once the precepts have become the established norm of your daily life, enlightenment will no longer stand apart from you as something to be sought. In such a liberated state one does not think in terms of moral laws or social conventions, of being either bound by or liberated from them. You move through social conventions and mores as though not moving through them—they are there yet not there. In the beginning one seeks freedom from feelings of oppression. Gradually, through zazen and observance of the precepts, the oppression which bound you within is dissolved. The price of this freedom, however, is long training and self-discipline.

Thomas Merton, recognizing this, said, "The Zen man's contempt for conventional and formalistic social custom is a healthy phenomenon, but it is healthy only because it presupposes a spiritual liberty based on freedom from passion, egotism and self-delusion." In this statement the word "contempt" is a poor choice, for the spiritually developed Zen man or woman is neither slavishly attached to nor disdainful of law and convention. Nonetheless it is true that Zen masters are known more for reforming than for conforming. Zen master Hakuin with his active pen flayed the powerful ruling classes of Japan for their oppression and exploitation of the farmers and serfs, with whom he frequently associated. The Buddha himself attacked the orthodox religions of his day for their superstition and authoritarianism even as he welcomed into his sangha of monks and nuns the Untouchables, the outcasts of Hindu society. That social justice and equality were able to advance through the efforts of the Buddha, Hakuin, and other masters is due to the transforming power of their spiritual freedom.

You ask, "How does Zen understand the consequences of not observing the precepts? How does Zen deal with the problem of guilt feelings which may arise from failure to fulfill the law of the precepts?" Feelings of guilt do not normally arise when one fails to keep the precepts because it is recognized that the ordinary person is unable to observe every one of the precepts at all times—only a buddha can do so. When one makes a sincere effort to live by these guidelines, repenting of failures and resolving to do better in the future, such lapses, while regrettable, are not fatal. What is fatal to one's spiritual progress is loss of faith in the Buddha's assurance, emerging from his supreme awakening, that each of us is inherently pure and whole and is able, through spiritual discipline and training, to realize this innate perfection.

The fundamental purpose of the precepts, then, is to enable one to steadfastly carry on Zen training with the aim of realizing one's intrinsic buddhahood. Without the equilibrium which their observance provides, few could walk the Way with energy and conviction. Actions abjured by the precepts should be renounced, not simply for moral or ethical reasons, but because one cannot put himself deeply into zazen while leading a wanton, thoughtless life, just as one cannot be asleep and awake at the same time.

Doesn't all behavior condemned by mankind as evil arise from a strong sense of self-and-other, from a vehement assertion of the ego-I? To the extent that one is able to banish this dualistic mirage and the self-centeredness it inevitably fosters, and to bring one's inner vision into single focus so that there is neither self nor other, feelings of opposition and antagonism, of resentment and anger, gradually evaporate.

"Right" action in a given situation, then, whether the issue is abortion, euthanasia, or any other complex moral dilemma, can emerge only when self-transcendence has taken place. More than this, for one who has awakened to the indivisibility of all existences and thoroughly integrated this awareness into his daily life, the concept "right action" disappears. A Zen master of old put it this way:

> Die while alive
> and be completely dead.
> Then do whatever you will,
> all is good.

The precepts in their relative-absolute subtlety and depth can be understood on many levels. When you undertake Zen training, and a natural restraint and purity emerge as you gain greater control over your mind and emotions, your understanding of the precepts will deepen. Thus it will be unnecessary to strain to follow them, for gradually your conduct will fall into accord with them. The precepts transcend morality, yet they do not exclude it.

It is the transforming power of zazen, and not the precepts imposed from the outside, that brings about purity of heart. Outward conformity to the letter of the precepts is far less significant than is the compassion growing out of zazen; and yet in the beginning an effort to follow the precepts is essential, for zazen can falter in the face of long-standing habits and daily temptations.

Having answered your letter, I urge you now to begin zazen, for it is clear to me that behind all your questions about the precepts is an emerging need for Self-realization. Once you awaken, all my words will seem like so much dross.

Yours,

Philip Kapleau

2 / " MEDITATION IS AN ESCAPE— WHAT ARE YOU DOING TO HELP SOCIETY?" /

DEAR ROSHI, it has been some time since I last saw you, and since it is very difficult for me to get to Rochester to speak with you due to my job, it seemed best to write you. In case you don't remember me perhaps I should mention first that I've been a member of the Center for about a year and have been sitting regularly with the Denver affiliate group.

Recently a very painful situation that has been going on for some time has come to a head. It concerns my parents and I simply don't know how to deal with it. I am quite close to both my father and mother, who are educated and intelligent people. We have always communicated freely and I have great respect for them, so you can understand how disturbed I was to finally realize that not only do they not approve of my doing zazen, they also are openly opposed to it. Roshi, I really don't know what to do. You may think me immature or even' foolish for being so concerned about what my parents think. After all, I am old enough to make my own decisions and follow through with them. But I suppose what is really happening is that my parents' hostility to this "Eastern religion," as they call it, has affected my own faith in the Buddha's dharma.

I have tried many times to explain to my parents why I am doing zazen—that my enlightenment, when it comes, will help not only myself but others too—but they cannot even begin to understand or accept this.

My parents say, "You're not doing anything to help society. You are using meditation as an escape and nothing more. If you really want to change yourself, you'd be better off seeing a psychiatrist." These accusations hurt and confuse me. True, I'm not the best judge, but I do feel that there have been certain changes in me for the better: I feel a greater clarity and calmness than I used to and am much more tolerant of others. Roshi, I respect and love my parents, as I said, and of course they know me well. Could they be saying such things if there were absolutely no validity to them?

When I started doing zazen, I really felt that sitting, and of course awakening, was the best if not the only way to help people. But now I must admit that sometimes I do feel guilty that I'm no longer involved in political reform and other causes that used to interest me. Is it really true what Dogen said, that when even one person sits in zazen he becomes one with all things throughout the universe and guides all beings to enlightenment? How I wish I had the faith to deeply believe that!

Rereading this letter just now, it is clear how weak my faith must be in zazen practice to even ask these questions. I am sorry, Roshi, for bothering you with all this. But if there is anything at all that you could say to help me clear this confusion, I would be extremely grateful.

With deep gassho,

Lynn

A Reply /

DEAR LYNN, your state of siege in defense of Zen that you describe in your letter reminds me of one of the legends about Bodhidharma, the first patriarch of Zen. He is doing zazen in a cave when three small boys stumble upon the entrance and peer inside. There they see a dark, menacing shape and run off alarmed. Curiosity draws them back, however, and from a safe distance they survey the immobile form, speculating as to its nature. "It looks like a human being," whispers the first boy. "But it can't be," replies the second. "No man can sit that long without moving. It must be a bear." "No," the third boy chimes in, "it doesn't have fur." Again they study the strange form. Emboldened by the "thing's" immobility, the three begin tossing small stones at it, but still it makes no sound or movement. Drawing closer, one boy, braver than the rest, runs up, quickly touches the form, and dashes back. Still no reaction. Vexed, the boys retreat to pool their conclusions. "It's definitely not a rock," says the boy who touched the shape. "It was soft, without fur, so it must be a man sitting up." "But why would any man sleep that way? It's not natural," the other boys insist. "Why didn't it move when it was touched?" The more they ponder the mystery the greater grow the boys' perplexity and annoyance. Suddenly one of them picks up a large rock and in a gesture of defiance hurls it at the inert form, striking it squarely on the head. Now at last the form begins to move—slowly—first the head, then the arms, legs, and body. Then it roars. The boys flee in terror, and Bodhidharma continues to roar—with laughter—then to shake with tears. The rock had precipitated his awakening, his great enlightenment.

Human nature has changed little since Bodhidharma's day. A person meditating quietly in his or her room or at a Zen center still encounters suspicion and even resentment. Your situation is typical in that the worst of this usually comes from close friends and family, the same people who sometimes advise psychotherapy. It is a curious phenomenon that an individual who regularly sees a psychiatrist is seldom criticized for trying to improve himself rather than society. On the contrary, his family and friends generally applaud him for his willingness to try to work through his confusions and anxieties. And if his recovery proceeds slowly, as it must if it is to be real and enduring, neither he nor the treatment is condemned out of hand.

But he who sets off on the path of zazen seldom receives either encouragement or understanding. If he is not ridiculed by his family and friends for this "aberration," he is expected to become perfect overnight—another buddha. Should his behavior seem unchanged—and how many skeptical critics are open enough to perceive the subtle changes in him at first?— they pounce upon him with the same irritation you have been facing at home. When you tell your parents that you are doing zazen with the hope of becoming enlightened one day, naturally enough they see Zen practice as an all-or-nothing proposition based on enlightenment; until awakening, they would suppose, you are just waiting, getting nowhere. They don't realize that in Zen the point is not to "go" but to *be*—more aware, loving, and self-reliant. How can they know that as your conceits, resentments, and stubbornness fall away through regular zazen, your innately pure, unstained nature will reveal itself?

What you say about feeling greater clarity and calm, and more accepting toward other people, is something every person doing serious zazen soon experiences. Do not be discouraged if your family and friends seem unaware of these changes in you. Remember, your parents' minds are clouded, too, and having grown so close to you over the years they have many fixed images of their daughter that will take time to overcome. Just as it is hard to see your own nose, it is difficult for a family busy solving its own problems and hangups to notice at first the metamorphosis of one of its members. But the strong intuitions of a mother eventually prevail. It may take longer for your father to pick up on them, but the subtle benefits of your zazen will begin to show through to both your parents. They will notice less irritability and defensiveness in you, as well as less remoteness, and they are bound to be positively affected by your thoughtful gestures and compassionate concern for their welfare. This is really your way of requiting their years of sacrificing for you. And if you continue sitting, in time you will contribute toward a loving, harmonious family. This would be no insignificant contribution to society, for after all, the home is the basis of society— its discord or goodwill inevitably are reflected in society.

Leaving aside the question of whether your parents are themselves doing anything to help society, is there any validity to their criticisms? Are you, in spending several hours a day sitting in zazen, evading your responsibility to society?

Before this question can be answered fairly it must be asked, "What does it really mean to 'help society'?" Do your parents know exactly what they mean by it? May it not be just some catch phrase, as nebulous as it is provoking, that they throw at you out of frustration? After all, you work at a full-time job, as do the doctors, housewives, carpenters, secretaries, musicians, and others who are also members of the Zen Center. What more would your parents have you do? Why does it bother them that you are using your leisure time to discipline yourself through zazen? Quite likely they sense the exertion and sacrifice demanded in your training, and, respecting you for this, feel guilty that they can't do the same, and then hate themselves for feeling guilty . . . and finally resent your zazen as the genesis of these unlovely feelings. This may account for the attitude of a parent who not long ago approached me upset about his daughter. "First it was drugs," he said, "then TM, and now Zen. What will it be next?" Often, too, those who wag their fingers at others for "doing nothing for society" do so out of feelings of guilt for their own selfish involvements, or out of uncertainties about their own values. Or it may reflect a frustration that certain hopes and ideals they long ago fastened onto have still gone unrealized.

So again: What does it mean to "help society"? Political activists thought they knew what it meant when in the sixties they grappled with the law and other external forms of society, yet today many of them declare that without working on oneself no meaningful changes can occur. "Do-gooders" no doubt feel that they are helping society as they officiously push themselves into others' affairs, force-feeding them with their own formula for happiness. Clearly, then, the phrase "helping society" is a haze, nothing more than a vacant slogan, at least when construed in terms of any particular activity or line of work.

If there is to be true helping of any kind, it must work from the "inside," improving the inner fiber of a person and every aspect of how he relates to life. In this sense you will unquestionably be helping others if you do zazen seriously. To the degree that you cleanse your mind of greed, anger, and self-seeking and develop a quiet, compassionate heart, you will become a better daughter, sister, neighbor, and employee. Continue sitting dedicatedly and you will gradually dissolve egotistical thoughts, stubborn prejudices, and false notions about yourself and the world. How could these benefits not be felt by those around you and by society as a whole?

Far from escape from life, the aim before you and anyone seriously practicing Zen is to more fully become one with it. A great Chinese master told his disciples: "Do not permit the events of your daily life to bind you, *but never withdraw yourself from them.*" Another Zen master warned: "The man who clings to vacancy, neglecting the world of things, escapes from drowning but leaps into the fire." Understand, then, that zazen is not an escape from the problems of the world but a liberation that gives us wisdom and strength to pursue whatever we are called upon to do. In Zen we are not coveting the peace of the grave but working to develop an inner stillness and clarity of mind through active involvement in the affairs of life. Genuine peace of mind is won not by avoiding conflicts but by confronting and working through them with the sword of struggle.

Very likely what's troubling your parents is the notion, deeply embedded in our Western way of thinking, that to be productive an individual must be "active." In *The Art of Loving* Eric Fromm examines the word "active" as it is commonly used in our society. He emphasizes that *what* a person does is less important than the motivation behind his activity. Someone driven to incessant work by insecurity, loneliness, or greed, for instance, is a slave to such passions, a passive object being acted *upon.* On the other hand, the person sitting in concentrated meditation is engaged in "the highest activity there is, an activity of the soul, which is possible only under the condition of inner freedom and independence. . . ."

Seen this way, even your parents may agree that if we are to preserve our mental equilibrium in the face of the mounting tensions and conflicts of modern life, we have no alternative but to give ourselves to this "highest activity of the soul." And not for our own sake alone. Buddhism teaches that the mind of one man is the mind of all men. Society is after all our own creation and nothing but the manifestation of the collective mind of all the individuals who make it up. Since the "outer" faults of society are really within our own minds, it follows, as you rightly sense, that we each must shoulder the responsibility for the conditions of man. How then can anyone who feels responsible to his fellow man neglect to undertake his own purification? How can he afford to overlook those defilements of body, speech, and mind that issue from himself?

So it is that the effect of one person's enlightenment on the collective world psyche is immeasurable. On the level of the unseen it unleashes a veritable stream of light and clarity into the darkness of others' minds. On the level of the seen, the power of a disciplined, purified, and awakened mind to affect and transform others is immense. And just as lighting even a few candles in a huge, pitch-black cave lessens the darkness to some degree, hundreds of thousands of persons meditating ego-lessly would obviously create a tremendous force for peace and harmony in the world.

For your own sake and others, Lynn, I hope you will persevere in your practice and experience yourself the miracle of Zen.

Yours,

P.K.

3 / "DO I HAVE TO ABANDON MY FAMILY TO GET FULLY INTO ZEN?" /

DEAR ROSHI KAPLEAU, since meeting you some months ago in Costa Rica I have been reflecting on some of the things that we talked about, and now that I have decided to attend a training program at the Zen Center, I would like to try to communicate to you some of my feelings related to this decision.

First, I have been reading about Zen, as well as other types of self-realization philosophies and disciplines, on and off for many years. Initially, I considered this interest nothing more than that, something that caught my fancy and fascinated me with descriptions of far-off places, exotic disciplines, the curious attitudes and behavior of assorted wise men, gurus, swamis, and masters, illogical, indecipherable references to Truth, Reality, Mind, the Infinite, and the Ultimate. But even if I did not comprehend it all, something had caught my attention and I kept going back for more.

Then, as time went on and I became more of an adept (at least at reading), the subject became more compelling and, as I found myself being attracted more strongly as well as developing a "feel" for what was being said, it all began to have more significance. I came to realize that all this "exotic philosophy" had a very direct relation to me, to my life, and I saw myself begin to change and move in a definite direction. Slowly but surely I arrived at many (for me) deep and significant realizations that altered the course my life had been taking up to that time. This process has continued up to the present where I now find myself in a situation that requires a resolution that will enable me to live the rest of my life serenely, convinced beyond any doubt that I have found what I was looking for.

What has happened over these years is that I have become much more aware, which has helped me to live and work more tranquilly and positively. However, this same process of awareness has also contributed to a deep sense of confusion, frustration, and anxiety, because I now have the unshakeable feeling that I have caught a glimpse of some Reality or Truth, something that is of a completely different order from what is readily apparent. And now I want to know what this other reality is. I want to get the full view instead of just a glimpse, and to achieve a breakthrough that will dissolve or eliminate once and for all whatever it is that I feel is separating me from this other dimension or reality of existence. During the past year or so I have made several unsuccessful attempts to accomplish this alone, with the result that I am even more intrigued, while my frustration and restlessness have increased. It would seem that to become enlightened without the help of an enlightened teacher is a very difficult if not impossible accomplishment.

And now that I have decided to take this next step, to attend a training program and put myself in direct contact with you, who might be able to eventually help me achieve enlightenment, I am experiencing new doubts and anxieties. On the one hand, I am sure that if I do not do this I shall continue to live in conflict. But, on the other hand, I have the feeling that I am setting out on a kind of final stage of a journey in search of the ultimate meaning of my life, and that there will be no turning back. And this idea of "no turning back" makes me wonder where exactly I am going, what will happen to me, and what the outcome of this step might be. Also, while I do not want to continue to live with this conflict and anxiety, nor die in such a state of confusion, I can see that a deeply rooted reluctance to give up what I am and what I have is also working in me.

To live this way is very difficult, because I constantly have the sensation that I am functioning very superficially, or in a very limited way, on the "outside" of some Reality in which all relationships and the solutions to all problems would be unequivocally clear to me, and yet it keeps eluding me. I also sense a potential energy locked up inside me, but I am unable to release it and realize what I feel to be something like my "true nature."

And, of course, another source of doubt and anxiety is my family. What about my wife, my children, their education, our work together, etc.? What will happen to all these very real and binding relationships and responsibilities if I set out on a path upon which it would seem there is no turning back? Such questions and doubts might appear to be unrelated and beside the point, or not really any cause for worry from your enlightened point of view, but for me they are precisely the type of obstacle that has caused me to hesitate and has kept me in a state of limbo. Or to phrase the question in a more general way, can I get fully into Zen without abandoning these relationships? Although my wife, who is an exceptionally mature and comprehending person, does not openly admit to being anxious about this point, I am aware that she is—a natural enough reaction—and I do not want to hurt her in any way. Nor can I conceive, at this point, of abandoning my children. The problem appears to be one of wanting to eat my cake and have it too, but I doubt if it is as simple as that.

These are not questions that I expect to be answered directly, but are more like considerations. I suppose it is highly probable that most of these doubts and anxieties will be resolved quite naturally as I go along, and so I have decided to just go ahead with the next step, which is to go to Rochester and begin training and let the process begin to work and the chips fall where they may.

This has been a rather difficult letter to write, especially where I have tried to express intuitions, feelings, processes, etc., that really cannot be described or captured in words. Nevertheless I am certain you will grasp the essence of what I am trying to say.

I hope all is well with you, and I am looking forward to seeing you again.

Sincerely,

David

A Reply /

DEAR DAVID, you are quite right—once your True-nature has begun to stir with the urging to come up to consciousness, there is no turning back. No doubt you are aware that Freud and other psychologists speak of the great harm done to the psyche when sexual desire cannot find an outlet. But far worse is the frustration of the primordial need to know who and what we are and the meaning of our life and death. These questions are barriers you yourself must penetrate; on the other side of them is the Reality that you sense. But it is not separate, this Reality—how can there be more than one Reality? When the silt of your delusory thoughts settles, you will gaze into fresh, clear water that is really the same water purged of dirt and impurities.

You are now hovering around the age of forty, are you not, David? This puts you at a crossroads where you must ask yourself, "Will I continue to follow the path of least resistance, which is comfortable in one way and painfully unsatisfactory in another, or will I enter upon a new life course leading to true freedom?" It may be your last chance to fulfill your hopes and master your fears, for you might find added to the usual middle-age anxieties a self-loathing for not having undertaken what pressed upon your heart so strongly. Sadly enough this is the plight of many thousands who, once filled with vitality and hope, find in later years their energies siphoned off in a spate of activities or drained by corroding fears of life and death in the face of which they feel impotent. Jung wrote that he never had a patient over forty for whom the underlying problem was not the fear of death. It is satori—awakening to your essential nature—that will dissolve this fear and allow you to live with zest and die with dignity.

Consider a prisoner serving a life term who comes up for parole. If he has been behind bars for many years and has made a comfortable niche for himself in the prison community, he may well have grown afraid of facing the responsibilities of life on the outside. If in such a man the vital life force has been stifled, he will decline the parole or do little to obtain it. If, however, he has served only a few years and his natural instinct to be free is healthily operating, he will do everything in his power to be released.

Similarly, your readiness to enter an upcoming training program shows that your spiritual vitality is strong. Were you to put off your decision, your active quest for Self-realization could get postponed until finally the urge for freedom became muted in you. Muted, but never eradicated. For though you might temporarily paper over your frustration and restlessness with diversions of every kind, there would be no real peace. Even your moments of greatest pleasure would be soured by a hollow ache of longing for Self-realization.

So I congratulate you on your momentous decision and look forward to having you with us in Rochester.

Your concern for your wife and children, their education, and your work together is commendable and shows how solid and viable your relationship with them is. In situations such as yours it is usually the wife whose fears are strongest. If she is not doing zazen herself—and I understand your wife is not—the feeling will arise in her that if you continue to develop yourself in Zen, eventually you will become a monk and leave her and the children. As you must know, this fear of being abandoned by a loved husband is strong in most women. The only way you can truly reassure her, and the children, too, since they inevitably pick up on the mother's anxieties, is to become more loving toward them. Not determinedly so, for this would be contrived and only betray your own worries. Rather, just put yourself wholeheartedly into Zen training—which means, remember, putting yourself fully into every aspect of your daily life—and you will naturally become more loving. That is to say, your intrinsic lovingness will be freed to emerge and express itself more and more. When you are with your wife and children, be fully there with them; likewise when at work do not leave part of yourself at home; when shaving just shave, when reading just read, and so forth; this is the true practice of Zen in your daily life. Continue this and before long you will find yourself becoming more understanding and patient with your children, knowing intuitively when to be firm and when to yield. You will become more sensitive and responsive to your wife's needs, too, and to those of everyone around you.

Finally, I would caution you not to think in terms of "hurting" and "not hurting" your family. Fretting about this will only make your behavior toward them forced and artificial. Instead, have faith that anything that helps you cannot but also, in the profoundest spiritual sense, help them. In the beginning this may not seem so, but as your practice deepens, the truth of this will be driven home to both you and your wife. Until then do all you can to reassure her—not through words but by your actions.

Thank you for writing, and if you have no objection I should like to read your letter in my next formal talk; many are bound to find it instructive and inspiring.

A warm welcome and hard work await you.

Yours,

Philip Kapleau

II / DIALOGUES / 1 / DOES AWAKENING PROVIDE THE SOLUTION TO MORAL DILEMMAS? /

QUESTIONER: Does enlightenment solve all of one's life problems?

ROSHI: What once were problems will no longer be problems.

SECOND QUESTIONER: What about moral dilemmas? It is clear enough that one should not kill or steal or lie. But sometimes no matter how much you think about what you ought to do in a certain situation, there seems to be no "right" answer. Does satori allow one to see through these moral problems so that the right action is apparent?

ROSHI: Moral dilemmas still have to be faced even by the deeply enlightened. Years ago my teacher told a story in a lecture of a moral challenge confronting a Zen master that provoked in the sesshin participants one of the most emotional reactions I've ever witnessed. This is what he said, as I remember it:

A certain Zen master in ancient times had a deep yearning to become a monk from the time he was a boy. But as his father had died he had to support his widowed mother by selling firewood. Unable to put aside for long his deep-seated wish to follow a religious life, when he had managed to save a little money he left it all for his mother with a note saying, "Forgive me for leaving, but I must find a spiritual master." The mother heard nothing more of her son.

Many years elapsed and the mother was now old and blind in one eye. She desperately wanted to see her only child before she died. One day she chanced to meet an itinerant monk who had been in a monastery in a remote part of the country, and he told her he had every reason to believe that the head of that monastery was her son.

Buoyed by the news that she might yet be able to see her son, she set out to find the monastery. After years of travel and many hardships, she found what she believed was the monastery described by the itinerant monk. By now very weak, she tremblingly approached the gate, where she was met by a monk who politely questioned her as to her mission. She told him the story of her son and how she had reason to believe that the abbot of this monastery was he. Could she please see him just briefly? She did not have long to live and would die in peace if only she could see her son once more.

The monk asked her to wait and went to speak with the abbot. After an interval he returned and said, "I am terribly sorry. I related to the abbot everything you told me and he said, 'She must be mistaken; I am not her son.' "

With these words the whole zendo erupted into tears. Men and women alike, including the roshi, wept openly.

Although I had followed the story in Japanese, it was unclear what had triggered the emotional outburst. On the way home (the sesshin had been held in the northern part of Japan) I was able to sit next to the roshi on the train and had a chance to review with him the particulars of the story and to question him about the weeping.

"Why did everyone suddenly burst out crying at the point where the abbot said he was not her son? He was her son, wasn't he?"

"Yes, he was her son, all right," replied the roshi. "Remember, he had not seen her since leaving home many years earlier. He knew that she would be old and frail and that upon seeing her he would be overcome by the desire to embrace and take care of her. But he was responsible for the spiritual training of some five hundred monks. If his mother were to live in or near the monastery, he would want to be with her and thus he would have less time to devote to his monks' training. We can only imagine the agonizing struggle that went into the reply he finally gave the monk to deliver. And because the anguish of the abbot in yielding to his duty instead of his heart was acutely felt by everyone in the zendo, they all wept."

THIRD QUESTIONER: Couldn't the abbot at least have sent word to his mother that he was her son and was well, but that it was impossible for him to see her?

ROSHI: If he had done that, wouldn't her anguish have been worse?

FOURTH QUESTIONER: Why was his duty to the monks greater than his duty to his aged mother? I have always heard that Asians, especially the Japanese, are devoted to their parents and take good care of them. Isn't this attitude very much part of their culture?

ROSHI: What the abbot did in this case reflected his particular sense of duty. One roshi I trained under in Japan had his aged mother living with him on the monastery grounds and visited her frequently. Perhaps because there were twenty monks in his monastery instead of five hundred, he felt that his relationship with his mother did not interfere with his responsibilities to his monks.

SECOND QUESTIONER: What about the mother? What was her reaction to the abbot's refusal to see her?

ROSHI: It doesn't take much imagination to guess, does it? But there is a sequel to this story.

After she had passed away, the abbot had a vision in which he saw his mother in the Pure Land. She was radiant, and with hands palm to palm told him that she forgave him, for she now understood why he would not see her. The abbot, realizing that his mother had had an awakening, wept for joy.

2 / ZEN IS ABOVE MORALITY BUT MORALITY IS NOT BELOW ZEN /

QUESTIONER: In the newsletter of a certain Center I read a dialogue that raised many disturbing questions in my mind. I'd be grateful if you would give me your reaction to it. I brought the newsletter with me. May I give you the gist of it, as it's rather long?

ROSHI: Yes.

QUESTIONER: Once when the master of a poor Zen temple in the country was away, his head monk talked the other monks into selling the monastery cow to buy wine, meat, and good food, after which they stayed up all night carousing. When the master returned the next day for the morning sitting he found the students all asleep amid the debris of the party, and the cow gone. Angry, he called everyone together in the main hall and demanded that the cow be returned. At this the head monk took off his clothes and crawled around the room on all fours, bellowing "Moo!" Delighted, the master hit him thirty times on the ass and said, "This is not my cow. This one is too small!" All were relieved and the subject was not brought up again.

I have several questions, but first of all, what is your reaction to this story?

ROSHI: What the master did was all right. Had I been there, though, I'd have grabbed his stick and cracked *him* over the ass.

QUESTIONER: Why?

ROSHI: For keeping a cow.

QUESTIONER: That was my next question. Do Zen monasteries usually keep cows or other animals?

ROSHI: No, they don't. Animals have to be fed and cared for, often at odd hours, and this could interfere with the monks' schedule for zazen and study. But more important, Zen monasteries don't keep cows or drink their milk for the same reason the Buddha himself didn't drink milk—it deprives the calves of it.

SECOND QUESTIONER: What about the monks' behavior?

ROSHI: Highly evolved Zen people have done some pretty astounding things—astounding, that is, to the unawakened—but only undeveloped, obviously deluded monks would steal the master's cow, sell it, buy liquor and meat, and go on a binge. Monks who behave in this fashion are called *namagusu bozu*— unholy men who smell of rotten fish.

SECOND QUESTIONER: Don't the Buddhist precepts prohibit drinking alcohol and eating meat? Are Zen monks exempt from the precepts?

ROSHI: Zen monks are also Buddhists.

SECOND QUESTIONER: Let me play devil's advocate. Zen is supposed to teach freedom. But how can you be free if you're hemmed in by a fence of precepts? And why shouldn't Zen people eat meat or drink liquor or take drugs if they want to? What's wrong with that if you do it in moderation?

ROSHI: In itself, nothing.

SECOND QUESTIONER: Are you implying that enlightened Zen people ignore the precepts when it suits them to do so?

ROSHI: Those advanced in their practice are not attached to the precepts, nor do they break them to prove how liberated they are. The precepts are like a scaffolding: necessary to erect a large structure, but who would insist on the scaffolding remaining when the building is completed? Remember, the precepts are not moral commandments handed down by an omniscient or divine being. Rather they reveal how a deeply enlightened, fully perfected person, with no sense of self-and-other, behaves. Such an individual doesn't imitate the precepts; they imitate him. Until you reach that point, however, you would do well to observe the precepts, for unless your mind is free of the disturbance that heedless behavior produces, you will never come to awakening. That is why the precepts are the foundation of spiritual training.

Let's return to the story you mentioned a moment ago. You said that when the master returned for the morning sitting he found all the monks asleep. Observe that they did not meditate that morning—no doubt because they were too hung over—nor probably that night either. Coming to enlightenment requires a clear head, concentrated energy, and a strong will, and these evolve from the discipline of zazen; they can only be weakened by drinking and eating in excess.

This story also illustrates how the breaking of one precept leads to the breaking of others. Had these monks not violated the second precept—not to take what is not given—they would not have broken the fifth precept, not to take drugs or liquor that confuse the mind.

Meat-eating, incidentally, is not specifically prohibited by the precepts. Nonetheless, the Lankavatara and Surangama sutras—both Mahayana scriptures—are quite eloquent in their condemnation of meat-eating.

SECOND QUESTIONER: What reasons do they give?

ROSHI: That there is not one being which, in its karmic evolution and devolution through countless rebirths, has not been our mother, our father, husband or wife, sister, brother, son, or daughter—not one being whose kinship with us, even while living in the animal state, has not continued. How then can any spiritual person who approaches all living things as if they were himself eat the flesh of something that is of the same nature as himself? Seen this way, isn't all flesh-eating a form of cannibalism? How can anyone who seeks liberation from suffering inflict pain directly or indirectly on another creature? Those who eat the flesh of an animal obviously enjoy it, so in effect they are deriving pleasure from the death of another living being.

When you stop to think of it, aren't the killing and the eating of cows acts of base ingratitude? The cow is foster mother to the human race. Her milk and its by-products nourish man and his children at the expense of her own offspring. But when she is too old and depleted to supply him with them, how does man show his gratitude for her years of service to him? By letting her live out her declining years in ease and contentment? No! He destroys her, often brutally, consumes her flesh, and then fashions footgear from her hide, in effect adding insult to injury by trampling her underfoot. And yet moralists say that man with his elevated nature is the only animal that can know gratitude.

SECOND QUESTIONER: If you don't kill the animal yourself and it is not slaughtered for *your* benefit, why is it so bad?

ROSHI: The slaughterhouse may be concealed by a graceful distance of miles, as Emerson says, but still there is complicity. But regardless of whether an animal has been destroyed specifically to provide food for you, if you put its flesh into your belly you are an accessory after the fact to its gratuitous slaughter. Why gratuitous? Because it is certainly easy enough to live and function quite well without animal protein.

You have asked me several questions. Now let me ask you a few. Why are you so concerned with the precepts?

SECOND QUESTIONER: I don't know.

ROSHI: Are you looking for a connection between morality and Zen enlightenment?

SECOND QUESTIONER: Well, that does bother me.

ROSHI: In what way?

SECOND QUESTIONER: I suppose it's my Christian upbringing. I've read that Zen is beyond morality, but without ethical behavior, without a sense of right and wrong, wouldn't the world be in an even worse mess than it is now?

ROSHI: Zen transcends morality but does not exclude it. Or to put it more Zen-like, "Zen is above morality but morality is not below Zen." The moral man knows right from wrong, or thinks he does, but he does not know *who* it is who thinks right and wrong. Such deep understanding requires Zen training and awakening.

The Japanese word for Bodhidharma and for an unlicensed, free-lance prostitute is the same—*daruma*. Here they are portrayed in a reversal of their usual attitudes: the prostitute in a reflective, self-assured pose soothing Bodhidharma, who appears nonplussed. The artist seems to be saying, "In their fundamental nature is there a difference between these two darumas?"

"Bodhidharma and a Prostitute," by an unknown seventeenth-century Japanese artist.

3 / BROTHELS AND BUDDHISM /

QUESTIONER: I just finished a class in Buddhism in which we read several sutras. One of them tells how the Buddha's chief disciple, Ananda, who was supposed to be a celibate monk, went to a brothel and was about to be seduced when the Buddha, learning about this through his psychic powers, rescued him. Another sutra—I think it's called the Vimilakirti—says that Vimilakirti, a famous Buddhist, often frequented brothels. And in still another sutra—I can't remember the name—there's the story of an enlightened woman who became a prostitute. There seems to be a strong relationship between brothels and Buddhism.

ROSHI: Vimilakirti was a layman whose spiritual stature was said to be second only to that of the Buddha. For one so deeply enlightened, teaching is as natural as breathing. Does this give you a clue as to why he visited brothels?

QUESTIONER: Obviously you're implying he went to brothels to preach Buddhism. But why to brothels?

ROSHI: Why not to brothels? Sages and harlots alike have the power to awaken to True-mind. The enlightened woman you mentioned—bodhisattva is a better name for her—became a prostitute in order to emancipate men from their base passions. And to try to enlighten the dark and ignorant minds of prostitutes and the men who patronized them, Vimilakirti frequented brothels. Yes, there was and continues to be a strong relationship between brothels and Buddhism.

QUESTIONER: You haven't mentioned Ananda. What about him?

ROSHI: Ananda no doubt was a novice monk at the time of the incident you mentioned, and novices do get into predicaments at times. Shall I tell you what happened when my roshi led several monks and me to a brothel and later took me to a geisha house?

VOICES: Yes! Yes!

ROSHI: First you need to be told about a spiritual discipline called *takuhatsu*. A group of monks walk through the streets in single file chanting "Ho" ("Dharma"), each one holding a wooden bowl and wearing a cloth bag around his neck. Into the bowls children and adults place monetary offerings and into the bags food donations, after which donor and receiver bow

to each other, hands palm to palm, in mutual respect and gratitude. Although the word takuhatsu is often translated as "beg-
ging," the monks do not "beg." They offer up to the public
the Buddha's teachings in the example of their own lives and
in return are given food and money to sustain themselves. The
monks are trained to view all donations with the eye of equality—
that is, not to make such judgments as, "He is generous, she
is stingy." Similarly the donors, if they are contributing with a
mind of equality, will be free of such thoughts as, "I will gain
spiritual merit for making this contribution."

One day in February, after I had been in the monastery for
three months, the roshi told me, "Tomorrow you may accompany us on takuhatsu." It was to be my first takuhatsu and I
looked forward eagerly to this new dimension of my training,
even though it meant several hours walking through snow and
ice in straw sandals and flimsy monk's garments.

"Where are we going on takuhatsu tomorrow, Roshi?"

"To the next village. After takuhatsu we will have a memorial
service in a garden."

"What kind of garden?"

"A garden of lotuses of the night."

"But . . ."

"No more questions! Be patient, Kapleau-san. You will see,
you will see."

The next day a group of ten of us went on takuhatsu, led
by the roshi. As we approached a rundown section of the village,
still chanting "Ho," the roshi signaled us to stop in front of a
shabby house. He rang the doorbell and we all waited in the
foyer, where we were soon greeted by a coarse-looking woman
who seemed surprised to see us. Evidently we had come earlier
than expected, but she made no mention of this and merely
apologized for the condition of the house, as would have any
hostess. Laughing, the roshi said graciously, "We're always too
early or too late." She bade us follow her. As we entered the
large front room the music and reveling of half-dressed women
and drunken men ground to a halt like a record player abruptly
disconnected.

"It's a cat house!" The words tumbled from my lips before
I could stop them.

Two disheveled drunks were rolled into an adjoining room

and the sliding doors closed on them. The madam scurried off and soon returned with green tea and cakes. We ate in silence. Following this refreshment we lined up on our knees Japanese fashion, together with the madam and the girls, before the "family" Buddhist shrine, hands palm to palm. On the altar, next to the buddha, were a number of photographs, evidently of deceased relatives of members of the "family." With the absorption of a scientist examining a rare specimen, the roshi lit a stick of incense and placed it alongside offerings of food and tea before the buddha in the shrine. Resuming his place at the head of the group, the roshi intoned the first few lines of the Heart of Perfect Wisdom sutra, after which everyone joined in the chanting. I glanced at the women. Time had fallen from their faces. Suddenly they were little girls attending their first communion. With childlike innocence and purity they chanted, "Form here is only emptiness/ emptiness only form. . . ."

After some fifteen or twenty minutes of chanting, the memorial service was over. Once again we were served tea and cakes, this time everyone laughing merrily as the roshi and the monks chatted and joked with the madam and her girls. Instead of the customary dinner we were given a monetary donation, after which a limousine provided by the madam returned us to the monastery.

A couple of weeks after this incident the roshi came to my room and cheerfully asked, "How would you like to accompany me this evening to a geisha house? Come to my quarters in thirty minutes if you wish to go."

This was my first social invitation from the roshi and he seemed eager that I accompany him. But why to a geisha house? The visit to the brothel had been part of takuhatsu and included the monks; this invitation obviously had another significance. Was it to be some kind of Zen test? If so, what was I to be tested for?

"If you go," I told myself, "you may be sure that whatever else happens there will much drinking of saké and beer and perhaps hard liquor." Alcohol, I knew from painful experience, was bad for my stomach as well as my practice, and I had promised myself and the old abbot to give it up. The roshi's invitation was my first temptation in that direction. Perhaps *this* was to be the test. I recalled a story about Gurdjieff,[34] who one night invited several ex-alcoholic disciples to a soirée in Paris. During the evening he repeatedly offered them cocktails and champagne, and although they protested that they were on the wagon and didn't want to get off, he egged them on. At last they broke down and drank themselves sick. The next day, filled with remorse and self-hatred, they bitterly reproached him. "Why did you force us to drink?" they demanded.

"Was anyone pointing a gun at you?" Gurdjieff asked calmly. "You didn't have to drink, did you?"

As thoughts of this story and its possible connection with the invitation were running through my mind, I looked at my watch: the thirty minutes were almost up. With mixed feelings I found myself walking toward the roshi's quarters.

"Glad you're going with me, Kapleau-san," he said as I entered. "It'll be a jolly evening."

And off we went to the geisha house.

Upon our arrival there was a merry exchange of greetings. An elegantly dressed geisha accompanied us to a low round table in a large entertainment room where there were other guests. We were quickly joined by three other geisha, one of whom brought the first of what were to be many trays loaded with beer and saké. My meager efforts at moderation met with little success. At one point, after trying unsuccessfully to restrain a geisha from pouring me a shot of Suntory whiskey that one of the guests wished to present to the American "because Americans prefer straight whiskey," I looked to the roshi, silently pleading for rescue. He threw back his head and roared with laughter, then once again turned to the geisha, who were swarming around him like bees at a fragrant flower, savoring the nectar of his witty sallies.

From one corner of the room a record player was loudly grinding out American dance tunes, clearly a sensitive bow to the foreigner. To celebrate my presence fittingly, the geisha suggested that instead of performing their traditional Japanese dances we all dance Western style. At once we launched into a medley of foxtrots, waltzes, tangoes, and rhumbas. To further cement American-Japanese relations we sang "Swanee River" and "The Beer-barrel Polka," followed by the nostalgic *"Kojo no tsuki"* ("Moon over the Castle") and "Silent Night." The American numbers were sung by me first in English and then, surprisingly, by the roshi and the geisha in Japanese.

As the night wore on, the dance floor became crowded, and between songs we were fast becoming acquainted with a group of three Japanese businessmen and the geisha with them. One of the men, evidently a friend of the roshi, took a special interest in me. The man grew increasingly friendly and boisterous until, like a big puppy with muddy paws, he became quite a nuisance. As the singing and carousing reached a peak, he somehow maneuvered me into a small private room off the main hall. The room was empty except for a bed. What was he up to? Before I could figure out his intention, in waltzed a coarse-looking, heavily painted young woman, who smiled at me invitingly— not a geisha but obviously a member of the world's oldest profession. She began to undress. My "friend" stumbled out of the room, and I was alone with the girl.

Was *this* to be the test in the roshi's scenario? "Why doesn't he tempt me with one of the beautiful geisha instead of this ugly whore?" I wondered. "That would be a *real* test." As these thoughts were running through my mind, the girl suddenly pushed me to the bed and started pulling at my clothes. I shoved her away. She retreated, looking hurt and puzzled. Through an alcoholic haze I glared at her. I felt like the Zen monk in the koan who is hanging by his teeth from a branch high up in a tree.[35] Were he to open his mouth to answer the serious question being asked him by someone from below, he would fall and hurt himself badly. But not to answer would fail the questioner. "If you let go and fall into her arms," I told myself, "you may also fall into the roshi's hands—his trap. But if you beat a retreat you will be ducking out of the roshi's test."

What should I do?

As yet my Zen training had generated in me little faith in the teaching of the Lotus sutra that one in distress will be aided if he calls the name of Kannon with reverence. But I now found myself beseeching Kannon to rescue me from this predicament. He must have sensed my appeal was a test case, for his response was immediate. It came in the form of three husky monks from

the monastery who calmly but briskly strode into the room,
brushed aside the girl, and seized me. One took hold of my
head and shoulders and the others a leg each. Like pallbearers
they bore me solemnly aloft through the entertainment room
to the doorway and down the stairs. My master, encircled by a
merry band of geisha, was laughing so hard that tears streamed
down his face.

Outside a crowd of villagers had gathered to watch, faces im-
passive as though this were an everyday spectacle. The monks,
confident of success, had brought a bicycle for me. In silence
we pedaled to the monastery.

Back in my room I began sorting out the questions crowding
into my mind. How had the monks learned of my plight? Had
the roshi's scheme been bungled by the clumsy antics of the
drunken businessman, forcing him to send an SOS to the monks,
or was the businessman playing an assigned role? Is it possible
that the monks themselves, with their sensitive spiritual anten-
nae, could have picked up my distress signals? Or that the abbot,
learning at the eleventh hour of the roshi's shenanigans, had
dispatched the monks to my rescue? Perhaps my humiliating
rescue from this tight squeeze was the intended outcome of
the drama after all.

More than any other this question nagged at me: What role,
if any, did the abbot have in this Zen play? Although eighty-
four years of age, he was still active and very much in charge.
Would the roshi, who was aware of the abbot's personal interest
in me, have dared take me to the geisha house without the abbot's
knowledge and approval? It seemed unlikely. And why would
the abbot, who never touched liquor except for a sip or two
of saké at a monastery celebration, sanction my visiting a geisha
house, where he knew there would be much drinking and merry-
making, unless it was to test me? The Zen story came to mind
of the boy whose father, a master burglar, set out to teach him
the profession. On their very first burglary together they heard
footsteps on the walk outside. Unhesitatingly the father grabbed
the boy, pushed him into a trunk, banged down the lid, placed
heavy books on it, then made his own escape. Several hours
later the boy returned home, ragged and exhausted.

"Father," he cried angrily, "why did you put me into that trunk? If I hadn't been made desperate by thoughts of prison, I *never* would have escaped!"

The father smiled. "My son," he said, "you have had your first lesson in the art of burglary."

The difference between that boy and me is that he pulled himself out of his predicament unaided, while I had to be rescued by the monks.

What grade did I receive on this test, if test it indeed was? I never learned, for the incident was never mentioned either by the old abbot, the roshi, or the monks.

Tell me, you students, why do you think the roshi took me to that geisha house?

FIRST VOICE: He was trying to teach you a Zen lesson.

ROSHI: Yes, but what lesson?

FIRST VOICE: That sex is natural, so why suppress it?

[Laughter]

SECOND VOICE: He wanted to show you the contrast between monastic discipline and a life of wanton pleasure.

THIRD VOICE: He wanted to dramatize the value of awareness—how quickly and surely the monks acted in rescuing you.

FOURTH VOICE: He was testing you to see if you were ready for the monk's life or were still hanging onto worldly habits like drinking and carousing.

QUESTIONER: Roshi, tell us what *you* think now about this whole episode.

ROSHI: Zen masters are always teaching their students.

QUESTIONER: But what did it teach you?

ROSHI: That if you stand apart you are only a part; that cutting yourself off from anyone is cutting yourself in two; that oneness is life, separation is death.

SECOND QUESTIONER: Then why didn't you sleep with that prostitute?

ROSHI: Because at that time I hadn't yet learned that fundamental truth.

THIRD QUESTIONER: Even if you had learned that oneness is life and separation death, could you really have become one with that prostitute just by sleeping with her?

ROSHI: Had I been more spiritually developed I could have had relations with her without using or abusing her and so have become one with her and transcended the act of sex. But as a beginner in Zen I made the novice's fatal mistake of separating myself by judging—that is, despising—her. In effect I was holding up to her, not her noble true nature but her untrue gross nature. By rejecting her advances I was denying the inherent purity and dignity of a human being who happened to be a prostitute, and in so doing I was defiling both of us.

To me she was no more than an "ugly whore." To the roshi she was a "lotus of the night." In Buddhism the lotus is a symbol of True-mind, for just as the lotus grows from mud and unfolds a lovely blossom, so our True-mind, unsullied by ignorance and turbulent passions, reveals its purity and beauty in awakening. We were both using labels, but his were gentle and compassionate, mine crude and judgmental.

FOURTH QUESTIONER: Could a celibate Zen monk show compassion in such a situation without sacrificing his celibacy?

ROSHI: He could, and the following story is a case in point.

A Zen master was walking through a large city when he heard someone call out his name from a second-story window. Looking up, he saw a woman who was obviously a prostitute. He was surprised she knew him, and when he asked her about this she replied, "Many years ago, when you were a boy, our farm was next to yours. Not long after you entered the monastery there was a bad harvest, and this is what became of me." The master entered the house to talk with her, and she asked him to spend the night there.

He paid the usual house fee and gave her additional money. They talked for many hours about their homes and families until it was time to retire. As the woman prepared the bed the master began to do zazen. "Why are you meditating?" she asked. "You have been very kind and I would like to show my gratitude. No one will be the wiser."

The master didn't move but simply said, "Your job is to sleep, mine is to sit. So go to sleep and I'll continue to sit." And that is what he did for the rest of the night.

When a Zen master was asked to write some words of wisdom on the back of a picture of a prostitute, he wrote:

The Buddha sells the doctrine,
the patriarchs sell the Buddha,
the great priests sell the patriarchs,
she sells her body,
that the passions of all beings may be quieted.
Form is Emptiness, the passions are Bodhi.[36]

If you truly understand these lines, you will know that there
is no "good" to seek and no "evil" to avoid.

III / A DHARMA TALK / THE FIRST PRECEPT: NOT TO KILL BUT TO CHERISH ALL LIFE

/ Tonight my talk will be on
the first of the ten precepts, or items of good character: not
to kill but to cherish all life. The others are 2) not to take what
is not given (but to respect the things of others); 3) not to engage
in improper sexuality (but to practice purity of mind and self-
restraint); 4) not to lie (but to speak the truth); 5) not to cause
others to use liquors or drugs that confuse or weaken the mind
nor to do so oneself (but to keep the mind clear); 6) not to
speak of the shortcomings of others (but to be understanding
and sympathetic); 7) not to praise oneself and condemn others
(but to overcome one's own shortcomings); 8) not to withhold
spiritual or material aid (but to give it freely where needed);
9) not to become angry (but to exercise control); and 10) not
to revile the three treasures of buddha, dharma, and sangha
(but to cherish and uphold them). The spirit of all the precepts
being essentially the same, if you grasp the essence of the first
you will comprehend them all.

To intentionally deprive any living thing, but especially a human being, of life will produce (except under conditions to be
discussed later) painful karma. Human life is foremostly precious
because, among other reasons, it is only from this state that
enlightenment can issue. Animals, for example, do not share
man's ability to attain formlessness and liberate themselves from
the binding chains of birth and death. In the Buddhist cosmol-

ogy, by the way, man is not the most evolved creature; he stands between a hungry ghost and a buddha.[37]

Slaughterers as well as hunters and fishermen—especially those motivated by sport alone—inevitably incur a heavy karma. Those who do experimental research on animals, often depriving them of their lives, also risk painful karma. The destruction of animals in such experimentation is justified on the ground that it is the only way by which to gain information vital to the health and welfare of human beings. Unfortunately, much animal experimentation today is undertaken without consideration of alternative, more humane methods. Such an unfeeling attitude may arise from a belief that animals, being less developed than man, suffer less. But who would deny that animals, too, suffer pain acutely and try to avoid it as much as humans? And precisely because their minds are less complex than man's and they are more intuitive, animals are more sensitive to impending violence and pain, which generates in them fear that prolongs their suffering. Porphyry, a Greek philosopher of the fourth century, wrote that anyone who had heard the scream of an animal being slaughtered could never again eat animal flesh. Confucius, many centuries earlier, made the same observation.

Is it not supreme arrogance for man to manipulate, mistreat, or destroy at his whim creatures who have a right to share this planet with him? Dr. Albert Schweitzer insisted, "We have no right to inflict suffering and death on another living creature unless there is some unavoidable necessity for it." Even more, since animals are dumb and cannot speak for themselves, they can be regarded as a sacred trust to us.

What about the killing of flies and mosquitoes? Those who would hesitate to kill even a frog often have no compunction about snuffing out the life of insects. With billions upon billions of insects, the death of one or two may seem utterly inconsequential. Yet consider: For all of man's ingenuity and complex technology he has yet to re-create the life of even a flea! One flea, as Whitman said, is miracle enough to stagger sextillions of infidels.

Maliciously or thoughtlessly to destroy insects and small animals is censurable for other reasons. Such pointless killing breeds an insensitivity to the sufferings of higher life forms as well. Sociologists have pointed out that a common thread in the early life of criminals is cruelty toward animals and the wanton killing of them.

Flesh eaters sometimes chide vegetarians, saying "You say you don't eat meat because you don't want to cause the killing of an animal, but what about the vegetables you eat? What is the difference between depriving a vegetable of its life and killing a cow or a chicken for food?"

There is all the difference in the world when these acts are weighed on the human moral scale—that is, from a *relative* point of view. According to these moral values, taking the life of a human being is far worse than taking that of an animal, and killing an insect is not as reprehensible as destroying, say, a fish or a bird. On the same scale, the life of a vegetable is less valuable than that of an insect. But plants, while not as developed as animals or insects, do have consciousness of a sort and an instinct for survival. This has been established by such outstanding botanists as Luther Burbank, George Washington Carver, and Sir Jagadis Bose. To cut down a tree or pluck a flower carelessly—that is, unnecessarily—is therefore contrary to the spirit of the first precept.

All life forms, in their never-beginning and never-ending karmic evolution and devolution, have been plants, insects, animals, demons, human beings, *devas.* Each existence is what it is by reason of the law of cause and effect; the place each occupies in the evolutionary chain is the product of its own unique karma. How then can we repudiate one expression of the Buddha-nature, our common element, in favor of another when we are all rooted in the same reality?

Yet the right to life is not absolute, and individual life may unavoidably have to be sacrificed to preserve the health and welfare of society. Consider a dog maddened by rabies approaching a group of children. To protect the health and possibly the lives of these children, he might well have to be shot. The same principle holds, for example, when a man with a gun goes berserk, begins to shoot wildly, and a policeman or bystander trying to restrain him takes his life.

Whether painful karma would accrue to one depriving an animate being of its life, even when the killing was motivated by concern for the common welfare, would depend foremostly on one's mind state. If the act were done no-mindedly, beyond *self-conscious* awareness of one taking life and a life being taken, no painful karma would be incurred, for in the profoundest sense there would be no killer and nothing killed. Let me hasten to add that only a highly developed individual could act in this way. At a lesser level, placing the hands palm to palm in a gesture of contrition and repentance when faced with the unavoidable necessity to take life denudes the act of malicious intent.

Although on a relative, moral level we discriminate the value of one form of life from another, from the absolute aspect of our Buddha-nature no such distinctions can be made. From the perspective of this all embracing True-mind—from the viewpoint of the universe, so to speak—everything is equal; the life of an Einstein is no more or less valuable than that of a carrot. The point is, we exist on both levels simultaneously, and unless we have experienced kensho (the realization that the relative and the absolute are not two) there is bound to be confusion and endless uncertainty as to "right" or "wrong" in a given situation. One who has seen into the absolute side of his True-nature does not cling to the relative, ever-changing world of phenomena and moral values, but sees it as an aspect of the unchanging absolute.

In a discussion of the first precept the subject of abortion is bound to arise. The issue of abortion, as you know, has long been the subject of bitter public debate. At one extreme are those who insist, "All life is sacred, even a human embryo!" These people rage against the "murderous mind" of those who would deny "the right of life" of the unborn child, insisting that "since only God can give life, only He can take it away." It may be asked: Are these same individuals just as vociferous in demanding a decent life for those *already* born who are under-nourished and exploited?

On the other side are those who insist that the pregnant woman alone has the right to decide whether to bear the fetus. To women who cry, "This is *my* body, I can do with it as I please!" I would ask, "How can you say it is *your* body when you cannot control the circulation of your blood or your heartbeat, your thoughts, aging, or death? Clearly your body has its own laws, which it obeys independently of your wishes. True, in a limited sense it is your body, for it is the outcome of your karma, of your volitional thoughts and actions in this life and previous ones. But don't forget that your karma also includes your biological inheritance from your parents. Moreover, it is not just by chance, as you may think, that the particular fetus within you was conceived. In the profoundest sense its conception is the expression of the karmic affinity between you: your need to provide it with a body and its need to be reborn through you."

Make no mistake, abortion is a grave matter. Even when the danger of the mother's physical death is remote, as in a modern clinic, the spiritual dying that accompanies an abortion can be real and painful. For a spiritually sensitive woman who realizes she is the means through which a particular being can be reborn in human form—that form which is so hard to obtain—to ac-quiesce in the aborting of that incipient life can be a soul-scarring experience, just as bearing a wanted child in happy circumstances can be a source of tremendous joy. Many women, and men too, have asked my advice about abortion. I have seen and heard the delight of those who, though having contemplated an abor-tion, decided to have the child, and I have observed sorrow etched in the faces of many who did have an abortion.

Sometime ago a couple consulted me about a possible abor-tion. They were not advised to act one way or the other; I simply pointed out certain karmic consequences that I felt would flow from each course of action. As a result of the discussion they decided to have the child. Recently this letter came from the woman: "Yes, our child is quite a fellow. How grateful we are that he chose us as his parents. More than one person has re-marked, 'He is the happiest baby I have ever seen.' Perhaps more noteworthy is his wonderful responsiveness and alertness and adaptability. How can we ever thank you, Roshi, for the advice you gave us so many moons ago when our child was just a speck inside me! That we once toyed with the idea of abortion is now UNBELIEVABLE [her emphasis]—a bad dream. . . ."

Having heard this, you should not conclude that abortion in

all circumstances is a violation of the first precept, for this would be a grievous misunderstanding. While Buddhism on the whole decries the destruction of any form of life, the Mahayana experience nonetheless sees the right to life as not absolute. This of course applies to abortion as well. To fully comprehend this statement, consider the contemporary state of the world. Demographers say that at the present rate of growth, by the year 2030 the present world population of four billion will triple.[38] A report by several organizations concerned with the population explosion points out: "The list of fallout problems from the population explosion includes oceans being overfished and polluted, air pollution, and a profusion of new chemicals endangering animal and plant species and causing human environmental illnesses, including cancer." Economists and other experts predict that when the struggle for dwindling food supplies becomes desperate, famines, pestilence, chaos, and wars—with untold suffering and death—are inevitable. This assessment, mind you, comes not from doomsday alarmists but from sober scientists. With such catastrophes looming ahead, how can women and men continue to beget *many* children without increasing the burden of humanity—even the burden of those very children, who will have to live and suffer in this starving, polluted world?

Already the welfare rolls in the large American cities are staggering, placing a tremendous burden on society. The economic, health, and moral problems created by irresponsible sexuality— the enormous increase in crimes of violence committed by fatherless youngsters and the spread of venereal disease—likewise are undermining the stability of society. No mother of several children who is faced with the birth of another, unwanted child can ignore these realities of life in the twentieth century. Unrestrained breeding is a self-indulgence that our floundering society can no longer tolerate without willing its own destruction. The law sanctioning abortion obviously takes cognizance of this dismal state of affairs.

At this point some of you are undoubtedly thinking, "You have discussed the pros and cons of abortion, but if I am faced with an unwanted pregnancy, on what should I base a decision? How can I be certain that what I decide to do is right and will not produce painful karma?" There is no absolute right or wrong, no clear-cut solution. If your mind is free of fear and of narrow, selfish concerns, you will know what course of action to take. Put yourself deeply into zazen—look into your own heart-mind, reflecting carefully on all aspects of your life situation and on the repercussions your actions might have on your family and on society as a whole. Once the upper levels of mind, which weigh and analyze, have come to rest, the "right" course of action will become clear. And when such action is accompanied by a feeling of inner peace, you may be sure you have not gone astray.

If having gone through the foregoing steps you are convinced that an abortion is unavoidable, let the two of you sit before a figure or picture of a buddha or Kannon and sincerely repent what you feel has to be done. In doing so you open yourself to the support and aid of buddhic forces. Try to face the abortion no-mindedly—that is, without fear or guilt or any other worrying emotion. Meditate on the fact that all life is phoenix-like, re-creating itself again and again from its own ashes. Understand that in the profoundest sense neither the doctor's instruments nor anything else can destroy the real life of the fetus, for its ever-abiding Buddha-nature is indestructible. Thus your burden will be lightened.

Let us now consider war in relation to the first precept. Besides causing the destruction of life and resources, war inflicts cruelties and untold suffering. To live in peace is an ideal of Buddhism, as indeed it is of all religions. To whatever Buddhist country you go, the figure of the Buddha is the supreme symbol of inner and outer peace. No religious war has ever been fought in the name of Buddhism.

The Buddha taught that all egocentricity is born of greed, hatred, and delusive thinking, and although the causes of war are many, in substance they can be reduced to the same three elements. The greed for power and possessions, the hatred arising from feeling thwarted or put upon, the deluded notion of a "manifest destiny" apart from others—all these strengthen individual ego, which emerges on a collective level as nationalistic self-interest. This self-interest must then prevail at any cost. Given an international conflict of interests and a combustible mixture of social, political, and economic conditions, war erupts—but always it is fueled by greed, hatred, and delusion. The genesis of war is the human heart.

I once asked a Ceylonese Buddhist master who made frequent trips to Vietnam whether Vietnamese Buddhist monks concurred in the view that their sufferings as a nation in the Vietnam war were a form of karmic retribution. He responded that all the monks he had questioned in Vietnam had unhesitatingly replied in the affirmative, citing in particular an unusually cruel act of aggression by the Vietnamese several hundred years ago in which they invaded the territory of one of their neighbors. This, he was told, was a collective karmic debt that the Vietnamese were now obliged to repay in the form of terrible sufferings.

Hearing this, some of you may wonder, "How can innocent children who die in an air raid be considered responsible for their own death?" But don't forget that children come into this life with their own karmic burden even as they are linked with the karma of their parents. Because of this connection they are compelled to suffer for the sins of their parents just as parents must suffer for the vices of their children. Although most people would have little trouble accepting the law of karma in terms of individual responsibility, collective karma is more difficult for them to acknowledge. Human nature is such that while we willingly identify with our nation's karma when its achievements are being praised, we quickly disassociate ourselves from it when our leaders' actions place the country in a bad light. Thus when American astronauts were the first to reach the moon, we exulted, "Hurrah—*we* beat the Russians to the moon!" But when our President ordered the saturation bombing of a Vietnamese city, with untold destruction of life, we disclaimed responsibility for his act.

After a talk on karma in which I referred to the statements of the Ceylonese master, someone asked, "Doesn't it follow, then, that any aggressor could justify his aggression by claiming he was repaying his victims for the sufferings they had once inflicted on others—that he was in fact helping them expiate past karma?" If it were true that one could willfully kill or maim and not suffer retribution in this or a future existence, would that not be flying in the face of the law of cause and effect? The fact is that the workings of karma ensure that those who intentionally inflict pain on others will one day suffer themselves. Thus every aggressor ultimately becomes the victim of his own aggression.

Because the law of karma, with its implication that we are responsible for our sufferings, is not understood or accepted, anger and the desire for revenge dominate the minds of most victims. So the violence, cruelty, and devastation of war, with its unleashing of demonic forces, continue to reverberate in the minds and hearts of the victims long after the fighting has stopped, perpetuating deep hatreds from generation to generation. Few realize that such powerful negative forces also contaminate the atmosphere and upset planetary equilibrium, sometimes even contributing to such phenomena as earthquakes.

In a less technological age earthquakes were described as "acts of God," but now scientists say that when the stresses experienced by the earth become too great the tension is relieved by a shifting of the "plates" of the earth's crust, and that this produces an earthquake. At the same time geophysicists admit that the how and the why of earthquakes are still pretty much a mystery.

From the Buddhist point of view, earthquakes and similar phenomena are neither acts of God nor caprices of nature; they are causally related to the thoughts and actions primarily of human beings. Man and his environment are not separate, they are mutually conditioning—two aspects of one reality. Each of our thoughts pulsates with the heartbeat of the cosmos, and the universe in turn is affected by and reflects our thoughts and actions. We cannot ravage and pollute the earth, upsetting the balance of the forces of nature—our own nature—without repercussions from the earth. C. G. Jung is quoted in an article in the New York *Times* in 1971 as saying (following the 1960 earthquake that destroyed many Chilian cities), "Even though today's scientists may reject the idea, the earth seems to be in tune with the destructive fury of mankind." But this is only half the equation. Through man's pollution of the atmosphere and the soil (such as happened in the Vietnam war), the very air man breathes and the food he eats poison him, eliciting from his body a similar protest in the form of pollution diseases, the foremost of which may be cancer. Thus the circle of destruction is complete.

Although war is the ultimate vehicle of human slaughter, many feel that killing in a war of self-defense is justified. Yet taking the life of another human being under any circumstances runs counter to the deepest instincts of man. The natural tendency of men and women free of fear and hatred is to gravitate toward one another in loving embrace, not to murder each other. Because of this instinctive aversion to kill a fellow creature, soldiers have to be taught to make a hated object of the "enemy," the enemy who is out to "kill you first."

What does the individual Buddhist do when, let us say, his country is at war and he is drafted for military duty? Does he serve the "common welfare" by unqualifiedly refusing to participate in the destruction and carnage war brings? In our own country there were innumerable opponents of participation in the Vietnam war who refused induction, preferring imprisonment or loss of citizenship. Many Americans applauded them for their stand, but many others condemned them.

How many of you remember the words of Stephen Decatur from your high-school American history? "My country! In her intercourse with foreign nations may she always be in the right. But my country, right or wrong." Compare them to those of another American, Carl Schurz: "Our country, right or wrong. When right, to be kept right; when wrong, to be put right." Which of these expresses the loftier ethic? And on what should we base a decision of moral right—the individual's conscience or that of the lawmakers? Is one's primary duty to his country or to humanity as a whole?

Especially in times of war these burning questions demand unequivocal answers. In seeking a resolution of these issues one must consider both the individual karma one would reap from his actions and the collective karma of the nation, for which each one is also to an extent responsible. Ultimately one's conscience and deepest intuitions must be his guides. As with the question of abortion, one must dig deeply into oneself through zazen, beyond the level of intellect, until there bubbles up the decision that banishes fear and uncertainty.

In the Vietnam war many Buddhist monks and others refused to take the lives of fellow human beings labeled as the "enemy," even though the penalty for refusal was often torture and even death. In refusing to despise and murder other human beings these Buddhist monks and laymen demonstrated a fundamental teaching of the Buddha: Hatred breeds more hatred, and he who kills another digs two graves. In so acting they affirmed that the human heart can free itself from fear and hatred and assert its natural love and compassion.

In Vietnam there were also monks, nuns, and laymen who burned themselves to death to dramatize the intense sufferings of the Vietnamese people. This self-immolation must be clearly distinguished from suicide, which of course is contrary to the first precept of nonkilling. In ordinary suicide where there is no mental disturbance, the individual does not really want to die, he wants to live, but in a way that he feels is being frustrated by his family, his friends, his work, or his society; or else his life is tedious and, he feels, devoid of meaning. Too weak to struggle to achieve what he desperately longs for, he loses all courage and hope. His barren, pain-producing life becomes unendurable, and in his overwhelming despair he kills himself. Suicide always has a strong element of ego in it: "*I* can't live *my* way, so *I* would rather die." The act of self-destruction is the suicide's supreme gesture of defiance, a symbolic thumbing of his nose at society—the society that at the same time he is dramatically accusing of having failed him rather than he it. But death is not the end, and wherever he is reborn and in whatever form, he will have to face the karmic consequences of his self-slaughter.

That the self-burning of Buddhist monks, nuns, and laymen in Vietnam sprang from entirely different motivations is clearly seen in the letter of Thich Nhat Hanh [39] to Martin Luther King: "What the monks said in the letters they left before burning themselves aimed only at alarming, at moving the hearts of the oppressors, and at calling the attention of the world to the suffering endured by the Vietnamese. To burn oneself by fire is to prove that what one is saying is of the utmost importance. There is nothing more painful than burning oneself. To say something while experiencing this kind of pain is to say it with the utmost courage, frankness, determination, and sincerity. . . . The Vietnamese monk by burning himself says with all his strength and determination that he can endure the greatest of suffering to protect his people. But why does he have to burn himself to death? The difference between burning oneself and burning oneself to death is only a difference in degree, not in nature. A man who burns himself too much must die. The important thing is not to take one's life but to burn. . . . To communicate one's feelings by burning oneself therefore is not to commit an act of destruction but to perform an act of construction—that is, to suffer and die for the sake of one's people. This is not suicide. . . ."

To sacrifice one's life in this manner calls for extraordinary courage and unusually strong samadhi power, which in turn require long spiritual training. Who can forget the news media photographs of the elderly monk who had himself set on fire while sitting in the lotus position? The sight of the half-incinerated body toppling over generated tremendous shock waves in the West, particularly in the United States. This reaction was due in part to the realization that behind this act were fearlessness, egolessness, and a degree of self-control almost unknown in the West today.

Another self-controlled death different from suicide is that of the Zen masters who allowed themselves to die when they became too old and infirm to continue to teach or work. A notable example in modern times is the late abbot [40] of the monastery where I first trained. When he was ninety-six and half blind, he stopped eating. When questioned by his monks, he replied that he had outlived his usefulness and was being a nuisance. They told him, "If you die now, in January, when it is so cold, everyone will be uncomfortable at your funeral and you will be an even greater nuisance, so please eat!" He thereupon resumed eating, but when the weather became warm he again stopped and not long afterward quietly died.

No commentary on the first precept would be complete without a discussion of euthanasia. Euthanasia is defined as "an easy and painless death," or "the act or method of causing death painlessly so as to end suffering." The morality of euthanasia, like that of abortion, has agitated the hearts and minds of thoughtful men and women for centuries. Not long ago the problem was dramatically brought to public attention through the case of a young woman who had been comatose in an intensive-care unit for some time, kept technically alive by a mechanical respirator and the cool efficiency of medical technology. Because of extensive damage to her brain, medical opinion was that even were she to awaken from the coma she would have to be institutionalized for the rest of her life. Her parents petitioned the courts to allow their benumbed and betubed child to die a "natural" death, but as the law in its majestic equality, to paraphrase Victor Hugo, forbids the healthy and desperately sick alike from taking their own lives or having them terminated, the hospital doctors continued to employ the drugs and mechanical devices necessary to prolong her life. The respirator was finally disconnected following a court ruling that authorized such action when the attending physician and a panel of hospital officials agreed that there was no reasonable hope of recovery.

This much-publicized case aroused considerable interest and elicited strong emotional responses. Those sympathetic to the parents' viewpoint argued that since this young woman could never be restored to even a semblance of normal life, she could only continue as a burden to herself, her family, and society. They maintained that compassion and the concern for human dignity, as well as the prohibitive cost of keeping her in an intensive-care unit, justified her being permitted to die without "unnatural" efforts being made to prolong her life. On the other side of the issue stood those who contended that because it is so unique and precious, human life in any form must be preserved at all costs, and that to break the fragile thread by which her life hung would be sacrilegious. In the middle was the medical profession, legally and ethically bound to prolong life and by reason of a highly sophisticated technology able to do so to a degree never before possible.

What is the Buddhist view of euthanasia? There is no "official" position, only the understanding of individual teachers growing out of their spiritual experience and that of scholars derived from their studies. Each individual is free to accept or reject such understandings. The guidelines are expressed in these famous words of the Buddha: "Don't believe solely because the written testimony of some ancient wise man is shown you . . . and don't believe anything on the mere authority of your teachers or priests. What you *should* accept as true and as the guide to your life is whatever agrees with your own Reason and your own experience, after thorough investigation, and whatever is helpful both to your own well-being and that of other living beings."

My own feeling is that the same considerations apply to euthanasia as to other modes of life-taking. If the sufferer intentionally ends his own life, he is commiting suicide and must one day face all that entails in terms of karmic retribution. In the same way, someone who enables the sufferer to die, even by request, is culpable, although the mind state in which such an act is performed vitally affects the resulting karma.

Nagging questions remain. Is it not selfish to be thinking of one's own karma when someone dear to you, terminally ill and in excruciating pain, implores you to end his or her life? But then, might not a refusal to respond to the patient's entreaties be kinder, karmically speaking, since the sufferer's karma is also involved? In any case, would a sufferer who understood the meaning of pain and its relation to karma—that is, the grateful acceptance of pain as a means of paying karmic debts—ask for euthanasia?

When I have been asked, "What would *you* do if someone asked you to end his life?" I have remained silent or said, "I don't know," for until one is faced with a specific situation one *doesn't* know, and such questions are academic. Regular zazen develops calm understanding that enables one to act or refrain from acting without remorse or self-doubt.

So far we have been talking about willful killing. What are the ramifications of unintentional taking of life? Suppose that while driving you run over a dog and it dies. Are you karmically responsible? In one sense, yes, inasmuch as you freely drove the car and were responsible for its being in a position to kill the dog. But the negative karma resulting from such an action would be less if you truly repented having caused the animal's death.

Or suppose that the car you are driving collides with another and that passengers in both vehicles are killed. Are you karmically responsible for their deaths? Or consider an airplane crash in which many are injured and killed. Is the pilot karmically responsible if he was not negligent? The following story and comment by my teacher may provide some answers to these questions.

While I was in Japan there occurred a head-on collision of two trains in which many people were killed and injured. The day following the crash there was an all-day sitting. Several of those present had been passengers on one of the trains, and after lunch a lively discussion began about karmic responsibility. In reply to a question, my teacher stated that each one who died in the collision was, from a karmic standpoint, at least 50 per cent responsible for his death (quite apart from the engineers' legal responsibility), since he had chosen to be on one of those trains at that particular time. The workings of karma, you see, are enormously intricate.

Another aspect of the first precept that ought to be mentioned is that not all killing involves the taking of life of an animate being. The first precept also forbids destroying the equanimity of the individual or the community through abusive words, malicious gossip, or other spiteful means. Also included within this precept is a prohibition against killing time—that is, against idleness and sloth.

To sum up: Animals have just as much right to life as we on this earth that we share in common, and therefore we have no right to destroy them at our whim. Moreover, since in our ascent and descent of the ladder of innumerable lives (according to causes and conditions) our Buddha-nature assumes many forms—all of which are aspects of oneself—to destroy any life form is to destroy a part of oneself. Human life is most precious because only from this state can we have the liberating experience of enlightenment, through which alone the truth of the indivisibility of all existences becomes a matter of personal experience. Where the taking of life is unavoidable, however, and is accompanied by feelings of contrition and repentance, the karmic retribution is always lessened.

AFTERWORD—A PERSONAL NOTE /

What makes a man in his middle years give up a secure job and comfortable income, family, and friends for the austere rigors of a Zen monastery and the uncertain life of a "homeless one"? Is it some outer traumatic circumstance or a compelling inner need? These questions were asked me dozens of times in Japan and almost as often in America. In my own case it seemed at times that what had motivated me to surrender my middle-class comforts and values to undergo Zen training was the desire to find relief from painful tensions and an exhausting restlessness. At other times I felt it was a need to understand the appalling sufferings I had witnessed in Germany, Japan, and China just after World War II. Eventually I realized that the answers to the foregoing questions lay in one word—karma, a term embracing the whole concatenation of causes and effects that is one's life. And it was karma, too, that brought me many years later, at the age of fifty-two, to the city of Rochester, New York, a place I had never set foot in previously, to find myself the head of a Zen Center. Before my contact with Asia and Zen, in the remotest flights of my imagination I had not pictured myself living the life of a monastic, much less becoming a teacher of Buddhism.

As I look back with greater understanding of the workings of the law of causation, it is clear that certain events and circumstances directly shaped the karmic pattern that eventually propelled me into Zen. As a child I had stubbornly refused to accompany my mother into what she called a "House of God," to attend Sunday school, or take any formal religious instruction. When she pressed me I asked, "If God is only in a church or temple, why did he create the rest of the world?" While on the whole the substance and spirit of the Bible felt remote and alien, some parts—for example, the Psalms—stimulated my interest. This reading and the study of other Western religious literature eventually coalesced into a burning question that was to obsess me for many years: "Why did the Jews repudiate Christ, who said he was fulfilling the Jewish religion, and why did Christians, who professed to love Christ, revile the Jews, his people?"

To find an answer to this question I attended Protestant, Catholic, and Jewish services and approached ministers, priests, and rabbis. Their initial reactions were invariably an embarrassed silence and then—perhaps because I was only thirteen at the time—a patronizing solicitude, which left me as perplexed as before, only now with resentment added to confusion. No clergyman ever gave me a response that satisfied either my intellect or my heart.

Disillusioned with the Judeo-Christian religions, I became first a freethinker, then an agnostic—"a know-nothing," as my churchgoing classmates branded me—and then the ultimate: an atheist. My heroes were Dostoevsky, Voltaire, and Robert Ingersoll, all of whose writings I read avidly. I quoted again and again Dostoevsky's pronouncement, "How terrible to watch a man who has the Incomprehensible within his grasp, doesn't know what to do, and sits down playing with a toy called God," although I scarcely understood its deeper implications.

In high school I formed The Atheists' Club and became its first president. The year was 1928, and the dramatic trial of John Scopes in Tennessee three years earlier for teaching the Darwinian theory of evolution in his biology class had generated ripples felt throughout the country. Our school dean was in no mood to countenance anything as anti-establishment as atheism and warned, "Unless you disband the club you will be expelled from school."

Years later, after opening my Mind's eye to some extent, it became clear that my zealous espousal of atheism was evidence of a religious sensibility beginning to stir. What is more, I realized that my boyhood heroes were on such intimate terms with God that they would not insult him by name-calling.

During World War II I was working as a reporter in the courts of Connecticut, having been deferred from the draft for medical reasons. This rejection did not leave me disconsolate, for I had not relished the thought either of killing or being killed. Then in mid-1945, as the war in Europe was ending, the newspapers reported that the United States, Great Britain, France, and the Soviet Union, the four occupying powers of Germany, were planning to set up in Nuremberg "The International Military Tribunal for the Prosecution of Axis Criminality," and would soon begin recruiting the personnel necessary for the conduct of the trials. I applied to Washington for a position as court reporter, and after a series of physical, mental, and performance tests, was accepted. Soon after, in October, I found myself on a plane bound for Nuremberg. The city of Nuremberg, once the glittering showplace of Nazi power and the scene of mass rallies led by Hitler himself, lay in ruins, the aftermath of heavy Allied bombing. Virtually every other large city in Germany had suffered the same fate. The Germans were reaping the whirlwind for having blindly followed Hitler. Yet from all that appeared most Germans were still unrepentant. Not long after my arrival in Nuremberg, *Stars and Stripes*, the U. S. Army newspaper, reported that when Pastor Martin Niemoeller, a prominent religious figure in postwar Germany, spoke to a large audience at Erlangen University, stating that German redemption lay in openly confessing her war guilt and repenting of it, he was booed and driven from the podium with tomatoes and rotten eggs.

The testimony at the trials was a litany of Nazi betrayal and aggression, a chronicle of unbelievable cruelty and human degradation. Listening day after day to victims of the Nazis describe the atrocities they themselves had been subjected to or had witnessed, one was shocked into numbness, the mind unable to comprehend the enormity of the crimes.

This grim evidence of man's inhumanity to man, plus the apparent absence of contrition on the part of the mass of Germans, plunged me into the deepest gloom, and my boyhood spiritual questionings, which had lain buried under concerns of study, work, and travel, suddenly burst again into full consciousness. And there arose other insistent questions: If "music hath charms to sooth the savage breast," why hadn't the music of the great German composers—music that held a special place in the hearts of so many Germans—restrained the Nazis in their brutality? Why in a land that gave birth to Protestantism, to Luther and Goethe, to Dürer, Heine, Hegel, and Kant, hadn't religion, art, and philosophy acted as civilizing influences? And why hadn't Italy's great culture and strong Catholicism, as well as the Pope's presence, arrested the cruel thrust of fascism there? A statement of Nietzsche's came to mind: "Art, religion, and philosophy are illusions invented by man as weapons in his struggle to prevail over himself and his fellows." As though to confirm Nietzsche's point, testimony was presented in court of the practice at one concentration camp of making lampshades from the skin of the victims of its gas chambers, while in the same camp the commandant and other personnel had formed a string ensemble that played Bach, Brahms, and Beethoven after the day's work.

The trials, now in their ninth month, were drawing to a close. In Tokyo, meanwhile, preparations were under way to try General Tojo and other Japanese leaders charged with major, or "Class A," war crimes. I had never been to Asia, and this was a chance to see Japan and perhaps other Asian countries, as well as to take part in war crimes trials in another area of the world. But there were other reasons for my desire to leave Germany. The frightful trial statistics, the self-pitying despair of the Germans, the widespread black marketing involving soldiers and civilians alike, my bondage to the "joyless pursuit of pleasure"—all these eventually induced in me a mood of black depression tinged with shame and guilt. At a deep level I felt somehow that I, too, was responsible for the overwhelming sufferings reverberating from the war. Japan could not be worse than Germany, I told myself, and it might prove to be better. So I applied for a transfer to Tokyo and got it.

The International Military Tribunal for the Far East had already commenced its operations when I arrived. Here again gruesome testimony spilled forth: the rape of Nanking, the "Bataan Death March" in the Philippines, and other atrocities committed by the Japanese Army. Yet the atmosphere prevailing at the Tokyo trials was relaxed, a far cry from the bitter tensions of Nuremberg. Inevitably the temper of the people of an occupied country is reflected in the behavior of its occupiers, and since the Japanese on the whole had accepted the war's aftermath with remarkable restraint and composure, the Tokyo courtroom mirrored this mood.

What lay behind so striking a difference between the attitude of the Japanese toward their postwar sufferings and that of the Germans? No doubt the traditional acceptance of adversity by the Japanese had much to do with it. But what was that acceptance grounded in? "The law of karmic retribution," Japanese acquaintances told me. This notion of a law of cause and effect operating on the moral plane aroused my interest because it contrasted sharply with the self-justifications so often heard in Germany. In Japan it was not uncommon, for example, to hear of such statements in Japanese newspapers and conversation as, "Because we Japanese have inflicted so much pain on others, we are now reaping the painful harvest." I asked Japanese acquaintances where I could learn more about karma. I was told, "It is one of the cornerstones of Buddhism, so you need to study Buddhism to understand it."

"Who can you recommend as a teacher?"

"Dr. D. T. Suzuki. He is an authority on Buddhism and also speaks English."

Suzuki, it turned out, was living in the compound of a large Zen monastery in Kamakura. I went to visit the renowned philosopher. Having read the romantic novels *Lost Horizon* and *The Razor's Edge,* I expected to be greeted by a sage with long white hair and beard, flowing robes, and crooked walking stick. Instead I came upon a short, clean-shaven, almost bald Japanese who looked for all the world like an editor. His book-lined study, the visor shading his eyes, and his one-finger typing at an old Underwood all strengthened this impression.

Suzuki's informal talks on Buddhist philosophy were over my head. What brought me back again and again to his simple lodging was the desire not to fathom his recondite lectures, or even to learn more about karma, but to experience the deep serenity that seemed to radiate from the giant cryptomaria trees, the temple buildings, the faces of the monks and laymen, from the very earth itself. It was the memory of all this that helped draw me back to Japan five years later to enter a Zen monastery.

Except for the judgment of the court, the Tokyo Class A trials were over. Rather than sit around waiting for the court's verdict, I obtained three weeks' leave for a long-hoped-for visit to China.

When I arrived there early in 1948, the condition of the Chinese was wretched in the extreme. Corruption was widespread and inflation so severe that it required a small suitcaseful of paper money to fly from Shanghai to Peking. The eight-year occupation by the Japanese Army, the Soviet invasion and subsequent fighting, and the continuing struggle for power between the armies of Chiang Kai-shek and Mao Tse-tung had reduced the lot of the people to want and misery.

Although my trip to China was not motivated by a conscious desire to learn more about Buddhism, the misery and despair I encountered there forced me to reflect on what I had read was a fundamental teaching of the Buddha: that life is a bitter sea of suffering. On another level, my nascent interest in Buddhism was given a boost by the temples I saw in Peking, with their giant buddhas and bodhisattvas—whose significance I could hardly guess then—and by the unique culture of the Chinese as revealed in the many fascinating antiquities and incomparable palaces of this fabled city of exotic beauty.

Upon my return to the United States it was impossible to settle down again to the daily routine of life and work in a small Connecticut town. Hundreds of impressions and unresolved thoughts were hanging in the backyard of my mind, like so much wash that needed to be dried and sorted out. My vacuous life no longer had meaning, yet there was no other to take its place. "Suspended between two worlds, one dead, the other powerless to be born"—this described my condition perfectly. To shake myself off this dead center, I began going to New York on weekends to investigate the Asian religions. Since I knew of no reputable teachers of Zen or Buddhism in general in New York City, I began attending meetings of the Vedanta Society; for a while the Baha'i teachings also attracted me.

Then my interest began to wane. Too much emphasis was placed on reading and doctrinal study and not enough, it seemed to me, on the meditation I sorely needed. In addition to this, there were the same presumptuous statements as in the sermons of the ministers and rabbis: "God is good," "God is almighty," "God is . . ." Many years later, after having gained some Understanding, I knew that God is neither good nor almighty nor anything else. In fact, God isn't even God.

In 1950 Dr. Suzuki came to America to ignite the fuse that was later to touch off the "Zen boom." At Columbia University, where he taught a late-afternoon class in the philosophy of Zen Buddhism, scores of painters, composers, poets, psychiatrists, philosophy professors, and others crowded into his classroom. I was among them. My acquaintance with Dr. Suzuki dating back to Japan and my more-than-dilettantish interest in Zen earned me a place among the small hard-core group that loyally sat in attendance wherever he delivered a formal lecture or talk. The "yen for Zen" was then raging in New York, largely fueled by Suzuki's writings. Hardly a cocktail party was given at which some Zen *aficionado* did not spout his latest self-devised koan.

Suzuki's yeasty presence was a ferment in the spiritual-intellectual life of New York in the early fifties. But he was a *sensei* (scholar-teacher), not a Zen master, and he could not "teach the law with a lion's roar." Still, considering that he was in his early eighties at the time, his accomplishments are remarkable. Almost single-handedly he ushered in the first, intellectual phase in the Zenning of America.

My study of Zen philosophy was not baking bread. True, my intellectual horizons had been expanded, but with this increased knowledge came no greater serenity. In fact, my restlessness, irritability, and inner dissatisfaction had worsened, and now the affliction of pride was added—was I not one of the Zen *cognoscenti*, an apostle of Suzuki's? Why had I not acted on my growing feeling that meditation, not philosophy, was what I needed most?

Dr. Suzuki's arcane lectures, so tantalizing to the intellect, and the provocative after-class discussions with artists, writers, and psychiatrists had repressed this deeper need. The ache could be ignored no longer, however, and it was this that impelled me to seek an enlightened Zen master. But where to find him? Inquiries disclosed that there were no Zen masters in the United States. So it was back to Japan, a prospect both pleasant and dreaded. Dreaded because it was clear that my Zen play was over and that I must now begin the serious, hard work of Zen training if I truly wanted to transform my life.

After several months agonizing over this prospect, I gave up my work, disposed of my belongings, and set sail for Japan, determined not to return until I became enlightened.

One does not enter the same stream twice, and the Japan of 1953 was not the one I had left. The Occupation was over and a new Japan was emerging; without the security of the United States Government's presence it felt cold and alien. The few introductions I was armed with, however, gave me confidence that I would be accepted into a monastery even though I was over forty and could speak barely a word of Japanese. Yet two masters turned me down because of the inadequacy of my spoken Japanese. "But isn't Zen a teaching without reliance on words and letters?" I protested. The question evoked indulgent smiles. "You need words and letters to get beyond words and letters" was in effect the response of each.

My discouragement at these rejections was so great that I spent several weeks in Kyoto retracing my steps through the antique shops I had known during the Occupation; here at least were friendly merchants and familiar territory. I even seriously considered returning to America, and would have done so had I not burned all my bridges behind me. At this low point I met an American professor in Kyoto, a Fulbright exchange scholar who was also interested in Zen training, and together we knocked on more monastery gates—but to no avail. Having no more names of Zen masters, we then called on several scholars and religious leaders of the Pure Land sect. Once when we were talking about enlightenment with a leader of this sect, he suddenly pointed to me and said, "You will achieve satori if you work hard, because your karma is ripe for it. But I don't think that you," pointing to the professor, "are yet ready for it." This statement naturally upset my friend, but it brought me the up-surge of spirit I needed. Eventually, through a series of fortuitous karmic circumstances, I came to the "Monastery for Awakening the Bodhi-mind" (Hosshin-ji) and began serious Zen training.

I remained here in training for almost three years,[41] and then, because of failing health exacerbated by the austere and tense atmosphere and the poor diet, was compelled to leave. On the advice of Soen-roshi, my adviser, I became a disciple of Yasutani-roshi, a dharma successor of Haradi-roshi. Although an ordained master, he did not have a monastery, since all his disciples were laymen and women. Thus I was able to live in quarters of my own. Thanks to his excellent guidance, my Mind's eye was opened to some extent. He ordained me after I had been with him for five years, and I remained his disciple for another five.

On a ten-month pilgrimage to Southeast Asia in 1958 I de-cided, in a last-minute change of plans, to visit the Sri Aurobindo Ashram in Pondicherry, India. There I met a Canadian woman, a serious aspirant, who told me of her admiration for Zen and her dissatisfaction with the haphazard meditation of the ashram and its strong emphasis on reading and study. Because of her interest in Zen and my interest in her, I urged her to go to Japan for Zen training, and she did so. After she had been in Japan for some six months we were married in a Buddhist cere-mony. Our marriage produced one child, a daughter. But my wife's karma with India had not been exhausted and eventually it drew her back to the Hindu tradition and to the city of Toronto, where she became the leader of a spiritual group under an Indian teacher. As for our daughter, we like to believe she has, so to speak, the best of two worlds.

In 1965, thirteen years after I had gone to Japan to train in Zen, a strong longing developed in me to return to my own country. It wasn't simply that my teacher was traveling exten-sively in Europe and the United States and I therefore could have no contact with him. More, it was the feeling that I had been in Japan too long for one who had no intention of making it his permanent home. I had grown stale and needed to renew myself through daily contact with the sights and sounds, the forms and customs of Western society. Enlightened or not, every man is to a large extent hostage to the cultural milieu in which he is raised, and he cannot deny this relationship forever without doing violence to his spirit.

My intuitions that it was time to return to America coincided with invitations from several spiritual groups in the United States to establish Zen centers in their cities. After a few exploratory visits I settled in Rochester, an area in western New York where the rugged winters drive one inward, and where so many religions have arisen in the past.

My joy at being back in my own country was tempered by the realization that it would not be easy to adapt Eastern Zen to our Western society; the middle way had to be found between a Zen stripped of its essentials and a Zen barnacled with foreign cultural encrustations. I recalled what the former chief abbot of one of the large Soto Zen monasteries in Japan, had written: that when Dogen brought the Zen teachings from China to Japan they were slow to take hold because for Dogen only Chinese Zen was correct, and the people felt that a foreign religion was being forced upon them. It was only when another master, a century later, discarded the Chinese forms and Japanized Zen that it spread rapidly throughout the country.

It has also been pointed out by social anthropologists that every culture takes out of a new religion only what it can assimilate into its own mores and traditions, and that no people have accepted and practiced a new religion in the form in which it was offered them by teachers from an alien culture. The process of assimilation is subject at every stage to modifying influences growing out of the cultural needs of a particular society.

That the Buddhism of Japan is a unique expression of the cultural, historical, and climatic needs of the people of that country was brought home to me with great force when I went to Southeast Asia on my pilgrimage. In the ashrams of India and the meditation centers of Sri Lanka and Burma I learned why Japanese Buddhism had to be different from that practiced in those countries. Just as the Buddha figures of Sri Lanka, India, and Burma reflected the facial features of those countries' inhabitants, so the expression of the Buddha's dharma reflected the cultures of each of these societies. My experiences in Southeast Asia enabled me to put Japanese Buddhism in its proper perspective and to see that the Buddha's dharma was flexible enough to accommodate itself to widely differing cultures and to develop according to the spiritual climate prevailing wherever it is introduced.

What is needed to assimilate Zen Buddhism into Western modes of thinking and feeling? English chanting versions of basic sutras, distinctive Western dress permitting easy crossing of the legs for zazen, Western-sounding Buddhist names for those who became ordained or took the precepts, and ceremonies, forms, and rituals that are in accord with our Western traditions. When I proposed to my teacher, who was then in the United States, that our Center make an English translation of the Heart of Perfect Wisdom, chanted daily in Zen centers everywhere, to replace the Japanese version we were chanting, he objected strongly. The Japanese version had evolved from centuries of chanting, he said; it was fluent and could be easily learned; the meaning of the words was secondary. In short, there was no need for an English version. Why then, I wondered, did the Japanese, the Chinese, the Koreans, and the Tibetans each chant this sutra not in a foreign tongue but in their own?

My teacher took an equally dim view of my other proposals. There was no way I could communicate to him my visceral reaction to the outlandish sights I had seen at a number of spiritual centers in the United States: Americans with a Chinese teacher dressed as though they were refugees from mainland China; those with a Japanese sensei or roshi looking like samurai, and students of a guru from India like fakirs. And why when Japanese Zen students received Japanese Buddhist names were not Americans in their own country given Western-sounding Buddhist names?

If Zen was not to be looked upon in the West as a teaching and practice suitable only for Asians, it was imperative, I felt, that the process of filtering it through the idiom of our Western culture begin at once. This meant discarding many ancient Japanese forms and devising new Western ones. But how to distinguish the substance from the accidentals? My thirteen years' training in Japan would, I believed, preserve me from throwing out the baby with the bath water.

Because of my teacher's opposition to this Westernizing of Zen, and for other reasons, it became increasingly difficult for me to continue as his disciple, and I asked leave to withdraw. It was a painful step, for the relation between a master and his disciple is an intimate one, closer in some respects than the parent-child relationship. But the break was inevitable. Whatever pain I may have caused my master Yasutani-roshi I deeply regret. I owe him and my other masters a debt of gratitude that is immeasurable. Indeed, the only way such an obligation can be requited is for me to faithfully pass on to others the essence of the teaching I was privileged to receive. I can only hope that during the past thirteen years I have in some measure accomplished this and thus begun to repay their benevolence.

NOTES /

1 This illustrious event is regarded in Zen as the first direct transmission, "outside the sutras, without reliance on words and letters," of the dharma. In holding up the lotus flower the Buddha was revealing the very heart of his teaching, and Maha-kashyapa, by smiling back in acknowledgment, became the first successor in a long line of transmission from master to disciple that continues today. This incident became the sixth koan in Mumon's *The Gateless Barrier.*

2 For more detailed information about these activities of Japanese corporations, see "The Education of a Japanese Banker" by Thomas Rohlen in *Human Nature* magazine, January 1978.

3 Further comments on the Sixth Patriarch's awakening appear on pp. 130–31.

4 It is not unheard of to have more than one teacher, for there are valid reasons for changing teachers. The writer, too, had more than one. My first master was Nakagawa-roshi, abbot of Ryutaku Monastery, with whom I stayed for several months. For various reasons he felt that Harada-roshi, abbot of Hosshin Monastery, would be a better teacher for me and he took me to his monastery, where I remained

for almost three years. Harada-roshi's assistant, Sessui-roshi, was also a teacher to me. When my health no longer permitted me to remain at this monastery, which was located in the coldest region of Japan, Nakagawa-roshi, who was more or less my adviser, recommended that I practice under Yasutani-roshi, a dharma-heir of Harada-roshi. I remained as a disciple with Yasutani-roshi for some ten years. His assistant and dharma-heir, Yamada Koun-roshi, acted as my teacher when Yasutani-roshi was not in Japan.

5 For more information about *The Gateless Barrier*, see pp. 280–81.

6 See the revised edition of *The Three Pillars of Zen* for questions and answers, with sketches, relating to posture problems and how to eliminate unnecessary discomfort and pain.

7 One of the great advantages of the half- or full-lotus sitting posture is that when the hands and feet are brought together in one point with the hands resting on the heels of the feet, pulse, blood pressure, metabolism, and other vital functions are at their quietest. It should be noted, however, that though these physiological functions are greatly quieted, the Zen meditator does not sink into a trance state, unresponsive to the world around him. Rather, electroencephalographic studies have shown that one doing concentrated zazen responds immediately to external stimuli and, in fact, responds each time the same stimulus is repeated, whereas most people lose awareness of such repeated stimuli. Moreover, while the response appears each time on the EEG of one doing zazen, it also very quickly disappears. It can be said, then, that the person seriously practicing Zen meditation is fully aware of what is happening in the world around him yet does not cling to this awareness.

These EEG results with Zen meditators contrast sharply with those found among people involved in other disciplines. In Yoga meditation, for example, it was shown that the practitioner is, in a sense, tuned-out from the world around him, and does not respond at all to external stimuli. See *Altered States of Consciousness*, ed. Charles Tart (New York: John Wiley & Sons, Inc., 1969), pp. 489–506, hardcover.

8 *The Abhidharmakosa shastra* and *The Vijnaptimatrasiddi shastra.*

9 The full chanting version of the Heart sutra in English appears on p. 180.

10 This chart and the next are adapted from Yasutani-roshi's booklet *Eight Beliefs in Buddhism*, translated by Eido Tai Shimano.

11 For more information about Bodhidharma, see pp. 109–10.

[12] A list of the ten cardinal precepts of Buddhism appears on p. 244.

[13] Te Shan Hsuan Chien (J., Tokusan Senkan, 780–865), an outstanding Chinese T'ang master. Te Shan had been a noted scholar of the Diamond sutra, but abandoned his academic studies entirely after attaining enlightenment when his master suddenly blew out a candle.

[14] For more information about *The Blue Rock Record*, see pp. 280–82.

[15] Mu Chou (J., Bokuju, 780?–877?), who became teacher to Yun Men, having trained as a disciple of Huang Po.

[16] "What Is the Sound of One Hand?" is one of the initial, or "breakthrough," koans used in Zen. It was devised by Japanese Zen master Hakuin.

[17] An in-depth commentary on the koan "Mu" by Yasutani-roshi appears in *The Three Pillars of Zen*.

[18] For a full discussion of the Bodhisattva of Compassion (J., Kannon), see the dialogue beginning on p. 200.

[19] A full English translation of *Affirming Faith in Mind* appears on p. 184.

[20] For more information about Hakuin, see p. 181.

[21] This figure, combining as it does the infinite with the finite, is an example of the way in which Buddhist texts convey immeasureable dimensions of time and space without lapsing into abstract terminology. In the Buddhist view of the universe one thousand solar systems make up what is called one small universe, one thousand small universes comprise one middle universe, and one thousand middle universes make one—and only one—large universe. In Buddhist cosmology time, too, is seen as boundless, but again we are given "handles," through vivid and concrete descriptions, by which to grasp in some measure this infinitude. Thus a *kalpa*, or world cycle of time, is described as the time it would take one to empty a huge bowl of poppy seeds, forty cubic miles in size, by taking out just one poppy seed every three years. Note by contrast how the word "aeon" is defined in the dictionary: "an indefinitely long period of time."

[22] A reference to Hui K'e (J., Eka), who cut off his hand and offered it to Bodhidharma as a sign of his sincerity. He later became the second patriarch of Zen. See also p. 115.

[23] For an account of a kensho that occurred after a sesshin had formally ended, see p. 145.

[24] In Buddhism one of the six realms (q.v.) of unenlightened existence is that of hungry ghosts *(pretas)*, or beings who through their greed have condemned themselves to a life of craving and unfulfillment.

[25] This koan, "How Do You Step Forward from the Top of a Hundred-foot Pole?" is No. 46 in *The Gateless Barrier*. The pole here stands for full enlightenment.

[26] For further discussion of the significance of such rites, see pp. 191–96.

[27] Skt., *Prajna Paramita Hridaya*.

[28] "Here" refers to the level of transcendental wisdom.

[29] "Thought": literally, "perceptions."

[30] Included in the blanket term "choice" are mental dispositions, tendencies, impulses, volitions, etc.

[31] "Adulterated mass-appeal Zen" refers to the practice of combining the koan with the reciting of the Pure Land formula, or *nembutsu:* "I put my trust in the Buddha Amida."

[32] Ch., *Hsin Hsin Ming*.

[33] For an extended discussion of the rebirth process, see dialogue 25, pp. 65–73.

[34] G. I. Gurdjieff (1870–1950): an enigmatic spiritual teacher born in Russia and purported to have developed his methods and powers through contact with a variety of traditions in the Near and Far East. He founded the Institute for the Harmonious Development of Man in Paris, and had many followers in his day.

[35] See the commentary on "A Man up a Tree," p. 119.

[36] Quoted in Trevor Legget's *The Tiger's Cave*, p. 164.

[37] See "Six Worlds" in the Glossary.

[38] See also the population figures given by World Bank President Robert S. McNamara in "How to Defuse the Population Bomb," *Time*, October 24, 1977.

[39] Thich Nhat Hanh is a Vietnamese Zen monk, author, and poet, and one of the leading spokesmen of the Vietnamese Buddhist peace movement.

[40] Gempo Yamamoto, former abbot of Ryutaku Monastery in Mishima, Japan, who died in June 1961.

[41] For an account of the author's experiences in this and another Zen monastery in Japan, see his *The Three Pillars of Zen*.

ANNOTATED READING LIST /

(See also dialogue No. 11, "To Read or Not to Read")

This select list does not pretend to be all-inclusive. The emphasis, naturally, is on books of the Mahayana branch of Buddhism, and particularly those in the Zen tradition, that I have found to be inspiring and instructive. A few books in this category have been excluded because they are no longer in print, and others, relating to Buddhism in general, have been omitted in order to keep the list within manageable proportions.

In addition to *The Three Pillars of Zen* (Boston: Beacon Press, 1967, 364 pp., paperback; revised and expanded paperback edition to be published by Doubleday & Company, Inc.) and *The Wheel of Death* (New York: Harper & Row, 1971 and 1974), 110 pp., hardcover and paperback), the following books, listed alphabetically, are recommended. Sutras are listed separately at the end.

The Autobiography of Chinese Zen Master Hsu Yun, tr. Charles Luk (Rochester, N.Y.: Empty Cloud Press, 1974), 120 pp., paperback
    This small-press edition of the life of Hsu Yun is a remarkable chronicle of unremitting service to the dharma by one of the most illustrious of contemporary Chinese Zen masters. A man of deep

humility and boundless energy, Hsu Yun lived to a ripe old age, 119. Though sometimes rambling, this moving account of his long lifetime of devotion is recommended reading for all interested in Zen.

The Awakening of Faith, tr. Yoshito S. Hakeda (New York: Columbia University Press, 1967 and 1974), 128 pp., hardcover and paperback
Yoshita S. Hakeda has, in his technically accurate, annotated presentation of this brilliant Mahayana classic, done us all a real service. *The Awakening of Faith* was written in the sixth century, and its explicitly stated purpose is to help men attain awakening and free themselves from the bonds of suffering. The strong sense of religious conviction and dedication to this goal, as well as the practical attitudes and teaching that permeate the work, make it potentially a very helpful reading experience, especially for the intellectually-minded person.

The Blue Cliff (Rock) Record—see KOAN COLLECTIONS

A Buddhist Bible, comp. Dwight Goddard (New York: E. P. Dutton, 1952), 677 pp., hardcover; (Boston: Beacon Press, 1970), 677 pp., paperback, with an Introduction by Huston Smith
Within the almost seven-hundred pages of *A Buddhist Bible* there is the richest selection of writings from the southern and northern schools of Buddhism (Hinayana-Theravada and Mahayana) to be found anywhere, notably generous portions of these sutras: the Diamond, the Surangama, the Lankavatara, the Platform (of the Sixth Patriarch), and the Prajna-paramita, plus the Life and Hymns of Milarepa and other inspiring texts. The English is at times turgid and the book as a whole is in need of an editing and index, but these are really minor shortcomings in a translation project of such huge proportions.

The Buddhist Experience: Sources and Interpretations, by Stephan Beyer (Encino, Calif.: Dickenson Publishing Co., 1974), 274 pp., paperback
A refreshingly lively and personal vision of the Buddhist experience seen through a collection of Beyer's own translations of traditional and often little-known Buddhist writings.

The Buddhist Teaching of Totality, tr. C. C. Chang (University Park, Pa.: Pennsylvania State University Press, 1971), 263 pp., hardcover
The Hwa Yen teachings are some of the most lofty in all of Buddhism, and in this conscientious philosophic work Professor Chang ably presents and explains the essence of the Hwa Yen vision. A

good sense of the completeness and depth of Buddhist experience, expression, and religious aspiration is conveyed here through Professor Chang's writings. Also included are brief excerpts from the Avatamsaka sutra, the main inspiration of the Hwa Yen teachings, which is not available elsewhere in English.

Buddhist Texts Through the Ages, ed. Edward Conze (New York: Philosophical Library, 1954), 322 pp., hardcover; (New York: Harper & Row, 1964), 322 pp., paperback
A wide-ranging, comprehensive collection of significant Buddhist writings from both the northern and southern schools of Buddhism, newly retranslated and, in some instances, first translated in the early 1950s from the original Pali, Sanskrit, Tibetan, Chinese, and Japanese.

The Buddhist Tradition in India, China, and Japan, ed. Wm. Theodore de Bary (New York: Modern Library, 1969), 417 pp., hardcover; (New York: Vintage, 1972), 417 pp., paperback
This collection of well-organized and well-edited source material conveys a good sense of Buddhism as a living, growing tradition, sketching its emphasis, direction, and movement through twenty-five hundred years. In the course of doing so it provides brief yet nourishing biographical fare on Shakyamuni Buddha, Lin Chi (Rinzai), Dogen, Hakuin, and other great masters, and presents selections from their teachings as well.

Ch'an and Zen Teachings: First Series, tr. and ed. Charles Luk (Boulder, Colo.: Shambhala, 1970), 255 pp., paperback
Perhaps the strongest of Mr. Luk's works, the first half of this book comprises a series of Zen talks by the great contemporary Chinese master Hsu Yun. The commentaries, presented during the course of a one-week sesshin that he conducted in Shanghai in 1953, are stirring expressions of his unshakeable Zen spirit. They more than overcome the disconcerting awkwardness of the translation.

Dropping Ashes on the Buddha, comp. and ed. Stephen Mitchell (New York: Grove Press, 1976), 232 pp., paperback
This new work presents the teachings of the Ven. Seung Sahn, a Korean Zen roshi now residing in the United States. Readers will probably find the traditional mondo and Zen anecdotes, as well as Seung Sahn's own lively responses to his students' basic doubts, confusions, and questions to be pertinent and valuable.

The Essence of Buddhism, by John Walters (New York: Apollo Editions, 1964), 164 pp., paperback

> A practical, down-to-earth, and distinctly modern treatment of Buddhism seen in the light of the Theravadin teachings. The author, a British journalist who converted to Buddhism in the course of his travels in Thailand, includes a good brief account of the Buddha's life as well as straightforward discussions of the Four Noble Truths and the Eightfold Path. Though the chapter on meditation is a bit oversimplified, this work still provides a sound introduction for persons relatively unfamiliar with the Buddha and his teachings.

Foundations of Tibetan Mysticism, by Lama Govinda (New York: E. P. Dutton, 1960), 370 pp., hardcover; (New York: Samuel Weiser, Inc., 1973), 311 pp., paperback

> Here is an "inside" elucidation of the doctrines of tantric Buddhism. It is a work done with understanding and clarity of style by Lama Govinda, a German-born scholar-monk who has spent many years in India. One might also add that *Foundations of Tibetan Mysticism* contains one of the finest expositions in print of the Bodhisattva Ideal, which is the very heart of living Buddhism.

The Golden Age of Zen, by John Wu (Republic of China: United Publishing Center), 332 pp., paperback

> This book is a veritable treasure house of Zen mondo, teachings, writings, and dharma episodes drawn from the vigorous lives of those spiritual geniuses, the early Chinese Zen masters. Starting with Bodhidharma, the First Patriarch of Zen in China, the book proceeds through Hui Neng, the Sixth Patriarch, and on to the "golden age" of the T'ang era masters. There is a wealth of strong, sparkling Zen material here—but be warned! Wu, a pious Catholic, has obviously had no Zen training, and so while the translated material is excellent, his comments often leave much to be desired.

KOAN COLLECTIONS: *The Gateless Barrier* (J., *Mumonkan;* Ch., *Wu Men Kuan*) and *The Blue Rock (Cliff) Record* (J., *Hekiganroku;* Ch., *Pi Yen Lu*)

> *Zen Comments on the Mumonkan,* by Zenkei Shibayama (New York: Harper & Row, 1974), 361 pp. hardcover; (New York: New American Library, 1975), 366 pp., paperback; *Two Zen Classics: Mumonkan and Hekiganroku,* trans. with Notes by Katsuki Sekida, ed. A. V. Grimstone (New York: Weatherhill, 1977), 413 pp., hardcover and paperback; *The Blue Cliff Record,* tr. Thomas and J. C. Cleary (Boulder, Colo.: Shambhala, 1977), 3 vols., 656 pp., paperback.
>
> *The Gateless Barrier* and *The Blue Rock Record* are the two most

widely used books of koans in Zen training. *The Gateless Barrier* consists of forty-eight koans—cases or anecdotes that express the free workings of the masters' enlightened minds—compiled and arranged (with accompanying comments and verses) by Zen master Wu Men (J., Mumon) in the year 1229. Each of the one hundred cases of *The Blue Rock Record* has a short Introduction, or pointer, by Zen master Yuan Wu (J., Engo) and a comment in verse by Chinese Zen master Hsueh Tou (J., Setcho), who compiled the book in the eleventh century.

Both of these works, but especially *The Blue Rock Record,* are subtle and profound, demanding from a translator not only a precise knowledge of the Zen idiom of ancient Chinese but koan training under a qualified roshi as well. Shibayama-roshi, recently deceased, was one of Japan's most respected contemporary masters, and Katsuki Sekida, a layman, has disciplined himself in Zen for many years under more than one roshi.

Of the three texts, *Zen Comments on the Mumonkan* is the most complete. Each case, comment, and verse of Mumon is accompanied by a teisho (Zen commentary) by Shibayama-roshi. In addition to bringing alive the spirit and drama of the koan in contemporary idiom, these teisho are solidly aimed at encouraging serious Zen practice and religious awakening. Lacking in many of them, though, is a certain "muscle" or directness—a reflection, it would appear, of this statement in Shibayama-roshi's Introduction: "Although I use the term 'teisho' in English for European and American students, it is naturally different in its significance and purpose from the traditional teisho I give to the monks in my monastery in Japan." What a pity we could not have had the authentic rather than the watered-down version. Still, this is a clear translation and a fine book, useful to both the general reader as well as the more accomplished Zen student.

Some of the translations and commentary notes in *Two Zen Classics* strike this reviewer as arbitrary, and unfortunately many of Mr. Sekida's comments are too explanatory and thus tend to impair the value of the koans as exercises for Zen students. But on the whole the book is a product of herculean labors, wrought with dedication and understanding. The publisher has provided both of these classic texts in one volume at a fair price.

The Blue Cliff Record is the first English translation from Chinese sources of this fundamental Zen text, and as such is especially welcome. The authors have included commentaries by Zen master Yuan Wu on each case and each verse, but the value of these commentaries is more apparent than real. Since they are couched in the ancient Chinese idiom and highly condensed, only the advanced Zen student will get much out of them. But then this work was never intended for beginners in Zen.

Lin Chi (J., Rinzai)
The Record of Lin-chi, tr. from the Chinese by Ruth F. Sasaki and others (Kyoto, Japan: Institute for Zen Studies, 1975), 88 pp., plus 35 pp. of Chinese text, hardcover; *The Zen Teaching of Rinzai*, tr. from the Chinese by Irmgard Schloegl (Boulder, Colo.: Shambhala, 1976), 96 pp., paperback

Although the words of the illustrious Zen master Lin Chi have been widely read for centuries in the East, only a limited number of his sayings have been available in English. Here for the first time in English is a complete translation of the record of his teaching, in two distinct translations.

The translation by Ms. Schloegl may be described as somewhat exploratory; still, it is an accessible work written in nontechnical language and gives one a good sense of Rinzai's direct and wholehearted style.

Ruth Sasaki's work is a more finished presentation, having undergone years of careful revision and polishing. As such, it seems more adequately to convey Lin Chi's own unique personality and spirit. However, as the English portion of the text is well under a hundred pages and the book is available only in a relatively expensive hardcover edition, the economy-minded may still want to consider Ms. Schloegl's paperback work as a practical and satisfactory alternative.

Mumonkan: see KOAN COLLECTION

Namu Dai Bosa, ed. Louis Nordstrom (New York: Theatre Arts Books, 1976), 262 pp., hardcover and paperback

This handsome and well-edited work celebrates the founding of International Dai Bosatsu Kongo-ji—the newly completed country training center affiliated with the New York Zendo, now under the direction of Shimano Eido-roshi. The particular transmission of Zen manifested in the flowering of the New York Zendo and Dai Bosatsu Kongo-ji is presented here with grace, dignity, and reverence for the dharma.

One Robe, One Bowl, tr. and ed. by John Stevens (New York: Weatherhill, 1977), 85 pp., hardcover

In Japan, the poetry of Ryokan, a nineteenth-century Zen monk, is well known and, like the memory of Ryokan himself, respected and loved. This new book is an excellent presentation of Ryokan's writings, which give expression to a heart of compassion, a heart in touch with the sensitivities of children, the living rhythms of nature, and the day-to-day condition of the ordinary laboring man. This is a nourishing and gentle work that should find a wide audience among practicers of Zen as well as the general public.

The Practice of Zen, by C. C. Chang (New York: Harper & Brothers, and London, Rider & Co., 1959), 199 pp., hardcover; (New York: Perennial Library [Harper & Row], 1970), 254 pp., paperback

The value of this book lies chiefly in the instructive discourses of the Chinese Zen masters and their stirring biographies, carefully selected and ably translated. There is enough excellent material here to inspire anyone interested in the exertions and realizations of some great Zen figures.

A Primer of Soto Zen, by Reiho Masunaga (Honolulu: East-West Center Press, 1971), 119 pp., hardcover; (Honolulu: University of Hawaii Press, 1975), 119 pp., paperback

A Primer of Soto Zen presents some of the informal talks of the great Zen patriarch Dogen, the master credited with founding the Soto Sect of Zen in Japan and who is considered one of the most seminal minds in all of Japanese Buddhism. The talks were recorded by Dogen's chief disciple and dharma successor, Koun Eijo. Unfortunately the book lacks both an index and a meaningful table of contents, but for sheer concentration on the essentials of true practice, this collection of brief but pithy encouragement talks is hard to match.

The Record of Lin-chi, tr. from the Chinese by Ruth F. Sasaki and others—see Lin Chi

Shobogenzo
Shobogenzo, tr. Kosen Nishiyama and John Stevens, Volumes I and II of three. (Sendai, Japan: Daihokkaikaku, 1975), Vol. I, 165 pp., hardcover; (Tokyo, Japan: Nakayama Shobo, 1977), Vol. II, 205 pp., hardcover; *Zen Master Dogen,* by Yuho Yokoi with Daizen Victoria (New York: Weatherhill, 1976), 217 pp., hardcover and paperback

Zen master Dogen's monumental Shobogenzo is a uniquely profound work. Simultaneously practical and abstruse, lucid and subtle, it defies all limited viewpoints, rising above pedestrian views like a towering mountain. The projected three-volume series by Nishiyama and Stevens of all ninety-five fascicles of *Shobogenzo* is a work particularly difficult to appraise. Given the special nature of the work, the general adequacy of the translation leaves little room for minor criticisms. The flaw in this otherwise inspiring and valuable effort is its price. At twenty dollars a volume few of even those with a serious interest in Zen will be able to afford it.

Zen Master Dogen is the first appearance in book form of selections from Shobogenzo, and it gives one at least an introductory sense of the uniquely penetrating quality of Dogen's Zen. The deeply Buddhistic awareness and profound veneration of the Three Jewels—buddha, dharma, and sangha—here, as in other of Dogen's writings, stand out in bold relief, contributing to the value of this work for Zen students.

The Three Jewels, by Bhikshu Sangharakshita (Garden City, N.Y.: Anchor Press/Doubleday, 1970), 269 pp., paperback

Here is an authoritative introduction to modern Buddhism as well as to the twenty-five-hundred-year-old tradition of religious experience that underlies its present cultural and artistic forms. The author, a British-born monk-scholar of some twenty years' practice who has lived and traveled extensively throughout India, speaks both as an informed world citizen and an ardent Buddhist. Despite occasional lapses of style, perhaps simply the outcome of trying to cover a vast subject in a short book, it is a decidedly helpful and informative work.

To Forget the Self, by John Daishin Buksbazen, with photographs by John Daido Loori (Los Angeles: Zen Center of Los Angeles, 1977), 70 pp., paperback

This third volume in the Zen Writing Series is, as its subtitle suggests, a handbook on zazen. It moves gracefully from a brief account of the Buddha's own quest, on through clear presentations of Zen postures, breathing, and practices, to sesshin and daily life. Punctuated throughout by sensitive photographs, *To Forget the Self* is a fine addition to the works available on American Zen.

Two Zen Classics: Mumonkan and Hekiganroku—See KOAN COLLECTIONS

The Wheel of Life, by John Blofeld (London: Rider & Co., 1959), 263 pp., hardcover; (Boulder, Colo.: Shambhala, 1972), 291 pp., paperback

John Blofeld's spiritual autobiography as a Western Buddhist makes for fascinating reading, tracing as it does his life, sojourns, and travels in China, Mongolia, India, Thailand, and Tibet. Marked by many true marvels and haunting mysteries of the spirit, it is a religious odyssey that includes as well the lapses, failure, and disappointments encountered by the author. In the end it is the simple, compelling honesty with which his experiences, both inner and outer, are related, grounded as they are in a sincere respect for spiritual values and devotion to the dharma, which gives the entire narrative a significance for anyone interested in Buddhism today.

Zen and Creative Management, by Albert Low (Garden City, N.Y.: Anchor Press/Doubleday, 1976), 255 pp., paperback
This brilliant work explores with both persistence and insight the central conflicts of human existence as expressed in the world of twentieth-century management, and their resolution in Zen. Albert Low is a serious student of Zen with many years of practical experience in both management concerns and actual Zen training. His book should prove to be of value to one's growth at either societal or individual levels.

Zen Comments on the Mumonkan—See KOAN COLLECTIONS

Zen Keys, by Thich Nhat Hanh, with an Introduction by Philip Kapleau (Garden City, N.Y.: Anchor Press/Doubleday, 1974), 185 pp., paperback
Zen Keys stands out as an aware and scholarly presentation of traditional Asian Zen and its vital role in our modern world. The author is a Zen monk who has been a leading spokesman of the Vietnamese Buddhist peace movement for the past fifteen years. His Buddhism is actively engaged in the mainstream of twentieth-century life and has earned the respect of persons throughout the East and the West.

The Zen Master Hakuin: Selected Writings, tr. Philip Yampolsky (New York: Columbia University Press, 1971), 253 pp., hardcover
This edition of the vigorous, direct, and deeply human writings of Hakuin, noted Zen master, painter, calligrapher, and sculptor of eighteenth-century Japan, surely comprises one of the most central and compelling of all Zen works available in the United States today. A book of constant, energetic encouragement, Hakuin's clarion call to a life af active zazen still rings loud and clear.

Zen Mind, Beginners Mind, by Shunryu Suzuki (New York: Weatherhill, 1970 and 1973), 138 pp., hardcover and paperback
The late Shunryu Suzuki was the founder and, until his death in December 1971, abbot of the Zen Center, San Francisco and Carmel Valley. This short volume, which grew out of a series of informal talks he gave to a group of his students over a period of several

years, focuses on those very "attitudes and understanding," as the Introduction puts it, that "make Zen practice possible." A work of general interest and encouragement, the teachings of the Soto tradition of Zen are emphasized throughout.

The Zen Teaching of Huang Po on the Transmission of Mind, tr. John Blofeld (New York: Rider & Co., 1958), 136 pp., hardcover; (New York: Grove Press, 1958), 136 pp., paperback

The Zen Teaching of Hui Hai on Sudden Illumination, tr. John Blofeld (London: Rider & Co., 1962), 160 pp., hardcover; (New York: Samuel Weiser, Inc., 1972), 160 pp., paperback
> *The Zen Teaching of Huang Po* and *The Zen Teaching of Hui Hai* are first-rate presentations of the profound and direct teachings (dialogues and dharma talks) of two great T'ang era Zen masters, Hui Hai (or Hyakujo in Japanese) and Huang Po (Obaku). These lively, lucent works have style and distinction—both are gems.

The Zen Teaching of Rinzai, tr. from the Chinese by Irmgard Schloegl—see Lin Chi.

Zen Training, by Katsuki Sekida (New York: Weatherhill, 1975), 258 pp., hardcover
> This book is a valuable work. Though physiologically technical, it still remains personal and practical, focusing on the actual experience of zazen practice. Ultimately, however, it is the concentrated and serious spirit of the book that most tellingly establishes its value to those interested in Zen. And this is understandably so, for the author has been an ardent and well regarded practitioner of Zen for over fifty years.

SUTRAS

The Dhammapada, tr. P. Lal (New York: Farrar Straus & Giroux, 1967), 184 pp., paperback
> This modern edition of *The Dhammapada,* a series of 423 verses on the "Way of Dharma" attributed to the Buddha himself, is particularly noteworthy for the vitality, clarity, and felicity of its expression. Valuable too is the brief but well-done impressionistic Introduction, "The Buddha: His Life and Teachings."

The Lotus sutra
The Lotus Sutra, tr. Senchu Murano (Tokyo: Nichiren-shu Headquarters, 1974), 371 pp., hardcover; *The Threefold Lotus Sutra,* tr. Bunno Kato,

Yoshiro Tamura, and Kojito Miyasaka (New York: Weatherhill/Kosei, 1975), 383 pp., paperback

In Dogen's view the Lotus sutra is the king of all sutras, and Hakuin, too, from evidence in his autobiography, felt a special affinity for this sutra of the Lotus Flower of the Wonderful Law. One of the last sutras delivered by the Buddha in his forty-five years of teaching, the Lotus sutra has particular relevance to our own times, bringing as it does a message of hope. As a vast cosmic drama embracing endless worlds, beings, and time, the Lotus sutra offers a revelation of the eternal presence of buddhas and bodhisattvas working without cease for the welfare of all beings, even in periods of greatest darkness and planetary confusion.

The Threefold Lotus Sutra renders into English the original poetic depth and richness for which the sutra has so long been esteemed in the East.

The language of the version by Senchu Murano, the most recent, is more direct and concise—that is, prosier—than that of the ornate Kato, et al. version, and for this reason may prove to be the more accessible for many people. On the other hand, some of the resonance and richness and uniquely Buddhist flavor of the sutra is sacrificed. Still, this translation is a commendable work and clearly the outcome of genuine spiritual dedication to the Lotus sutra, its message, and the task of translation itself.

The Platform sutra of the Sixth Patriarch
The Sixth Patriarch's Platform Sutra, tr. with Notes, by Philip Yampolsky (New York: Columbia University Press, 1967), 216 pp., hardcover; *The Sutra of the Sixth Patriarch on the Pristine Orthodox Dharma*, tr. Paul and George Fung (San Francisco: Buddha's Universal Church, 1964), 187 pp., hardcover

The Sixth Patriarch's Platform sutra is one of the most highly respected texts in Zen, presenting as it does the life and teachings of Hui Neng, Sixth Patriarch of Zen in China, thirty-third in the line of transmission from the Buddha himself.

The Fung and Fung translation appears in a handsome edition and is noteworthy for the care with which it brings this clear, insightful, and eminently down-to-earth sutra to life. To those seeking direct exposure to the heart-mind of the Sixth Patriarch himself, this translation is recommended.

Philip Yampolsky's more scholarly edition of this text is accurate and precise, containing more complete introductory material and notes. Though as a religious work it is perhaps not as moving as the Fung translation, it is probably the most careful and technically correct text available.

The Vimalakirti Nirdesa sutra
The Holy Teaching of Vimalakirti, tr. Robert A. F. Thurman (University Park, Pa.: Pennsylvania State University Press in co-operation with the Institute for Advanced Studies of World Religions, 1976), 166 pp., hardcover; *The Vimalakirti Nirdesa Sutra*, tr. and ed. Charles Luk (Boulder, Colo.: Shambhala, 1972), 157 pp., hardcover and paperback

To understand the traditional popularity of the Vimalakirti sutra as a Mahayana text, one need only look to its "hero," who is neither the Buddha nor a monk but a wealthy householder-bodhisattva. Vimalakirti was a family man living fully in, but not of, the world, and his spiritual stature is said to have been second only to that of the Buddha. The sutra's profundity, its lively spirit and humor, and its constant emphasis on the nondual nature of ultimate reality have long endeared it to followers of Zen.

The latest version of the Vimalakirti sutra is Robert Thurman's careful new translation, a work characterized by a sincere concern for language and the subtleties of linguistic connotation. Accompanied by an Introduction, an Epilogue, a complete Glossary, and Notes, it is a fine contribution to the growing collection of dharma works now available in English.

Charles Luk's earlier translation has been until now the only complete text available in English. The spirit of the sutra comes through clearly here, and as a pioneering accomplishment offers much for which we can be grateful. However, the translation itself, while adequate in a popular sense with its immediacy and easy, nontechnical style, falls far short of Thurman's more exacting effort. Thus while Luk's *The Vimalakirti Nirdesa Sutra* may serve as an initial, not misleading, and essentially inspiring introduction to this text, Thurman's work is recommended for those looking for a more direct, in-depth presentation of the sutra.

GLOSSARY /

In this section are brief definitions and explanations of Zen and other Buddhist terms, as well as proper names and words and phrases associated with Zen that are mentioned in the text but not defined therein. English and foreign words of more common usage that are being defined or explained appear in roman, while foreign words considered unfamiliar to most readers have been put in italics.

The names of Chinese masters, some of which appear Japanized and others in their original Chinese, are entered in the glossary as they appear in the text. When Japanized, the original Chinese follows in parentheses.

Sanskrit words and names are marked Skt.; Chinese, Ch.; and Japanese, J.

Baha'i: a religion founded by Baha'u'llah (1817–92), a Persian who taught that God is unknowable except through his manifestation, the prophet; that divine revelation is continuous and progressive; and that all beings are in essence one.

Bassui Tokusho (1327–87): a great Japanese Zen master who from boy-hood on struggled with the self-inquiry, "Who is the Master?" (that is, the source, or controlling force) until he attained full en-lightenment. (For his "Dharma Talk on One-mind" and letters to his disciples, as well as more biographical data, see the author's *The Three Pillars of Zen.*)

bodhisattva (Skt.): literally, "wisdom-being" or "-hero"; anyone who, having attained enlightenment, dedicates himself to helping others do the same. Originally bodhisattva referred to any of the most highly developed disciples of Shakyamuni Buddha or to a being in the final stage of enlightenment. In the Platform sutra the Sixth Patriarch says, "Bodhisattvas are compassionate thoughts made manifest." In Zen, anyone sincerely working on himself and for the sake of others is often called a bodhisattva.

brahma (Skt.): in Hinduism, Supreme Reality manifested as the lord of creation.

buddha: lit., "enlightened one," or anyone who has awakened in some measure to the true nature of existence. A fully perfected buddha is said to appear only once each world cycle. In our age this was Siddhartha Gautama, or Shakyamuni Buddha (563–483 B.C.), who "founded" Buddhism in India and is often referred to as "*the* Bud-dha." Inasmuch as the mind of a full buddha is illumined to an immeasureable degree and encompasses the infinity of all uni-verses, buddha also carries the meaning of ultimate truth, or abso-lute mind.

Buddha Hall: a hall used for large assemblies, usually spiritual functions other than formal zazen, which is done in the zendo. Ceremonies are held and formal talks given by the roshi in the Buddha Hall.

buddhahood: Self-realization. Initial awakening marks one's entrance into the first stage of buddhahood, but countless more lifetimes of discipline and exertion are required to reach the spiritual stature of a full buddha such as Shakyamuni.

chain of causation: also called the chain of dependent origination. Each link gives rise to the succeeding one: ignorance leads to action, action leads to consciousness, consciousness leads to name and form (mind and body), name and form lead to the six sense organs, the six sense organs lead to contact, contact leads to sensation, sensation leads to craving, craving leads to clinging, clinging leads to existence, existence leads to birth, and birth leads to old age and death, etc.

Chuang-tzu: a Chinese Taoist sage of the fourth century B.C.

dera (Skt.): lit., "one who shines"; a heavenly being. The deva realm is one of happiness and ease, the highest of the six realms of unenlightened existence. When a deva's good karma becomes exhausted, however, he/she/it falls to a lower, more painful existence.

dharma (Skt.): Derived from the Sanskrit root "dhri," dharma means (1) the *law* or principle that supports and governs the universe. This law holds that (2) all *phenomena*, which also are referred to as dharmas, are subject to the law of causation, appearing and disappearing according to causes and conditions. The universal applicability of this law gives us the meaning (3) ultimate *truth,* and (4) *the Buddha's teaching,* which is an explication of this truth and from which derives (5) *Buddhist doctrine.*

Diamond (Skt., *Vajracchedika*) sutra: This highly venerated Mahayana sutra takes its name from the unexcelled cutting power of diamond. As a text dealing largely with the Buddhist doctrine of emptiness, it is so profound as to cut away every trace of conceptual bondage.

Dogen Kigen (1200–53): considered the founder of the Soto school of Japanese Zen, though he himself disavowed such distinctions as "Soto," "Rinzai," or even "Zen." After eight years of koan training, Dogen at the age of twenty-three journeyed to China, where he attained full enlightenment before returning four years later to introduce Zen to his native Japan. His prime teaching method was *shikan-taza* ("just sitting"), and he placed great stress on the tenet that "practice and enlightenment are one" as well as on the necessity for "sustained exertion."

ego: In Buddhism ego refers to the notion of oneself as a fixed and discrete entity separate from other selves and from an "outside world." Thus a silently stubborn or self-deprecating person may be said to have as strong an ego as one who is, say, proud and domineering. Through awakening the illusory nature of the ego is seen through.

emptiness: See *sunyata.*

Fifth Patriarch: Hung Jen (J., Obai)

Four Noble Truths: These were proclaimed by the Buddha in his first sermon, and comprise the cornerstone of Buddhist teaching. They are: 1) All life is suffering. 2) The origin of suffering is ignorance, which causes egoistic craving and attachment. 3) There is a way to the cessation of suffering. 4) This Way is the Eightfold Noble Path: right understanding, right thinking, right speech, right action, right livelihood, right effort, right mindfulness, right concentration.

gassho (J.): a gesture of respect, gratitude, and humility in which the hands are joined palm to palm.

gatha (Skt.): a set of verse, usually brief, that expresses insight into Buddhist teaching. Gathas have often been composed upon one's coming to awakening.

guru (Skt.): an Indian and Tibetan term meaning teacher or guide; some gurus are considered incarnations of God or the Absolute.

hara (J.): the area of the loins, including the stomach, abdomen, and hips, and the functions of digestion and elimination connected with them. In Zen, the hara—or more correctly the *tanden,* which is specifically the lower abdomen—is recognized as the body-mind's vital center, and by learning to focus the mind there and to radiate all one's activities from that region, one develops greater mental and physical equilibrium and a reserve of energy.

Harada Sogaku-roshi (1870–1961): Regarded as one of the outstanding Japanese Zen masters of modern times, Harada-roshi trained assiduously in both the Soto and Rinzai schools before blending the best of each into an integral school now referred to as the "Harada-line." (For further biographical information about him, see the author's *The Three Pillars of Zen*).

hatha yoga (Skt.): a system of discipline by which the physical body is purified and strengthened through various postures *(asanas),* controlled breathing, etc. Originally hatha yoga was intended to prepare the body for spiritual realization, but today it is often practiced as an end in itself.

Huang Po Hsi Yun (J., Obaku Kiun, ?–850): an heir of Pai Chang (J., Hyakujo), and one of the great Zen masters of T'ang China. Huang Po's methods were forceful and direct, and brought out the same qualities in his most famous disciple, Lin Chi (J., Rinzai).

Isan Reiyu (Ch., Kuei Shan Ling Yu, 771–853): an illustrious Zen master who was a founder of one of the "Five Houses" of Zen. Isan's temperament was gentle and patient, yet subtle and profound.

joriki (J.): samadhi power; the dynamic energy that arises from a mind unified through one-pointed concentration but especially from za-zen. Sensitive persons report having felt the joriki of a strong sesshin from hundreds and even thousands of miles away.

Joshu Jushin (Ch., Chao Chou Ts'ung Shen, 778–897): one of the leading Zen masters of the T'ang period, whose ingenious teaching may be seen in numerous koans, the most famous of which is "Mu," the "first barrier" in the koan system. Joshu attained kensho at the age of 18 and full awakening at 54, yet he did not begin formally teaching until 80, after many years of deepening and refining his enlightenment through "dharma combat" with other Zen masters in China. He lived to be 120.

jukai (J.): taking of the Buddhist precepts, a ceremony in which one is formally initiated as a Buddhist.

karma (Skt.): The doctrine of karma is subtle and exceedingly intricate, and only its basic workings can be sketched in so brief an explanation as the following. Reduced to its most elementary meaning, karma is action; it refers also to the fruits of action. It may be seen as the law of causation on a personal level, a combination of primary and secondary causes. In the case of a plant, for example, the seed is the primary cause, and the rain, wind, sunlight, etc., are the secondary causes. Similarly, every thought, utterance, and deed is a seed that ripens over time until, under suitable conditions, it comes to fruition as an event or circumstance. It is, moreover, a continuous process, for the way in which one responds to these circumstances determines the quality of his present life as well as future ones. Thus the doctrine of karma repudiates any notion of "fate" or "fixed destiny" inasmuch as these circumstances and our response to them are constantly changing. Clearly, then, everyone has the potential at each moment to alter the course of his future karma.

Within the period of a single lifetime, however, every being has in addition to its mutable karma a particular "fixed karma," as for example the species, race, and sex into which it is born. These karmic traits, though set for life, are then recast at the next rebirth, again in accordance with the individual's ever-ripening past actions.

Although we often speak of "good" and "bad" (painful) karma, the term is generally used in reference to the latter, as when selfish actions, for instance, are called "karma-producing." In recent years, as karma has become widely used in the West, several new usages of the word have arisen. Among these is the term "heavy karma," meaning an unusually large "debt" that must be expiated as a result of pain-producing thoughts and actions in this life and previous lives. It may also imply an evil bent of mind growing out of long-standing ego-dominated behavior. We may also speak of "having a karma" with someone, implying a mutual attraction or repulsion that exists as a result of a strong relationship from a previous life.

Karma means that everything that happens to us, without exception, we ourselves directly or indirectly, partly or entirely, have set in motion at some time in the past. The Buddha said, "If you want to know the past [cause], look at your present [effect]. If you want to know the future [effect], look at your present [cause]." The answer to the familiar refrain, "What have I done to deserve this?" is always "Plenty!" Yet suffering can also follow from collective karma, in which each member of a group reaps what the group as a whole has sown. And when the conditioning causes of one's karma, whether that karma is of hardship and disgrace or fortune and honor, are exhausted, it will disappear. (For an extended discussion of karma, see the author's *The Wheel of Death*.)

kensho (J.): seeing into one's own True-nature and hence the nature of all existence; a first awakening, usually shallow.

kinhin (J.): formal walking zazen done between periods of sitting zazen. Kinhin serves as a link between immobile zazen and zazen in motion (daily activities).

koan (J.): Most koans are formed from baffling sayings of the Zen masters, or from incidents growing out of the free working of their awakened minds. These have been recorded, systemized, and used for centuries to instruct and test students in formal Zen training. Every koan points directly to our True-nature that transcends all distinctions, and its perplexing formulation is meant to "throw sand in the eyes (the discriminating intellect)" of the student so that he is forced to open his Mind's eye. Koan literally means "public record," for by requiring a student to grasp the original spirit of a koan the teacher allows no false private understanding. Although there are some seventeen hundred recorded koans, the best koan is the perplexing inquiry that arises naturally out of one's own life experience and cannot be put aside until resolved.

"Kwatz!" (J.): an exclamation having no precise meaning but which, when uttered by one of spiritual power, expresses strong Zen spirit.

kyosaku (J.): a stick used for encouragement in the zendo; a wooden paddle, two to three feet long and flattened at one end, that has been used in Zen training for centuries as an aid to concentration. Each shoulder is struck twice on points corresponding to acupuncture meridians. The kyosaku (sometimes called *keisaku*), is of great help in rousing slumbering energies and a sagging spirit, especially during long stretches of sitting.

lama: a monk of the Vajrayana branch of Mahayana Buddhism. With a capital *L* it signifies one advanced in age or spiritual development.

Lankavatara ("Descent into Sri Lanka") sutra: a major Mahayana sutra comprising much metaphysical and psychological description.

Lin Chi I Hsuan (J., Rinzai Gigen), (?–366): a great T'ang master who, though timid and piestistic before enlightenment, became famous for his fiery spirit and forthright teaching methods. He was successor to Huang Po and founder of the Lin Chi school of Zen, in which his book *The Sayings of Lin Chi* is an important text.

Mahayana: the "Greater Vehicle," one of the two main branches of Buddhism. Also known as the northern school, Mahayana Buddhism spread from northern India to Tibet, Mongolia, China, Vietnam, Korea, and Japan. It has a broader and more progressive emphasis than its counterpart, the Theravada tradition. Thus the Mahayanist strives for enlightenment so as to better help others, and to this end has developed diverse forms to accommodate Buddhist teachings to fit particular cultural, social, and individual needs.

makyo (J.): *ma*, "devilish"; *kyo*, "objective world"): As generally used, this term refers to the visions, hallucinations, fantasies, illusory sensations, fears, and other mental and physical phenomena that may arise during zazen. In the widest sense, however, anything short of enlightenment can be called makyo. (For further information about makyo, see the author's *The Three Pillars of Zen*.)

mantra (Skt.): words or formulae of special sound vibrations used in tantric Buddhist and other forms of meditation. Mantras are transmitted from master to disciple at initiation, and through single-minded repetition can open the mind to insights. Only an enlightened master possesses the spiritual authority to assign a mantra.

maya (Skt.): illusion, or the phenomenal world as it is perceived through the veil of ignorance.

mondo (J.): a lively exchange of questions and responses, always pointing to ultimate truth, between two masters, a master and a student, or between two or more spiritually developed persons.

monjutor: a portmanteau word coined at the Rochester Zen Center to refer to the leader of formal zazen. It derives from the word "Manjusri," a bodhisattva usually shown wielding the delusion-slaying sword of enlightenment, and from the English word "monitor."

nirvana (Skt.): lit., "extinction"; the unconditioned state beyond birth and death that is reached after all ignorance and craving have been extinguished and all karma, which is the cause of rebirth, has been dissolved.

parinirvana (Skt.): lit., complete extinction. Parinirvana usually refers to the state of perfect emancipation reached by Shakyamuni Buddha upon his death.

prajna (Skt.): true wisdom or understanding, beyond the discriminating intellect and conventional truth, that emerges from the actualization of True-mind; the power and functioning of enlightened Mind.

Pure (Lotus) Land: The central doctrine of the Pure Land sect of Japanese Buddhism is that one who invokes the name of Amida Buddha with sincerity and faith in his saving grace will be reborn in his Pure Lotus Land of peace and bliss.

samadhi (Skt.): lit., "putting things together" or "union of the meditator with the object meditated upon." In Zen, samadhi is a state of intense absorption in which the mind has transcended all thoughts, visualizations, imaginings, etc. This is not a blank insensibility but a deep and illumined awareness.

samsara (Skt.): the endless cycle of birth-and-death in which all phenomena are in constant transformation; the world of suffering. Mahayana Buddhism regards samsara as the other side of nirvana, or enlightenment.

sangha (Skt.): originally, the Buddhist monastic order, but more generally the community of people practicing the Buddha's Way. The sangha is one of the three treasures, or jewels, of Buddhism, along with the buddha and the dharma.

satori (J.): enlightenment, usually deep; awakening to the truth lying beyond all dualism and discrimination. Far more than ecstasy or psychological or philosophical insight, satori is spiritual awakening that brings about a fundamental transformation of personality and character and a wholly fresh vision of the world.

Second Patriarch: Hui K'e (J., Eka).

sensei (J.): made up of the Chinese ideograms meaning "first" and "to be born"—hence, the first born, senior, one deserving respect, etc. A common English rendering is "teacher" or "instructor."

sesshin (J.): lit., "concentrating and unifying the mind"; an intensive training period in seclusion, usually lasting not less than three days and not more than seven. Strict sesshins are held in complete silence, with participants remaining on the premises from beginning to end.

silver mountain and iron wall: metaphors describing the seemingly insuperable obstacles that confront one striving for awakening. "Only he who attempts the absurd is capable of achieving the impossible."

six worlds: the six realms, or changing conditions, of unenlightened existence. In ascending order these are: the realms of hell, hungry ghosts *(pretas)*, animals, fighting demons *(asuras)*, human beings, and heavenly beings *(devas)*. These worlds, through which sentient beings are constantly evolving and devolving, may also be interpreted in a psychological sense, for all are One-mind.

Sixth Patriarch: Hui Neng (J., Rokuso-daishi).

sunyata (Skt.): Voidness, the dynamic substratum of all existence. All phenomena are essentially empty, or devoid of self-substance, in the sense that they are but fleeting manifestations in a stream of endless transformation. Though sunyata is without form, it informs everything; to see into this no-thingness of things is awakening.

Surangama (Skt.) sutra: one of the most esteemed of the Mahayana sutras, believed to have been written some five hundred years after the Buddha. Of principal value in the text are the instructions, conveyed through questions and answers, for training in the successive steps leading to supreme enlightenment.

swami (Skt.): literally, "lord," "master"; a title of respect for a Hindu religious teacher.

tai chi (Ch., T'ai Chi Ch'uan): an ancient Chinese health meditation-exercise that expresses Taoist principles of yielding, pliability, and circulation of *ch'i* energy (Skt., *prana*) through the body. Tai chi may also be developed as a martial art.

Tao (Ch.): the essence or Truth of the universe; the way of Truth ("the Way").

Tathagata (Skt.): one of the appellations of the Buddha, used by him in referring to himself. Literally it means "one who has thus-come (or gone)":—i.e., one who has come like buddhas before him. In Zen "thus come" has a somewhat different implication, as masters will frequently ask a newcomer, "What is this that thus comes?"—in other words, "Show me your Buddha-nature!"

ten directions: north, south, east, west, the four intermediate points, and the zenith and the nadir. In Buddhism this encompasses the whole cosmos.

Theravada: the southern branch of Buddhism, sometimes referred to as the Hinayana, or "Lesser Vehicle." This school has a more rigid and doctrinaire emphasis than the Mahayana. The Theravada tradition is maintained in the countries of Southeast Asia.

Vairochana (Skt.) Buddha: the "All-Illuminating One," the supreme nonhistorical buddha, symbolizing the "truth-body" *(dharmakaya)* or universal buddha-mind that pervades all time and space.

Vedanta (Skt.): a system of Hindu philosophy based on the four ancient sacred books of Hinduism called the Vedas.

Way, the: See *Tao*

Yasutani Hakuun-roshi (1885–1973): a highly respected Japanese Zen master; a dharma-successor of Harada-roshi. (For further biographical information about him, see the author's *The Three Pillars of Zen.*)

zazen (J.): lit., "sitting Zen"; to be distinguished from meditation, which usually involves a visualization or putting into the mind of a concept, idea, or other thought form. During true zazen the mind is one-pointed, stabilized, and emptied of random, extraneous thoughts. Zazen is not limited to sitting but continues throughout every activity.

zendo (J.): a room used for formal sitting zazen, which is often its exclusive purpose. Roughly equivalent to the sanctuary of a church, the zendo is the heart and the most important area of every Zen center.

"Zen macrobiotic diet": a diet based essentially on the belief that health is best maintained through eating natural, unprocessed foods in a certain balance of *yang* (alkaline-producing) to *yin* (acid-producing). It has no connection with Zen Buddhism.

INDEX / *Numerals in italics refer to pages where terms are defined or described in detail. Numerals in parentheses refer to footnotes.*